Counterweights
The Failure of Canada's German and European Policy, 1955–1995

Focusing on Canadian-German defence relations from 1955 to 1995, Roy Rempel examines the evolution of Canada's bilateral relationship with Germany in the context of the broader goals and objectives of Canadian foreign policy. He argues that Canadian decision-makers have often been ignorant of the important role played by the military in supporting these objectives and that, as a result, Canada's defence policy has often been ad hoc, ill considered, and badly implemented. Ultimately this has undermined and destroyed the Canadian government's attempts to construct a European political and economic counterweight to the United States.

Rempel traces pivotal events in the development of the bilateral relationship between Canada and West Germany, from Canada's policy on the admission of the Federal Republic to NATO in 1954–55, through Prime Minister Pierre Trudeau's 1969 decision to reduce Canadian forces in Europe by half, to Prime Minister Brian Mulroney's 1992 decision to withdraw Canadian military forces from Europe entirely. He looks at the development of the missions and functions of Canada's forces in Germany and assesses why Canada failed in its efforts to integrate the political, economic, and military dimensions of its foreign policy.

Counterweights highlights the profound implications of Canada's failure to develop a co-ordinated defence policy to support its international objectives for its present-day relations with both Europe and the United States.

ROY REMPEL is a policy analyst with the Intergovernmental Affairs Secretariat of the Government of Newfoundland and Labrador and lectures in international relations at Memorial University.

Counterweights

The Failure of Canada's German and European Policy, 1955–1995

ROY REMPEL

McGill-Queen's University Press
Montreal & Kingston • London • Buffalo

© McGill-Queen's University Press 1996
ISBN 0-7735-1507-0

Legal deposit first quarter 1997
Bibliothèque nationale du Québec

Printed in the United States on acid-free paper

This book has been published with the help of a grant from
the Social Science Federation of Canada, using funds provided
by the Social Sciences and Humanities Research Council of
Canada. Publication has also been assisted by grants from the
Publications Subvention Board of Memorial University of
Newfoundland and from the Centre for International
Relations of Queen's University, Kingston, Ontario.

McGill-Queen's University Press is grateful to the Canada
Council for support of its publishing program.

Canadian Cataloguing in Publication Data

Rempel, Roy Anthony, 1962–
    Counterweights : the failure of Canada's German and
    European policy, 1955–1995
    Includes bibliographical references and index.
    ISBN 0-7735-1507-0
    1. Canada – Foreign relations – Germany. 2. Germany –
    Foreign relations – Canada. 3. Canada – Foreign relations –
    1945–   . 4. Germany – Foreign relations – 1945–   .
    5. Canada – Military relations – Germany. 6. Germany –
    Military relations – Canada. I. Title.
    FC251.G4R45 1997   327.71043   C96-990022-8
    F1029.5.G4R45 1997

Typeset in Minion 10/12
by Caractéra inc., Quebec City

For my parents

Contents

Preface and Acknowledgments

This study examines the evolution and development of the bilateral relationship between Canada and the Federal Republic of Germany, particularly in the years after the restoration of German sovereignty and the FRG's entry into the North Atlantic Treaty Organization in 1955. Chapter 1 sets out the general themes of the study while chapter 2 offers an examination of the particular foreign, defence, and alliance policies of the two states. Thus, Part One of the volume explains, first, some of the most important elements and aspects of the postwar foreign policy objectives of the two countries and, second, assesses to what degree the broad interests of the two states have had the potential to converge at any particular time.

In Part Two I look specifically at the development of the bilateral political relationship between the two countries from 1955 until the mid-1980s. Chapter 3 focuses on the evolution of relations until the early 1970s. Here, the impact of Canada's foreign and defence policy review of the late 1960s on the relationship is examined, with particular reference to the relations between Ottawa and Bonn. Chapter 4 discusses the differing and coinciding dimensions and approaches taken by the two countries on the question of security in Europe. Finally, chapter 5 looks directly at Canada's attempt to broaden the bilateral relationship in the 1970s and to use it to help pursue the objective of deepening the country's economic and trading ties with Europe as a whole. It was in this period that Germany assumed the pivotal position in Canada's traditional search for counterweights in its foreign policy relationships.

Part Three examines the place and role of Canada's military commitment in defence of Germany and the central front in Europe. It will be argued that throughout the post–World War II period, strategic and military issues were central to the framework of German security policy. The role, both political and military, that Canada's forces played in this framework has for a long time required closer study. How did the Germans perceive the political and military role of Canada's forces in Germany? To what extent did the Canadian military commitment in central Europe support Canada's developing links with Germany? When and how did Ottawa's actions in relation to Canada's commitment undermine the positive evolution of relations between the two states? Thus, chapter 6 looks at the relative military and political importance that the Canadian military commitment to the Atlantic alliance had in the first two decades after it was made. It traces the extent to which a general Canadian commitment to the alliance had by 1955 become a specific commitment made by Canada to the Federal Republic of Germany itself. Chapter 7 then analyses the changing military roles of the Canadian Forces in the years from 1970 to the end of the Cold War with particular attention to the close interrelation of the military and political dimensions of the Canadian presence in Europe.

Finally, in Part Four, I examine the developments in relations between Canada and the Federal Republic in the post–Cold War era. Chapter 8 looks at Canadian-German diplomacy in the period leading up to Ottawa's decision in 1992 to withdraw all of its military forces from Europe, while chapter 9 sets out the principal circumstances confronting Canadian and German policy in the 1990s and into the twenty-first century. With the collapse of the Cold War order, the future of the transatlantic relationship is in question. As a product of the revolutionary events which have occurred since 1989 – and because of Canada's poor management of bilateral relations in the past – it seems very unlikely that the Canadian-German relationship will retain the importance which it had in the past, either in itself or as a dimension of Canada's traditional emphasis on counterweights in the making of its foreign policy.

This study was pursued over six years, between 1989 and 1995. In consequence, I owe debts of gratitude to a great many people who facilitated its progress in a variety of ways.

First, I with to thank the Department of National Defence, and most specifically the people in the Military and Strategic Studies Program. The financial assistance provided through the department's doctoral fellowship made possible this study and, in particular, my research in the Federal Republic of Germany.

Second, I deeply appreciate the assistance of the many individuals who agreed to be interviewed – some anonymously and some on the record. These interviews not only assisted me in the reconstruction of events but also helped to focus my own thinking on particular theoretical aspects of both the Canadian-German and the transatlantic relationships.

Third, I am grateful to the Department of External Affairs – as it then was – for the access afforded to classified documents under the department's programme for academic research.

I wish to thank all those officials in the Corporate Communications Division of the Department of External/Foreign Affairs, the Department of National Defence's Directorate of History, the National Archives of Canada, the Privy Council Office, the Political Archival Section of the German Foreign Office, and the German Federal Archives – Military Division who gave me invaluable assistance in compiling archival material. I am most grateful to the Stiftung Wissenschaft und Politik in Ebenhausen, Germany, which generously provided me with a home base for three months while I was conducting research in the Federal Republic.

I owe a special debt of appreciation to my dissertation adviser, Dr David Haglund of Queen's University, Kingston, who encouraged and greatly facilitated my research throughout the preparation of this study.

A number of people assisted me with other work related to the preparation of the manuscript. While all translations of German-language material (and any mistakes therein) are my own, Dr. Gunter Hartmann helped to review my citation of German-language source material. Gerard Gouthro assisted with assembling the index, Susan Lindberg drew the map, and I am grateful to Dr Christopher Dunn for suggesting the title. I also wish to thank Marion Magee for her great assistance in editing this manuscript and Peter Blaney and Joan McGilvray at McGill-Queen's University Press for their work in connection with publication of the book. I acknowledge with thanks grants in aid of publication from the Social Sciences and Humanities Research Council of Canada, the Publications Subvention Board of Memorial University of Newfoundland, and the Centre for International Relations, Queen's University.

Finally, and most importantly, I wish to thank my parents who have always supported my work.

December 1995
RR

The lord mayor of West Berlin, Willy Brandt (*left*), meets with Prime Minister John Diefenbaker during a visit to Ottawa in 1959. After a positive start to the relationship in 1955, relations between Germany and Canada became strained in the succeeding ten years because of clashes over a variety of political – and later military – issues. (National Archives of Canada (NA) PA 194910)

Lester Pearson (*right*) in conversation with Chancellor Ludwig Erhard during the latter's state visit to Canada in June 1964. By the early 1960s, the policies of Canada and the Federal Republic had moved to opposite poles within the Atlantic alliance. Pearson and Erhard, who both came into office in 1963, placed great emphasis on moving their respective security policies back into the alliance mainstream. The result was a closer bilateral relationship between the two countries in the 1960s. (NA PA 164840)

The German foreign minister, Willy Brandt (*right*), met with Canada's secretary of state for external affairs, Mitchell Sharp, in Ottawa in April 1969 in the immediate aftermath of Canada's decision to reduce substantially the size of its forces stationed in the Federal Republic. The decision brought bilateral relations to a low ebb. (NA PA 1949B)

Helmut Schmidt (*left*) travelled to Ottawa in July 1972 to discuss mutual defence questions with Canada's minister of national defence, Edgar Benson. While Schmidt was the German minister of defence (1969–72), Bonn placed great emphasis on restoring stability to its political relationship with Canada. (Canadian Forces photo unit)

The German defence minister, Hans Apel (*centre*), visited Ottawa in September 1978 for discussions with his Canadian counterpart, B.J. Danson (*left*). The Germans were lobbying strongly for Canada to purchase the European-built Tornado combat aircraft. Despite the boost such a purchase would have given to trade with Europe at a time when Canada was seeking to diversify its trading relations, the Tornado was eliminated from the competition for a new fighter in 1978. (Canadian Forces photo unit)

Chancellor Helmut Schmidt of Germany speaks to the press during his 1981 visit to Canada at the time of the G-7 summit in Montebello while Prime Minister Pierre Trudeau looks on. The friendship between the two men was an important anchor of the bilateral relationship from 1975 to 1982. (NA PA 194912)

Prime Minister Brian Mulroney (*left*) in conversation with Chancellor Helmut Kohl at the G-7 summit in Bonn in May 1985. Relations between the two countries seemed stable because Canada had just announced that it would increase the strength of its forces in Germany by 20 per cent. Within six months, however, Canada was proposing a complete withdrawal of its forces. (Embassy of the Federal Republic, Ottawa)

General Wolfgang Altenburg (*left*), inspector-general of the Bundeswehr, arrives at National Defence Headquarters in September 1985 for talks with General Gerard Thériault, Canada's chief of defence staff. In the autumn of 1985, the Germans successfully opposed a plan formulated in Canada's Department of National Defence to withdraw from Canada's commitment on the central front in Germany in favour of an enhanced commitment to NATO's northern flank. (Canadian Forces photo unit)

General Jean de Chastelain, chief of the defence staff, and senior Canadian and German generals review a contingent from the newly established 1 Canadian Division at Lahr in November 1989. The division had been established as a result of the decision in Canada's 1987 defence white paper to consolidate the country's military commitments to Europe in Germany. Established, ironically, in the month the Berlin Wall came down, the division commitment had already been gutted because of the impact of the sharply reduced appropriations for defence in the April budget. (Canadian Forces photo unit)

Canada's secretary of state for external affairs, Joe Clark (*left*), meets with Hans-Dietrich Genscher, Germany's foreign minister, at the time of a CSCE meeting in Paris in November 1990. With the end of the Cold War, the Germans were lobbying hard – though ultimately unsuccessfully – for a continued Canadian presence in Europe. (Bundesbildstelle Bonn, 88 380/25; fotograf, Stutterheim)

Prime Minister Brian Mulroney of Canada in conversation with
President Richard von Weizsäcker of Germany during the
former's state visit to the Federal Republic in June 1991.
Mulroney's promise to retain Canadian forces in Europe, made
during the visit, was broken in less than a year. (Bundesbildstelle
Bonn, 88 295/15; fotograf, Reineke)

Prime Minister Jean Chrétien of Canada accompanies Chancellor Helmut Kohl
(*right*) of Germany during the latter's visit to the Canadian Arctic following the
G-7 summit in Halifax in June 1995. Although residual political and military ties
still exist between Canada and Germany, the end of the Cold War and the withdrawal of Canadian military forces from Europe mean that Canada occupies only
a peripheral position in the hierarchy of foreign policy concerns of its European
allies including Germany. (Bundesbildstelle Bonn, 106 130/30; fotograf, Reineke)

PART ONE

Canada's Germany and Germany's Canada

1 The Context of
the Bilateral Relationship

An important and recurring theme in the study of Canada's foreign policy is the country's seemingly perennial search for "counterweights" to offset, politically and economically, the country's relationship with the United States. Even before Canada's confederation in 1867, the relationship of British North America with the republic to the south dominated much of the external focus of both Canada's political élites and its population. While the military threat from the Americans began to dissipate in the second half of the nineteenth century, the challenge that the United States (by virtue of its very size and existence) offered to Canada's independence and sovereignty continued to dominate the foreign policy concerns of the young dominion's leaders and people.

Until World War II, Canada's position as a dominion of the British empire and Commonwealth was the crucial support for its continued independence from the United States. After the war, however, the decline of British power and the advent of a new world order compelled the country's leaders to look for new ways to counterbalance the enormous potential influence of Canada's large (even if friendly) neighbour to the south.

Canada's international position and its historical relationship with the United States have meant that the counterweight principle has always had a prominent position on any list of Canadian foreign policy concerns and objectives. It was certainly instrumental in reinforcing the country's commitment to the principle of multilateralism and to its membership in international organizations such as the United Nations and the North Atlantic Treaty Organization (NATO). Multilateralism was seen as a vehicle for securing an effective voice for Canada on the international stage as well as an instrument for constructing the necessary alignments of interest with other states which could serve to counterbalance the dominant influence of the United States.

In the post–World War II period, the North Atlantic alliance soon emerged as the most promising and credible multilateral institution for both influencing and counterbalancing the influence of the United States. In the first decade or so after the formation of NATO in 1949, the focus of Canadian diplomacy was on the institution itself, headquartered in Paris, and on Canada's direct political relations with its two close wartime allies, the United States and the United Kingdom. Bilateral relations with other alliance members (save, to some extent, with France) took a back seat. However, as power in the alliance shifted and in particular as the influence of the continental European states grew in the 1950s and, especially, in the 1960s, the recognition of the potential importance of bilateral links with some of these allies also grew in Canada. In this respect, no power was more important to Canada than the Federal Republic of Germany (FRG).

Both politically and economically, the power and influence of West Germany increased steadily in the late 1950s and the 1960s. The so-called Wirtschaftswunder (economic miracle) had made the German economy the fastest growing one in Europe. Moreover, the country's pivotal position in the Common Market (created in 1957) ensured it a key role in the formulation of continental economic and trade policy. Likewise, German rearmament elevated the country's political position to that of a major power within NATO. This reality made the development of Canada's political relations with the Federal Republic highly desirable.

Closer relations with Canada were also of potential interest to West Germany, given the particular goals of its security policy. The West German state, which had been created in 1949, was very much a product of the Cold War. For forty years, the position and very existence of West Germany was consistently overshadowed by the overt and direct military threat from the Soviet Union. Until the collapse of Soviet power in 1989–91, Soviet military forces remained in de facto occupation of East Germany (the German Democratic Republic – GDR). Throughout this period they also maintained the capability to initiate offensive military action in central Europe on very short notice.

This threat, and the political conditions it created, ensured that security-related considerations dominated the policy-making of Germany's leaders. The Soviet threat also ensured that for some forty years external guarantees from its allies were the most important element in the maintenance of the Federal Republic's independence and security. The most significant of these guarantees was that provided by the United States. Indeed, the political importance of the American guarantee to the Federal Republic meant that almost every aspect of the transatlantic relationship acquired a greater political and symbolic significance than it would otherwise have had.

The centrality of this matter for the Federal Republic even extended to its relationship with Canada, the other North American country in the alliance. Because the societies of the two North American states were similar in so many ways and because their political, economic, and military relations were so close, events in Canada, and with respect to its relations with Europe, were viewed as indicators of possible trends in relations between the United States and Europe as well. Thus, the Germans always perceived a certain geostrategic unity in North America and regarded the collective commitment of North America to European and to German security as essential to counterbalance the Soviet control of the Eurasian land mass.

It was in this derivative context that the Canadian commitment to the North Atlantic alliance became important to the Federal Republic. The Canadian commitment was most directly manifested through the deployment of the country's ground and air forces in West Germany from 1951. This physical presence was the most tangible symbol of Canada's interest in the security of central Europe. By extension, it also became the single most important means for promoting the country's influence in Europe and giving significance to its diplomatic positions and interventions.

This military pledge, while initially made by Canada to the alliance as a whole, evolved into a commitment by Canada to West Germany most directly. Throughout the more than forty years that Canada's forces were present in the Federal Republic, the Germans showed a consistent and close interest not only in the continued presence of those forces but also in the details of this military commitment. The military configuration of the forces, where they were based, and the specific missions they were assigned were of tremendous interest to the Germans. As a result, Germany's own political leaders were prepared to go to some length to ensure a continuing and viable commitment.

Most Canadian leaders, however, never understood the full political worth of the country's military presence in Germany. In consequence, the value of that presence to Canada, both politically and economically, was never fully appreciated and therefore never fully exploited. Indeed, in many instances, the lack of understanding of the political importance of the Canadian military commitment in Europe ensured that Canada's diplomatic and military policies actually worked at cross-purposes.

The lack of appreciation on the part of Canadian leaders of all political stripes for the potential political utility of the country's military presence in Germany has deep roots. It rests on the fact that defence policy generally has had a low priority for Canada's political decision-makers. For the last century or so, there have been few direct and immediate threats to Canada's physical security and independence. As a result, most Canadians have only a superficial understanding of the purpose of military power and of its wider political and military usefulness and significance.

Historically, in the Federal Republic of Germany and most other Western countries, a "realist" approach to the conduct of international affairs has been dominant. Integral to such an approach is the recognition by the governing foreign policy élites that whatever idealistic impulses any particular state and society may have, the realities of the international state system mean that the pursuit of the larger political and security interests of the state must take precedence. Moreover, realist-based approaches to international affairs also recognize and appreciate the role played by military power in facilitating the achievement of larger political and security objectives. In Canada, such a realist-based foreign policy has been for the most part absent. Canadian decision-makers have been especially ignorant of the broader political role played by military power in international affairs with the result that Canada has not utilized defence policy effectively in pursuit of broader political and economic purposes. Most directly, the country's ability to construct a European counterweight to its relationship with the United States was undermined by a defence policy which was often ad hoc, ill considered, and badly implemented.

Thus, it will be argued in this book that the country's failure to develop a credible defence policy contributed much to the inability to develop the Canadian relationship with the Federal Republic of Germany to its full potential. This, in turn, has had profound implications for Canada's broader international position and for the nature of the relationship which exists today between both Canada and Europe and Canada and the United States. This failure in the area of defence has in fact been instrumental in contributing to a steady decline in Canada's influence with its most important allies and to its fading relevance internationally.

2 The Security Policies of Canada and Germany in the Cold War Era

The North Atlantic Treaty Organization, which came into existence in 1949, joined ten European states in a military alliance with two states in North America.[1] In the prevailing security climate both European and North American political leaders recognized the strategic necessity and political importance of a firm commitment on the part of North America to the security of Western Europe. The weakness of the states of continental Europe following the end of the Second World War and the spectre of a military, political, and ideological challenge from what was perceived to be an expansionist Soviet Union made this firm commitment by outside powers (which had traditionally shunned peacetime continental military entanglements) to Europe essential.

This union of North America and Europe in a common military enterprise to ensure their mutual security was (and remains) the essence of the alliance. North America became the strategic counterweight to the military weight of a Eurasian land mass dominated by the Soviet Union. Simultaneously, in a political and ideological sense, the commitment of North America (and the United Kingdom as well) reinforced, and reinvigorated, the confidence and resolve of continental European states to rebuild their societies in some semblance of security. This initial importance of Europe's relationship with North America was sustained in the subsequent years and decades. The union of North America and Europe in the North Atlantic alliance remained the key to Western Europe's continued freedom and independence.

In the early 1950s arrangements were arrived at in which forces from North America and the United Kingdom were stationed permanently on the continent of Europe. Although many in North America hoped and believed this deployment to be a temporary measure until the West European nations had been able to rearm and provide for their own security, by the late 1950s it had become apparent that the continuing military engagement of North America was regarded as an essential aspect of deterrence and the maintenance of the balance of power. Because of the bipolar character of the balance of power between East and West (that is, the existence of one state on each side of the East-West ideological divide which possessed a preponderance of power), the clear commitment of NATO's leading state, the United States, to its allies across the Atlantic was essential.

Within this context, the Canadian position in the alliance came to be unique. First, and most importantly, as the second North American country in the alliance, the Canadian commitment to NATO had a special quality. The strategic unity of North America was manifest to many observers of the North American scene. Canada was perceived as closely linked to the United States not only in military terms but also culturally and economically. Thus, Canada's position and actions within the alliance have often been thought to hold a wider significance for the very nature and character of the wider transatlantic relationship itself. In many ways, therefore, the deployment of Canadian ground and air forces in Europe from 1951 was seen as part and parcel of the more general North American commitment to deterrence and defence in Western Europe. The Canadian contingent deployed in Europe thus assumed a significance far beyond its simple military utility. In fact, it can be argued that its small size made the primarily political purpose of the Canadian military presence all the more manifest. As a result of this perception, not only the simple presence of the Canadian contingent but also its geographic location, its composition and configuration, and the degree of Canada's commitment to alliance strategies all took on an enhanced symbolic salience.

Second, the Canadian role in the alliance was perceived as important because of Canada's position as the second of only two North American states within NATO. This provided the transatlantic relationship with a multilateral dimension. Although this perception was somewhat at odds with the conception of North America's geostrategic unity, it nevertheless came to be a factor in the European view of the Canadian role within the alliance. Certainly, the notion of Canada as a "transatlantic bridge" or "linchpin" within the alliance has long been popular in certain Canadian foreign policy circles. While the perception among European alliance members of Canada's role in this sense may not have fully paralleled the perception which was popular among some Canadians, Canada was nevertheless viewed in some quarters in Europe as a voice of moderation or as a spokesman for the interests of the smaller powers. In Canada, the European powers had a North American state which often took political positions closer their own than to those of the United States.

Germany – The Alliance's Strategic/Political Centre of Gravity

While the union of North America and Western Europe was key to the achievement of the alliance's political and military objectives, the principal focus of those efforts was the maintenance of peace and stability in the central region of Europe. Throughout the post-1945 era this region was the centre of gravity in the East-West balance of power. For the alliance states most directly exposed to military threats in the central region (the Benelux countries, France, and the Federal Republic of Germany), the Atlantic alliance was the "strategic backbone" of their security.[2]

As the principal point of confrontation between East and West, Germany was the natural central focus for the alliance. Germany was vital in both strategic and political/ideological terms. Strategically, both East and West recognized that whichever side dominated, or alternatively was allied to, a unified Germany in all likelihood would dominate all of Europe as well. Thus, as the Soviet Union moved in the late 1940s and 1950s to consolidate its position in Eastern Europe and in East Germany and in the face of a continued large-scale and offensively oriented Soviet military deployment there, the Western position in West Germany became the principal focus of allied deterrence and defence policy. Germany became, in Josef Joffe's words, the "key prize" in the conflict between East and West. For both sides, therefore, the outcome of the struggle over Germany would determine the future of the continent of Europe and of the relationship between North America and Western Europe.[3]

In political and ideological terms, the "German Question" was at the heart of the problems dividing Europe and separating East from West and touched on the most important questions concerning the long-term stability of central Europe. Hence, the initial diplomatic efforts of the Western powers in the 1950s sought to anchor the Federal Republic firmly to the West so as to prevent any further westward expansion of Soviet influence. Anchoring Germany to the West also served as way of discreetly controlling Germany and securing a measure of stability for central Europe. While the evolution of a democratic and firmly Western-oriented Federal Republic to an extent diminished the emphasis on the second of these policy objectives, this dual emphasis nevertheless remained the essential basis of allied policy in central Europe after 1949.

The level of military engagement by countries of the alliance in West Germany was therefore considerable. As the occupying powers, the United States, the United Kingdom (joined by Belgium), and France continued to deploy forces in Germany after 1945; they were later joined by forces from the Netherlands and Canada (and for a short time from Norway and Denmark as well). Thus, half of NATO's member-states, and both of the alliance's North American members, were engaged in Germany. The unity and high level of integration of NATO forces in Germany symbolized and gave practical effect to the alliance's deterrent policy for some four decades.

The Canadian-German Partnership

Among the alliance's member-states there exists a vast number of dyadic relationships. Some of a state's many bilateral links are obviously going to assume greater importance than others. Some of these connections will be a product of fairly deeply held common or converging political, military, ideological, and even cultural factors. Other alignments of interest may only be temporary and issue-specific. In the former case, the longer term convergence of common perceptions and interests can contribute to an intensification of the level of mutual consultations and co-operative political interaction. What Roger Hill has described as "the quality of consultations" between alliance members is indicative of the importance attached by each state to its bilateral relationship with the other.[4]

In the case of Canada and Germany, there have been some important points of common or converging interests in an intensified bilateral political relationship. For the Federal Republic, Canada's importance would seem to have accrued most directly from its position as the second North American power in the alliance, while for Canada its long-standing interest in political and military stability in central Europe has made Germany an important potential partner in Europe. In addition, as the relative weight of the FRG, especially in the political and economic spheres, has grown, so too has Canada's interest in a closer bilateral relationship.

Moreover, in the period after Germany's entry into NATO in 1955, both states were closely engaged in the physical defence of central Europe and can be said to have belonged to the "core group" within the alliance. Collectively, they represented perhaps the most visible demonstration of the alliance's resolve. Divergence from NATO policy and strategy by any country engaged in central Europe (that is, the stationing states) generally had a greater significance politically than policy divergence by other alliance states. The visibility and importance of the deterrence mission on the central front ensured this response. Furthermore, deterrence and defence strategies on the central front and the military force postures adopted to implement those strategies had a wider political significance because of the centrality of Germany and the German Question in the wider European and East-West balance of power.

The potential intensity of the Canadian-German bilateral political and diplomatic relationship was enhanced by this common factor. Moreover, the close relationship which prevailed in the military sphere was bound to spill over into other areas of the bilateral relationship. While this was most likely to occur in the formulation and co-ordination of diplomatic positions on key issues of political interest, it was also likely to affect and influence other dimensions of the bilateral relationship. To determine the particular areas and actual extent of convergence between the interests and perspectives of the two countries, one must begin by examining the basic elements and key points of emphasis in the postwar foreign and alliance policies of the Federal Republic and Canada.

GERMAN SECURITY POLICY, 1949–1989

The formulation of German security policy after 1949 was governed and constrained by a series of international and domestic factors which arose from the country's geographic position and history. First, the country's status was very much a consequence of the emerging Cold War and of the division of Europe between the Western allies and the Soviet Union. As a result of the breakdown in co-operation between East and West over the governing of occupied Germany, the United States and the United Kingdom (followed more slowly and reluctantly by France) gradually merged their zones of occupation after 1946, ultimately sanctioning and supporting the creation of the Federal Republic of Germany in 1949. This division of Germany, through the creation of the Federal Republic in the West and of a separate Soviet client state, the German Democratic Republic, in the East, was thus a direct product of the Cold War.

Second, in addition to constraints imposed by the international environment, the German federal government had to contend with the reality of the country's internal political climate. The trauma engendered among the German people from all the horrors which occurred during the Second World War, as well as the subsequent defeat and military occupation of the country, left many Germans with a profound aversion not only to militarism but to any and all issues associated with military and defence matters. It is probably safe to argue that up to the early 1950s, a majority of Germans actually opposed the reconstitution of a national German army.[5] This aversion to matters military was also, at least partly, a product of the perception that German rearmament and the integration of the Federal Republic into the Western political and military bloc would sharpen and deepen the division of Germany (an argument strongly advanced by the opposition party in the Bundestag). Thus, while the nature of the Federal Republic's external relations with its Western patrons pointed to the logic of a firm integration of West Germany into the Western defence system, the dynamics of the FRG's internal politics seemed to be pushing in the opposite direction.

Compounding these paradoxical political dynamics, the reality of the division of Germany posed another dilemma for the construction of a viable German security policy. Any prospective German security policy not only had to ensure the security and safety of the Federal Republic itself but also had to seek to promote and maximize conditions under which German national unity could eventually be regained. In other words, the government in Bonn was from the outset torn between a strong desire to align the new state to the West and by the simultaneous political and constitutional requirement to press the issue of the country's reunification. In formulating its security policy, the West German government had always to consider not only the interests and needs of those Germans living in the western part of the country but also the interests and needs of Germans living in eastern Germany. Moreover, it had to do this without unduly alarming the country's neighbours, allies, or adversaries while simultaneously sustaining as broad a consensus as possible within the German population.

For some time historians, political analysts, and sociologists have concerned themselves with the issue of the place of Germany within Europe. The German Question effectively encapsulates the dilemmas confronted by Germans in constructing a new national security policy for their country in the aftermath of the Second World War. In the postwar period, the German Question has been defined in essentially three distinct ways.

First, most commonly, the German Question centred on the issue of German unity: the dilemma of how and under what circumstances to restore German national unity, and the implications of German division for continued peace and stability in Europe. This was, arguably, the most important issue in the East-West balance of power.

A second dimension of the German Question rested on and continues to rest on Germany's relationship to the rest of Europe. In the nineteenth century the unification of Germany under Prussian leadership made that country the strongest power in Europe. The strength of Germany after 1871 made the construction of a stable balance of power more problematical. Many Europeans perceived the growth of German power after 1871 as in large measure responsible for the two world wars fought in the twentieth century to prevent Germany from completely dominating all of Europe. At the end of the Second World War the problem of how most effectively to manage German power and ensure that Germany never again committed aggression against its neighbours was a prominent one. The German Question defined in this sense thus encompasses, on the one hand, the question of how Europe can be secured against German aggression and, on the other hand, the issue of how the German people can be made to feel secure in the centre of Europe surrounded by and vulnerable to the actions of other great powers.[6]

The final definition of the German Question was certainly the most complex and in many ways the most difficult of the three incarnations of this question to address, for it involved, as Ralf Dahrendorf noted, the very nature of the German character and of German society.[7] Germany emerged from the war not only as a defeated nation but also as one which was humiliated and reviled. The atrocities and mass murder committed in the name of the German people during the war led to a debate after the war as to whether Germany could ever again be fully admitted to the community of civilized nations.

Thus, the German Question encompassed the most fundamental of questions. Were the German people inherently aggressive? What was it within the German society, culture, and character that had made Auschwitz possible? Why had the German people turned in such massive numbers to National Socialism after 1933? Was there a natural inclination towards authoritarianism or totalitarianism in Germany?

In the aftermath of the war there was a great questioning of the philosophical value system which had underpinned the essential structure of German society. The German philosophical and political tradition had stressed values which were now seen to have contributed to the aggressive nature of German policy in the twentieth century and, ultimately, to the rise of Nazism. In particular, it was widely perceived that typically Prussian values of authoritarianism, militarism, and subservience and obedience to bureaucratic authority had created an inhospitable climate for the rise of liberal democracy in Germany.[8] It was thus the policy of the Western allies after 1945, and of the German government after 1949 (dominated by Western-oriented Christian Democratic politicians) to promote and instil within German society such values as individual rights, the rule of law, and tolerance of minority opinion. The American occupation authorities and West German Christian political figures believed the "re-education" of the German population and a moderation, if not elimination, of the Prussian influence over German society was the most effective way of addressing this aspect of the German Question.

Hedley Bull has drawn a distinction between the concept of the "international system" of which all states are a part and the notion of "international society" which is composed of those states which adhere to the principles, norms, and rules which were essential elements of Western civilization even before the advent of the European state system in 1648.[9] In 1945 the German nation and state was an outcast from this "international society." It thus became the principal objective of the German government's security policy after 1949 both to restore Germany to a respected place within the community of civilized nations and to re-establish full German sovereignty and unity without further endangering the security of the Federal Republic. To accomplish this objective, the government of Konrad Adenauer sought to address directly each of the essential elements of the German Question by firmly pursuing a security policy strategy which would integrate the Federal Republic into the Western political, military, and economic system. Their security policy, both in its content and in the means of its implementation, sought to reassure the country's allies and adversaries alike of the Bonn republic's modest and limited policy goals.[10]

Four Themes in Security Policy

The Adenauer administration, as the first German postwar government, sought from the outset to formulate an integrated policy approach which would successfully manage the German Question in each of its dimensions. The formulation of a new Western-oriented German security policy was an essential element of this broader philosophical approach to the problem of restoring Germany's position in Europe. The Federal Republic's security policy came to be structured around four principal themes:

1 Atlanticism (or the relationship with the United States);
2 Europeanism (in particular the relationship with France);
3 the quest for full sovereignty and equality in the context of an integrated Western community of states; and
4 Bonn's national and Eastern policy (encompassing until 1990–1 the question of national reunification and Germany's relations with the USSR).

In the first of these areas, through its relationship with the United States, the Germans promoted the important objective of seeking to ensure the security and stability of Europe and the Federal Republic by emphatically supporting the maintenance of a firm American political and military engagement on the continent. This commitment was vitally important to Germany in three particular senses. The first and most immediate involved the imperative requirement for an adequate deterrence and defence effort in the face of the Soviet threat. Throughout the Cold War period the Soviet Union deployed military forces with a strong offensive posture in East Germany, in Eastern Europe, and in the western military districts of the USSR. Soviet military power was thus used to support Soviet political and diplomatic objectives and to coerce Western Europe. The United States was the only country capable of counterbalancing the Soviet Union militarily.

Second, the United States, in the German view, provided Europe with vital leadership – political, economic, and moral. The leadership of the United States was perceived as a prerequisite not only for security and stability but also for European unity and reconstruction. In the environment of security created under the American umbrella, Europe could be reborn and its national differences put aside.

On a third level, Bonn perceived the United States as an important political ally. By the late 1940s, the Americans had come to be viewed as the most sympathetic of the Western powers to Germany's security needs and requirements.[11]

Throughout the post–World War II period, the Federal Republic remained politically and militarily reliant on the guarantee provided by the United States, the credibility of which was most directly symbolized by the continuous presence of American forces in Germany during that time. The Atlantic link or Atlanticism thus emerged early on as a crucial cornerstone of the Federal Republic's security policy. Indeed, in the course of the 1950s and into the 1960s, as the many important aspects of this relationship became ever more apparent, the consensus in support of the significance of the Atlantic dimension in German security policy strengthened.

The second theme in postwar German security policy focussed on reconciliation and pursuit of the goal of European unity which would integrate the Federal Republic firmly with its West European partners. France was the key state to be conciliated. Beginning in May 1950 with the proposal of the French foreign minister, Robert Schuman, that the entire production of coal and steel in France and Germany be placed under a joint international authority, France and Germany became the driving force (or "twin engines") of the movement towards European unity. The principal vision behind this movement was the belief that the construction of a European federation would bury Europe's history of war and conflict once and for all.

For the Federal Republic, the relationship with France also provided a necessary political and economic complement to the transatlantic relationship with the United States. However, for many in Germany and in France, a widening of the relationship to include a stronger military/security component also began to attract interest after 1955. From the late 1950s the strong support Gaullist France gave to the German position on Berlin underscored the wider political importance of Bonn's close relationship with Paris. Subsequently, in the early 1960s, when relations with the newly elected Kennedy administration in Washington were seriously strained because of differing military and security perspectives, the Adenauer government flirted with the possibilities of a closer alliance with France. This process culminated in the signing of the Elyseé Treaty in 1963 which set up a structure for closer political and military relations between the two countries.

However, the French conception of an independent Europe united from "the Atlantic to the Urals" excluded both the United States and Britain. Playing the French card as an alternative to the Atlantic link inevitably raised the anxiety level of Atlanticists in both Europe and North America. A closer German political relationship with France therefore came to be seen in Washington and London as running counter to the Atlantic relationship. Moreover, the nature of French security policy meant that any prospect of closer harmonization between the policies of Bonn and Paris would always raise concerns in Washington as well as London.[12]

The third objective of German security policy after 1949 was to move the Federal Republic in a multilateral and collective context to an integrated but fully equal position in the Western community of states. This was a diplomatically delicate undertaking, especially in the early 1950s, when European states (most particularly France) were reluctant to accord the Federal Republic a fully sovereign role in military affairs. For every German government, the restoration of full German sovereignty and the incremental removal of the legal discriminatory restrictions imposed on it remained, above all, an important question of principle involving a recognition of Bonn's symbolic equality. Right up until German unification in 1990, however, the four great power allies retained certain residual rights related to a final German settlement, the status of Berlin, and the stationing of their forces on German territory. Such was the delicacy of questions related to German sovereignty that even though the FRG had been a integral partner in the Western alliance for thirty-five years, the move of Germany to total sovereignty with its unification in October 1990 still raised the concerns of its neighbours. This was most evident in 1989–90 with regard to the states of Eastern Europe (particularly Poland).

The fourth theme in German security policy involved the government's Eastern policy. From the founding of the Federal Republic and of the Western occupation zones in 1949, Germans debated the question of how to balance the country's relations with the West with the goal of national reunification. The Adenauer government, supported by a majority of the German electorate in the 1950s, decided this question squarely in favour of Western integration. For the governing Christian Democratic leaders of the Federal Republic, the importance of orienting Germany to the West went far beyond its day-to-day political, military, and economic dimensions. Its ultimate purpose was to demolish the idea that Germany occupied a unique position between East and West and to bind Germans in a philosophical and spiritual sense to the West. The most important consequence of this orientation was that while reunification remained the declared policy of the federal government, its realization was tied to terms in which a united Germany would maintain all of its links with the West. Only under these terms did the goal of reunification receive the official backing of the Western alliance.

In an effort to force the Soviet Union to consider seriously the question of reunification on these terms, the postwar German government pursued a "policy of strength" (Politik der Starke) which rejected any improvement in the East-West relationship until the question of Germany's reunification had been settled. In essence, reunification became a prerequisite for East-West détente. The Federal Republic, of course, went even further and, under the Hallstein doctrine, pledged to break relations and all contacts with any state maintaining diplomatic relations with the German Democratic Republic. Only the Soviet Union itself was exempt from this policy out of the simple necessity of retaining diplomatic contacts with the Eastern superpower.

For a time the rigidity of Bonn's Eastern policy did serve to reassure Germany's allies that it would remain committed first and foremost to the alliance. Indeed, in the atmosphere of the 1950s, the American secretary of state, John Foster Dulles, certainly viewed German policy as complementary to the American objectives of containing communism and, where possible, "rolling it back." In this sense, Dulles viewed the Federal Republic as a "shining light" for the people of East Germany and thus a tremendous asset in such a strategy. Germany's relationship with Washington was extremely close in this period, with both sides pursuing an uncompromising policy toward the East. Indeed, Dulles apparently went so far as to tell Adenauer in 1956 that on this issue the United States and the Federal Republic were really the only "reliable" members of the alliance.[13]

Balancing the Four Themes

From the beginning the German government sought to maintain a balance among the principal themes of its security policy. Each of the policy themes – Atlanticism, European unity, the goal of sovereign equality, and reunification and relations with the East – sought to address one particular aspect of the process involved in restoring Germany to a position as a reintegrated and fully respected equal member of the international community. But the four themes were always seen to be interlocked and mutually supportive. Indeed, the rise of any one of them to a position where it seemed to overshadow the others inevitably provoked anxieties and suspicions about the ultimate direction of German policy. The need to balance themes was exacerbated by the fact that different political circles within Germany, as well as within Germany's neighbours and allies, often emphasized the importance and significance of one particular theme over the others.

Nevertheless, pushed by internal and external dynamics as well as by the changing perspectives of particular German decision-makers, the relative weight accorded to these themes would vary over the years. As a result, the construction of a permanent and stable equilibrium among them, one acceptable to each of Germany's neighbours and allies, would remain difficult.

Maintaining this balance became most difficult with respect to the Atlanticist and European dimensions of German policy. By the late 1950s and early 1960s the Germans had increasingly come to recognize their own vulnerability to fluctuations in American policy. By virtue of its dependence on American power and on the continued engagement of the United States in Europe, West Germany confronted an "entrapment vs abandonment dilemma"[14] when it assessed the most significant security and defence questions of the day. "Abandonment" entailed the risk and the fear that the United States might arrive at some form of accommodation or settlement with the Soviet Union which would not be in Germany's interests, while "entrapment" involved the prospect that American or NATO policy or strategy might evolve in a direction deemed incompatible with German interests.

Both prospects, abandonment and entrapment, raised the fear of a strategic singularization of the German security position within Europe.

Evidence of this entrapment/abandonment dilemma was observable both in intra-alliance political disputes, such as the Berlin crises of 1958 and 1961,[15] and in military policy conflicts and debates, such as that over the creation of a NATO multilateral nuclear force in the first half of the 1960s.[16] Some of these issues re-emphasized for many Germans the limitations inherent in Bonn's relationship with the United States. This "special" relationship would remain the cornerstone of Germany's security and defence as long as the Soviet threat existed, but it made the Germans exceedingly vulnerable to changes in American policy or strategy. In the course of the 1960s, therefore, there was a growing perception in Germany that the country had perhaps become overly reliant on the United States. Most especially, Germany's hard-line policy towards the Eastern bloc increased the risk of German singular-ization within the alliance now that American policy had shifted to a more accommodating stance.

Concerns over the consequences of American military and diplomatic policy helped contribute to the rising profile of the European dimension in German policy in the late 1950s and early 1960s. However, the European option and closer relations with France could never replace the security afforded Germany by the American guarantee. Thus, in essence, the evolu-tion of German policy in the 1960s was driven by the search for an Atlanticist-oriented security policy which would retain a European component (and thus limit the alienation of France) as well as limit Germany's vulnerability to any fluctuations or changes in American policy. It also increasingly reflected the need to develop a new approach to the East and the German national question which would, in the words of Foreign Minister Willy Brandt in 1966, "relax the situation in a divided Germany"[17] and also bring Germany's Eastern policy into the alliance mainstream which was increas-ingly emphasizing the desirability of a new relationship with the Soviet bloc.

Ostpolitik and the Strengthening of the Multilateral Atlanticist Dimension

In October 1969, shortly after becoming chancellor, Willy Brandt outlined the rationale for his government's new policy initiatives towards the East: "Twenty years after the establishment of the Federal Republic of Germany and of the GDR we must prevent any further alienation of the two parts of the German nation, that is, arrive at a regular modus vivendi and from there proceed to cooperation. This is not just a German interest, for it is of importance also for peace in Europe and for East-West relations." Simulta-neously, he emphasized the continued importance of the Federal Republic's Western links: "Our national interest does not permit us to stand between

East and West. Our country needs cooperation and co-ordination with the West and understanding with the East."[18]

Thus, the famous Ostpolitik of the Brandt government came to have three important dimensions:

1 The normalization of the FRG's relations with the Eastern bloc generally, and with the GDR specifically, from the basis of a strengthened German position in the West.
2 The emphasis on the principle of multilateralism in the Atlantic alliance which would ensure the widest possible support for German policy and simultaneously reduce the Federal Republic's vulnerability to the policy fluctuations of any single power.
3 A stress on the importance of a collective and unified allied approach to East-West issues – as the essential prerequisite to the success of German and allied policy initiatives.

The basis of this approach was set out in the alliance's Harmel Report of 1967. It sought to improve and relax relations between East and West working from a position of strength in which the formal objective of a unified Germany would not be compromised. Thus, the Federal Republic placed a great emphasis on the collective alliance setting as the most important framework for co-ordinating its own bilateral initiatives towards the East in the context of the multilateral diplomacy of the alliance as a whole. In this way the Federal Republic endeavoured to reassure its allies that its policy goals with respect to the German national question would not challenge the primacy of the Federal Republic's links with the West.[19]

This multilateral (as opposed to strictly bilateral) Atlanticist framework came to be perceived within Germany as crucial for both the promotion and the defence of German interests. In this sense, the occasional suggestions from the United States of a new special bilateral relationship with the Federal Republic were usually viewed with apprehension in West Germany as were, for instance, proposals for a more high-profile German political and military role in Europe.[20] Even in the 1970s and 1980s, the notion of substantially increasing the German weight in Europe was greeted by Germany's neighbours and other allies with concern and even alarm. For the Federal Republic then, Atlanticism provided the framework in which its particular political and security interests could be promoted within the alliance mainstream.

This policy approach achieved perhaps its strongest expression under the government of Helmut Schmidt (1974–82). Schmidt was fully conscious of the importance of the American military commitment to both Germany and Europe, yet he was also aware of the vulnerability of the FRG to fluctuations in American policy. Relations with the Carter administration in particular were often strained as a result of alterations in United States policy.[21] Then, during the Reagan administration, the German effort to maintain an open and co-operative relationship with the USSR and especially with the GDR, despite the collapse of détente, further damaged relations. The United States was particularly concerned with what it perceived as the Federal Republic's growing vulnerability to the Soviet Union, in particular in the aftermath of the FRG's decision early in the 1980s to fund the construction of a natural gas pipeline to Western Europe to supply the Europeans with Soviet natural gas.[22]

While the German government's Ostpolitik underscored the principle that interactions with the East could not and would not proceed at the expense of relations with the West, the national question had nevertheless come to assume greater importance on the German policy agenda. Indeed, the whole détente process had been perceived as an important vehicle through which the situation between East and West Germany could be normalized. Consequently, when the détente process came under pressure as a result of growing East-West tensions in the late 1970s, the Germans sought as much as possible to insulate their Deutschlandpolitik from the new divisions between the alliance and the Soviet bloc.

The ascendance of this perspective in German security policy coincided in the 1980s with a growing "angst" with respect to the policy orientation of the Reagan administration. These concerns related to the challenges within the United States to the concept of Mutual Assured Destruction (MAD). The fear that a doctrine which placed primary emphasis on deterrence would be superseded by new strategies which emphasized concepts of war-fighting was reinforced by concerns over implications of the Strategic Defense Initiative (SDI) which many in Europe saw as a move by the United States to insulate its territory from the effects of any war in Europe.[23] The German experience with the shifts in American policy over the deployment of intermediate-range nuclear forces (INF) also contributed to this general anxiety over the evolution of American strategy.

The long-standing German fear of abandonment had always been accompanied by a fear of being entrapped by the evolution of American or alliance policies or strategies which were potentially harmful to German interests. Certainly the fear of Germany becoming a Kriegschauplatz (or theatre for war) was a permanent feature of German domestic politics once NATO began its deployment of thousands of American tactical nuclear weapons on German territory in the mid-1950s. By the 1980s this popular sentiment at the grassroots level had been joined by similar concerns among the élites. By the late 1980s, therefore, Bonn's fear of entrapment had begun to outweigh even its fear of abandonment.

For France, all these developments, in particular the Federal Republic's strong emphasis on the sanctity of its Deutschlandpolitik, raised concerns over the drift of German policy. French initiatives from 1983 thus sought to tie West Germany more firmly to the West and to reinforce the credibility of the French commitment to German defence. Thus, closer co-operation with France on a bilateral basis and multilaterally with other European partners in the alliance again became an important aspect of the security policy of the Federal Republic. Bilateral political and military links with France on the basis of the Elyseé Treaty were reactivated and the long-dormant Western European Union was revived to strengthen the European pillar of the alliance.[24]

Some Conclusions

Throughout the period from 1949 to 1989, the conduct of German security policy demanded a delicate balancing act. The centrality of the German Question to the European balance of power meant that all powers maintained an intense and constant oversight on all the FRG's actions. Although the Federal Republic largely succeeded in integrating itself into the Western community of states in a position of full equality, the issues inherent in the German Question were never fully put to rest. In practice, this necessitated the maintenance of a balance between the Atlanticist, Europeanist, and national aspects of the Federal Republic's security policy.

In the 1950s, the tight bipolar balance of power, the relative weakness of both Germany and Europe, and the similar security perceptions of both the American and German governments resulted in the subordination of the Europeanist, Eastern, and national elements of security policy to the priority of close relations with the United States. By the 1960s, however, the perception of change in American policy, the fear of growing isolation within the alliance, and internal pressure for new initiatives on the national question caused a shift in German policy. Thus the ascendance of Atlanticism in the late 1960s and 1970s was a product of the desire to ensure that German policy remained in the mainstream, thereby reducing German vulnerability to shifts in American policy. Yet this sought-after "middle power role" became increasingly illusive, not simply because of the Federal Republic's own growing power but also because the FRG's Ostpolitik and Deutschlandpolitik, which had thrived in an era of détente, became matters of contention and suspicion when the international climate changed. In part as a response to this development, Atlanticism came under increasing challenge in the Germany of the 1980s. Nevertheless, the continued reality of the Soviet threat ensured its continuing place as the core element of German security policy.

It was in the period after 1969, when Atlanticism and multilateralism were the essential cornerstone of Germany's new Ostpolitik, that the Federal Republic's other transatlantic link – with Canada – acquired enhanced importance. The extent to which this relationship was developed was largely dependent on the orientation of Canada's own foreign and defence policy in this period.

CANADIAN ALLIANCE AND DEFENCE
POLICY, 1945–1989

When one examines Canada's defence and alliance policy from World War II to the end of the Cold War, it is important to place the period in a larger historical context. Between 1939 and 1945 Canada's position in international affairs was transformed. World War II resulted in the death of one international security system and sowed the seeds of another. It gradually became apparent after 1945 that the world was being divided into two principal blocs, one dominated by the United States and the other smaller bloc controlled by the Soviet Union.

This overarching international reality acted as a constraint on Canada's foreign policy options. Canada's wartime role as a junior partner in the larger allied coalition arrayed against Nazi Germany had reinforced the sense of the common values and common interests it shared with the United States and the United Kingdom. This was true of the population at large, but especially within Canada's relatively small foreign policy decision-making community. Canada's decision actively to participate in the Western coalition of free nations is thus not surprising. It was nevertheless a significant shift from Canada's pre-war foreign policy tradition.

Until 1939 Canada had played a very different role in international affairs, a role suited to a very different international system. In the pre-war international system Canada's leaders had believed that the country's interests were best served in the context of the British empire. The empire provided Canada with an opportunity to influence world affairs in a fashion which would never have been possible had it acted independently. This attachment to the empire was also, at least until after the First World War, a very strongly ideological and emotional one. In English-speaking Canada specifically it meant that Canadian interests were identified with those of Britain almost automatically. Canada developed its own foreign policy very slowly, with a Department of External Affairs being formed only in 1909 and full formal autonomy in international affairs only being achieved under the Statute of Westminster in 1931. These factors, combined with the country's relative geographical isolation, made it unnecessary for Canada's leaders or its population in general to concern themselves greatly with foreign affairs or security matters. When examining Canada's post–World War II foreign policy it is always important to remember that Canada is a relatively young state which has been largely spared many of the unpleasant consequences of power politics. These circumstances were to be influential in the way in which Canada formulated its foreign policy after 1945 and in the nature of the defence and alliance policies which flowed from that foreign policy.

Canada's foreign and defence policy has also been closely influenced by the minimal nature, or outright absence, of any direct military threat to the country for most of its history. The result has been a "non-military" political culture.[25] Canadian diplomacy thus lacks a tradition in which military power is seen or used as an active policy instrument, as an instrument designed to achieve larger political objectives. The realist approach to the conduct of foreign and defence policy has always had only a minority following within élite circles in Canada. This is exemplified, for instance, in the assertion by Kim Richard Nossal that "the utility of the CAF [Canadian Armed Forces] as a direct instrument of Canadian statecraft is exceedingly limited." Defence is hardly discussed in Nossal's book, which serves as a text for the study of Canadian foreign policy in many universities, and force is in fact described by the author as "relatively irrelevant" for most states in the international system.[26] The dominant perspectives of international politics in Canada borrow instead from the idealist and neo-realist theoretical approaches.

In his very thorough study of Canada's strategic and military history, Gerard Vano convincingly points out that Canada has always lacked an indigenously formulated strategic or military doctrine.[27] This deficiency has contributed to the creation of a foreign policy which has all too often been unidimensional in nature, unsupported by a complementary military effort. Indeed, the notion of military power as a tool of political policy has been either inadequately understood in Canada or dismissed as immoral and inappropriate for the country.

Likewise, Canada's military policy has always been formulated in terms of commitments to a larger collective effort – be it the British empire, the United Nations, or the North Atlantic alliance. Instead of basing the formulation of defence policy on national assessments of the security issues which directly and indirectly affect Canada, the country's leaders have usually relied on foreign assessments of security problems. The recognition of the need for the formulation of an independent Canadian security policy (combining both defence policy and other political instruments of the state in a single and overarching framework to secure and implement national security objectives) has never taken root.[28]

The absence of an independent Canadian security policy has meant that the country's defence policy has often been tailored to meet those security requirements defined as important by the dominant elements in the larger international groupings to which Canada has been committed. Dissatisfaction in Canada with the types of commitments then asked of the country by these larger international entities has in turn led to half-hearted efforts to sustain those obligations over the longer term. Examples in the Cold War era are numerous and include the nuclear roles grudgingly assumed by Canada in the early 1960s and then abandoned a decade later, the periodic reviews of Canada's military presence in Europe from the late 1950s onward, and the short-lived relevance of the three defence white papers produced between 1964 and 1987.

The paucity of independent strategic thought in Canada was already apparent more than three decades ago. In the 1960s, the Canadian defence analyst, R.J. Sutherland, noted that "Canada has no particular tradition of strategic calculation."[29] He argued that relatively constant factors (both strategic and economic) usually guided the formulation of any nation's security policy over the longer term. However, given Canada's vacuous strategic culture, other factors have traditionally been more important in determining the nature of the country's foreign and defence policies. The importance of pressures from allies and from the larger international groupings of which Canada has been a member has already been noted. The prevailing world-views of particular Canadian governments and leaders – or the lack thereof – have also been significant. In the crucial formative years for postwar Canadian foreign policy, it was liberal internationalism which emerged as the dominant world-view of that element of the national élite interested in foreign policy; and therefore it was upon liberal internationalism that Canada's foreign and defence policies were both based initially. The military commitments thus assumed by Canada were ones which fit into and fulfilled the liberal internationalist world-view.

Liberal Internationalism

In the years after World War II, liberal internationalism emerged as the dominant world-view of that element of Canada's national élite which was interested in foreign policy. Canada sought a constructive role in world affairs in the hope of bringing some measure of influence to bear to create a better international order. Canada's involvement in international organizations such as the United Nations and NATO was a product of this liberal internationalism. It was believed that in such organizations Canada could best work towards the construction of a more stable and more equitable world order.

The liberal-internationalist consensus constructed in the postwar period rested on a common set of beliefs held by the Canadian decision-making élite. For them, liberal internationalism was a response to the great events of the first half of the century. The experience of the two world wars had been a brutal shock for many Canadians. In the First World War some 60,000 Canadian soldiers were killed; another 40,000 would die in the world war that followed only twenty years later. The country's relatively sudden and brutal introduction to European power politics left a decidedly negative impression of the European order, as it then existed, particularly in the minds of many in the liberal Canadian establishment.

The experience of world war provoked two responses. One, which many North Americans embraced in the interwar period, was to try to ensure that North America generally, and Canada in particular, remained isolated and aloof from conflicts in the rest of the world. Mackenzie King, who was prime minister for most of the period from 1921 to 1948, was certainly sympathetic to this view. However, while King sought in 1939 to avoid the automatic commitment which Canada had given in response to the British declaration of war in 1914 by delaying Canada's own declaration of war by one week, he found that Canada was unable to simply stand aside in the face of a direct threat to the peace and balance of power in Europe. Most Canadians perceived Canada's interests to be affected directly by the events in Europe and believed the country could not remain aloof.

As a result of this experience, a second perspective attained a significant following among the national élite following the Second World War. This liberal-internationalist perspective rested on a desire on the part of the country's postwar leadership not to repeat the perceived mistakes of the interwar period. With the memory of war still fresh, Canada's political leaders sought to ensure that the country did all it could to contribute to a stable and peaceful world order.

This internationalist emphasis in Canadian foreign policy is often associated with the philosophical outlook of Lester B. Pearson who served as undersecretary of state for external affairs from 1946 to 1948 and secretary of state for external affairs from 1948 to 1957, before becoming prime minister in 1963. Pearson, as a Canadian soldier in the First World War and a Canadian diplomat in the Second, had seen the ravages of war at first hand. His perspective was that of the liberal humanist. Man, Pearson believed, was essentially a good creature and could contribute positively to the building of a better world. "I believe," Pearson stated, "that there is a higher proportion of men of good-will in the world today than ever before, and that the dazzling technical and scientific developments of our age may be accompanied by an increase, rather than a decrease in that number."[30] Many "Pearsonians" in the Department of External Affairs came to see the nation-state as an institution that had failed. "In any rational analysis," Pearson said, "sovereign power, exercised through the nation state, which came into being to protect its citizens against insecurity and war, has failed in this century to give them that protection. The rationale for change has been established."[31]

The road to change was, in the Pearsonian view, to use the state as a vehicle for the promotion of wider co-operation in international organizations. The two principal international organizations with which Canada became closely affiliated, the United Nations and the North Atlantic alliance, were seen by Canadian decision-makers not only to be promoting altruistic goals connected with the construction of a better world order but also as fitting in closely with the country's own national interests. In short, through involvement in large multilateral organizations it was believed that Canada could make its voice heard and maximize its own influence. In particular, working to ensure that both the United Nations and NATO maintained adequate consultative rights for smaller members came to be an important Canadian concern.

It was through the multilateral framework of NATO that Canada sought, and to some extent achieved, its highest levels of postwar influence. It was also in the North Atlantic alliance that many of Canada's political leaders placed their hopes for the construction of a better world order. Canada's idea that NATO should be more than a military alliance – that it should develop strong political and economic aspects and eventually transform itself into a Western "community of states" – was the most important manifestation of this hope.[32]

Canada's enthusiasm for NATO was also a product of the relatively high level of influence that Ottawa was able to acquire within the alliance. This development was due to the crisis atmosphere of the Cold War which predominated after the outbreak of war in Korea in 1950. Since most of the European allies were unable, initially, to make a major contribution to the collective defence of the West, the Canadian military contribution became that much more significant. As a result, the country was by the mid-1950s devoting nearly 10 per cent of its gross national product and 50 per cent of its national budget to defence.[33] This huge peacetime effort resulted in regular armed forces of some 115,000 to 120,000 personnel, with an additional 60,000 or so in the reserve forces.[34]

However, this "herculean" defence effort, as it was termed by one of Canada's leading historians of defence policy, James Eayrs, rested on the continued acceptance of three key premises: first, that the Canadian effort was necessary to contribute to collective deterrence against a possible Soviet attack on the Western community; second, that an impressive Canadian effort was "buying" the country a continuing influential voice in the alliance's highest decision-making councils; and, finally, that the Atlantic alliance contained within it the seeds for the eventual creation of a Western community of states.

By the late 1950s the international environment had changed. The Soviet threat was perceived as much reduced and the relative weight of the European powers was on the rise. The government's willingness to sustain Canada's defence effort began to erode. Serious cracks appeared in Canada's liberal-internationalist foreign policy consensus; these cracks would widen in the course of the 1960s.

The Collapse of Consensus – Defence Policy Begins to Drift

The change of government in Canada in 1957 was to have a major impact on the conduct of the country's foreign, alliance, and defence policies. The Conservatives who came to office after an absence of twenty-two years did not have the same commitment to the notions of liberal internationalism as the previous Liberal administration under whose auspices it had flourished.

However, the Conservative government of John G. Diefenbaker did not have any concrete alternative concepts on which to construct a new Canadian foreign and defence policy either.

The original deployment of Canadian military forces in Europe in 1951 was to have been a temporary and emergency measure. By the late 1950s the military efforts of Canada's West European allies would dwarf its own small ground and air contribution. Prior to the election of the Conservatives, the Liberal government had already begun to give serious consideration to withdrawing its military forces from Europe. In a top secret memorandum issued in February 1957, the Liberal minister of national defence, Ralph Campney, expressed the hope that this day would soon be at hand. He noted that the American secretary of state, John Foster Dulles, had apparently recently informed the NATO Council that the Europeans "would soon have to expect to provide conventional forces on the continent alone." The memorandum, summarizing Campney's view, stated:

No replacement was planned for the F-86 aircraft. Once it became obsolete there would be little point in continuing to station the Air Division in France and Germany. With the build-up of the German ground forces, the significance of the Canadian Brigade group would be marginal ... Only bringing the Air Division and brigade home would involve very little saving, but disbanding them would mean a reduction in expenditures of $150 million annually.[35]

On the surface and from a strictly economic point of view, it seemed to make little sense to maintain a small contingent of Canadian forces in Europe at the end of a 3000-mile supply line and at considerable cost when the Europeans could provide much larger forces at a much lower cost. However, the Canadian military presence in central Europe had taken on a political importance which made withdrawal difficult. As a result, after its election in June 1957, the incoming Diefenbaker government soon committed itself to maintaining Canada's forces in Europe. However, as will be discussed in chapter 6, little consideration was given to evaluating whether the types of ground and air commitment now being asked of Canada by the allies were really suited to the country's long-term economic capabilities and political interests; it soon became apparent that they were not.

On other military-related issues, a similar "question of relevance" arose during the tenure of the Diefenbaker Conservatives.[36] The most salient of these concerned the CF-105 Arrow fighter aircraft programme. The Arrow had been envisaged and designed as the Canadian air defence fighter for the 1960s and beyond. However, the decline of the bomber threat to North America and the soaring costs of the fighter's development led the government to make the controversial decision to cancel the programme and to purchase cheaper American-designed air defence systems instead.

This decision had a major, and one might argue decisive, political and psychological impact on Canadians. After the cancellation of the Arrow in 1959, an increasing number of Canadians began to question the relevance of any Canadian military effort. Indeed, the decision to cancel the Arrow, coupled with the signing of the Defence Production and Development Sharing Arrangements between Canada and the United States the previous year, oriented Canada's defence procurement firmly towards the acquisition of equipment from the United States. This was to have far-reaching political repercussions. To some degree these were already evident to observers at the time. A *Globe and Mail* editorial of the day argued that those countries which "draw their entire supply of modern weapons from one of the Great Powers ... find themselves bound to support the policies of their armorer ... A nation in that position may be independent in name, but it has no real independence in fact." Similarly, *Maclean's* magazine asked whether "Canada itself" was "obsolete as a military nation." It answered the rhetorical question with a definite "yes."[37] As Vano has argued, the failure to build weapons systems in Canada of "special significance to the Canadian situation" was directly related to the "doctrinal hiatus" in Canada's military policy-making.[38] It was also clearly linked both to the continuing underdevelopment of Canada's strategic and military culture and to the subsequent rise of a stark question of relevance in Canadian defence policy.

In general, the transition from an era when resources for defence were abundant to one in which resources were scarce was very badly managed. The Diefenbaker government, on whose shoulders it fell to make this transition, proved to be poorly informed on many of the key international and military questions of the day. This fact alone was largely responsible for the major crisis in Canada's relations with its allies which erupted in the early 1960s.[39] The key defence decisions taken by the government were badly thought out and their implications never completely considered. When the Conservatives were defeated at the polls in 1963 (in an election precipitated by the crisis generated by the government's refusal to carry through on its pledge to equip the Canadian forces with nuclear weapons as allied strategy directed), the government of Lester Pearson considered itself, not unjustifiably, to have earned a mandate for remaking the country's foreign and defence policies.

The Pearson government's efforts to restore a foreign and defence policy consensus based firmly on an internationalist footing were centred on an effort to recapture Canada's past influence in the United Nations and NATO. In the latter case, this task involved rebuilding the credibility which had been damaged in the Diefenbaker period but attempting to do so on a much smaller budget – one which no longer enabled the Canadian military to carry out many of the expensive and high-profile roles that they had had in the past.

Neither the international environment nor Canada's domestic political climate in the 1960s was conducive to this effort. On the one hand, the "question of relevance" had become a permanent element in the Canadian defence policy debate; specifically, the idea that Canada could not make a contribution of any real military relevance to the defence of North America or Europe had become widely accepted by both the majority of the Canadian public and many decision-makers. The Pearson government's plan to rebuild Canada's defence effort through the creation of a mobile force which would be readily available to either the United Nations or NATO (a policy announced in the white paper of 1964) was an attempt to overcome this reality by finding the country a militarily viable role within the two most important international organizations of which it was a member.[40] However, the doubts concerning the necessity of this effort became evident as the ability to create a viable mobile force foundered in the face of budgetary restrictions which meant a steady decline in the real dollars devoted to defence throughout the 1960s.[41]

At the same time, neither the United Nations nor NATO was enjoying the same support in Canada that they had had in the previous decade. Because the divisions between the superpowers had made it difficult for the United Nations to act, there were serious questions in Canada by the mid- to late 1960s about the viability of basing the country's defence policy in large measure on commitments made to that organization. Somewhat paradoxically, the North Atlantic alliance was also being challenged. Many Canadians (on the left in particular) perceived NATO as an American-dominated institution which had determined the nature and content of Canada's defence policy since its founding. Thus, by the time Pearson resigned as prime minister in 1968, it was evident that the effort to build a new policy consensus on the liberal internationalism of the past had failed.

Pearson's successor, Pierre Elliott Trudeau, approached defence policy from a different perspective. Trudeau believed that Canada's internationalist-driven foreign and defence policy did not properly reflect or serve Canada's own interests. He believed that foreign and defence policy had been driven by Canada's NATO commitments. This he was resolved to change.

Essentially, the foreign and defence policy review of 1968–9 determined that in the past Canada had devoted too many of its resources to defence and that it was in the country's overall interest to downgrade its defence effort significantly. The question of relevance was in essence taken to its logical conclusion. If the automatic security protection afforded by the United States limited the relevance of a major military effort by Canada, and if the value of Canada's forces in Europe in an era of détente was under serious challenge, then large-scale expenditure on resources for defence was a largely futile exercise. This line of thought was not only dominant within the Trudeau cabinet but was also to be found among a large segment of academic opinion.[42]

Thus, in place of the traditional missions envisaged for the forces, the defence review of 1968–9 led to the famous decision to reduce the strength of Canada's forces in Germany by half and to move the importance of NATO down in the hierarchy of defence priorities. The value of the Canadian Armed Forces was now to be cast in terms of their contribution to the protection of Canadian sovereignty and, more generally, to the goals of the Trudeau government's overall national policy. Thus, the 1971 white paper, *Defence in the 70s*,[43] stated that "the Armed Forces combine effective command and organization, high mobility, great flexibility and a range of skills and specialties broader than that of any other national organization. These provide Canada with a resource which may be used to carry out essentially non-military projects of high priority and importance to national development." The white paper also noted that the forces made an important contribution to Canada's identity and would serve the government's purpose in that regard by bringing "Canadians from all parts of the country, from all walks of life, from the two major linguistic groups and other origins, into an activity that is truly national in scope and in purpose." Thus, the Trudeau government's defence policy de-emphasized traditional military tasks in favour of new roles which were, in many ways, non-military in nature.[44]

In the 1964 defence white paper, the maintenance of Canada's forces in a front-line NATO role had been justified on the basis of their symbolic contribution to alliance unity and cohesion.[45] Picking up on this argument, the Trudeau review concluded that if the nature of Canada's commitment was primarily symbolic, then a much smaller and cheaper force would suffice. However, this line of thought proved superficial in that the *political* signals sent by the decision to reduce the country's forces in Europe by 50 per cent were never adequately considered. Nevertheless, despite the impact on Canada's alliance relations, the decisions taken in 1969 were confirmed in the 1971 white paper.

The problem which arose almost immediately after the release of *Defence in the 70s* was that the Trudeau government's de-emphasis of NATO was soon recognized to be seriously out of step with its larger foreign policy goals in Europe. After the Nixon shocks of August 1971, in which the United States imposed a 10-per-cent surcharge on all imported goods, Canada initiated an economic and trade policy programme – the Third Option – to reduce the country's vulnerability and reliance on trade with the United States. The principal focus of this trade diversification strategy was on the European Economic Community (which in 1973 would expand to include the United Kingdom – Canada's largest trading partner in Europe).

The events of this period probably offer the most glaring example of Canada's defence and other policy objectives working at cross-purposes.

While Canada's trade policy was re-emphasizing the importance of Europe, the country's defence policy seemed to be doing exactly the opposite. The evident linkage between defence policy issues and the trade diversification strategy gradually forced the government to revise its defence policy and, by the mid-1970s, to accord NATO a higher priority.[46]

Despite this lesson and the "rediscovery" of the value of NATO in the mid-1970s, the political purpose served by defence policy and military power was still not appreciated. In fact, after the election of the Progressive Conservatives in 1984, the "drift" in Canada's defence policy became even more pronounced in many ways. An examination of the Mulroney government's defence and alliance policies reveals in large measure the same schizophrenic tendencies that the policy of the Trudeau Liberals had exhibited. Unsure of the direction it wanted to take the country's defence policy, the Mulroney government first discussed (in 1985) with its allies the option of completely withdrawing its forces from Europe. (This was to be compensated for by a more credible "northern orientation" in the country's defence policy.) However, after these ideas met with a negative response from the allies, the government abruptly altered course and in the 1987 white paper announced instead a major effort to enhance the Canadian military commitment in Germany. Less than two years later this policy itself fell victim to new budgetary priorities which all but cancelled this build-up.

Competing Foreign and Defence Policy Perspectives

Since the 1960s, Canada's defence and alliance policies have been very vulnerable both to fluctuations in the nation's foreign policy outlook and to currents at play in the country's domestic politics. The root of this problem lies in the lack of any unifying perspective on the country's foreign policy position which might create and sustain a consensus within the national élite in the way the internationalist perspective did from the late 1940s to the 1960s. Instead, since the 1960s various perspectives have vied for ascendancy in setting the Canadian foreign policy agenda.

One perspective, which still retains a considerable following, is based on the traditional internationalist ideas so popular in the postwar years. Defence and alliance commitments are undertaken, to a large extent, so as to help create a more stable and generally better international order. In particular, Canada's co-ordinated action with other like-minded nations in international organizations such as the United Nations and NATO is an essential element of such a policy. However, from the 1960s onward, the original enthusiasm many in Canada had felt for these organizations faded. As tensions between East and West declined in the 1960s, the perceived importance of investing in collective defence was called into question. Meeting the country's military commitments was viewed less in military terms and more as a symbolic or political exercise. As a result, Canada's military capabilities and its ability to meet its commitments eroded significantly. Even after the mid-1970s, when Canada's commitment to NATO received renewed emphasis, military spending programmes were limited to relatively small and largely symbolic purchases of equipment.

A second perspective on Canada's role in world affairs emphasizes the desirability of moving in a more independent direction internationally, especially in terms of the then existing East-West conflict. Since the late 1960s, when the New Democratic Party (NDP) formally adopted the position that Canada ought to withdraw from NATO and the Trudeau Liberals moved to reduce significantly the country's military role in the Atlantic alliance, this perspective has assumed a position of greater importance in the Canadian defence debate. According to some polls during the 1970s and 1980s, around one-quarter of the Canadian electorate was supportive of the concept of neutrality for Canada.[47]

Naturally, those who lean towards a more independent Canadian foreign policy are a fairly diverse group, and they include socialists on the left of the NDP as well as individuals more to the centre of the political spectrum. The 1971 defence white paper reflected the Trudeauvian manifestation of this perspective. Although economic nationalists in the 1960s may have seen NATO as an American-dominated alliance with which Canada should have "no truck or trade," Trudeau's vision was not an anti-American one; rather it simply sought to place greater emphasis on defence priorities closer to home. Nevertheless, the belief that Canada has become unduly constrained by its alliance commitments is common to all who hold this perspective.

The defence component of this independent Canadian policy approach differs depending on the school advocating it. Often, defence is virtually ignored. Others advocate a significant cut in defence spending with a transfer of the saved resources to foreign aid.[48] A minority believes defence policy is an important policy tool, if utilized to facilitate a more independent Canadian foreign policy. Before the 1988 election, for instance, the NDP (influenced by its right wing) suggested a policy under which Canada would withdraw its troops from Europe but increase its defence spending to provide a more effective military effort in North America. In spite of this unique approach, defence policy is generally a low priority for adherents to this second perspective.

A final perspective on Canada's role in world affairs corresponds more closely to realist approaches to international politics. Within this tradition, some neo-realist/liberal–oriented analysts who have looked at Canada's international situation have sought to emphasize its rising position in international affairs. This has especially been stressed in an economic sense and by virtue of the country's role within certain international forums such as the Group of Seven (G-7) major industrialized countries (even if Canadian membership in this "club" was mostly due to a desire of the United States in the 1970s to have a supporting North American voice at the table when dealing with Europe and Japan). This assessment has led some to describe Canada as a "foremost nation" or a "principal power."[49] Defence policy and military power are of little importance in this perspective.

Traditional or "classical" realists have rejected this liberal/neo-realist view of Canada's role in world affairs as inflated and unrealistic. At the same time they believe both the internationalist and the neutralist approaches to Canadian foreign policy to have serious shortcomings. While they regard Canada's alliance relations to be of continuing importance, these analysts also argue for a more assertive and self-reliant foreign and defence policy, with an improved Canadian capability to manage its own immediate strategic environment. This view emphasizes an improved capability to defend the air and sea approaches to Canadian territory and bases the country's defence policy more concisely on strategic and political imperatives.[50]

The influence of this approach could be divined in the goals of both the 1985 defence review and the 1987 defence white paper. Both placed great emphasis on the importance of Canada itself having the forces to control the sea approaches to its territory and to make a more viable contribution to continental defence. This was to be accomplished in part by building up Canada's naval power to establish a truly effective maritime capability in each of Canada's three oceans. There also appeared to be a clear desire to assume a more active military role in the East-West balance of power.

This approach attracted little support, however. In fact, when one examines the ultimate fate of the 1987 white paper, those advocating this approach (particularly within the Department of National Defence) lacked the necessary backing to sustain the policy for even two years.

The failure to establish consensus on Canadian defence policy is the product of a variety of factors. However, the general perception in the majority of these policy perspectives that defence policy is simply not relevant must rank as one of the most critical factors. By and large, much of the political élite in Canada is completely indifferent to the issues surrounding the country's defence policy.

For this reason more than any other, none of the three defence white papers produced between 1964 and 1987 was able to command any sort of consensus in Canada for more than a few years. Partly for this reason as well, the defence portfolio in cabinet has, for the most part, not attracted the interest of the "rising stars" of Canadian politics. Many of those politicians who have served as minister of national defence have gotten out as quickly as possible. Indeed, from 1955 to 1995, Canada had twenty-five permanent and acting defence ministers (an average of one every 21 months). Since most ministers are only in the position for a short while, there is little time for them to develop any real expertise in defence policy. In this regard, General

Gerard Thériault, chief of the defence staff from 1983 to 1986, noted that a great deal of time is absorbed in simply helping a minister to become familiar with the issues of the day. It is not uncommon for a minister to be moved to a new cabinet position just as some expertise has been developed.[51]

Germany, by way of contrast, had fewer than half that number of defence ministers in the same period (only eleven). This no doubt relates to the centrality of defence and security policy questions in German politics. Defence is not now (nor is it likely in the near future to become) an area of any significant interest for those who govern Canada. This fact has had far-reaching implications and consequences for the country's position and standing internationally.

Canadian-German Relations and the Counterweight Conundrum

For most of Canada's postwar history, its governments have placed some emphasis on counterbalancing, to varying degrees, the country's relationship with the United States. Michael Tucker, for instance, has argued that Canada was forced into a continuous balancing act in the conduct of its foreign policy relations in order to offset the influence of the United States. This he has described as the country's "counterweight conundrum."[52]

After the 1960s the search for counterweights and for greater balance in Canada's external relationships became more pronounced. This activity was driven in part by concern over the political implications of the ever growing economic relationship with the United States and by the mounting American "presence" in the Canadian economy. It was also influenced by the increasing attention the country's leaders gave to the problem of national unity. The rise of Quebec nationalism in the 1960s had an impact on the conduct of Canadian foreign policy. A more assertive Quebec, which began to make its own presence felt on the international stage, moved the Canadian government to initiate policies designed to diversify the country's international relations and to give greater expression to the French fact in its foreign policy. Thus, the theme of building a more independent and distinctively Canadian foreign policy became increasingly prominent in this period.

Europe was the obvious focus of this endeavour, and the position of the Federal Republic of Germany in relation to the rest of the continent made that country a natural centrepiece in any counterweight strategy pursued by Canada. Given West Germany's own emphasis at this time on multilateral Atlanticism and the general importance of the Atlantic alliance in the German security policy framework, Canada's military links with the Federal Republic through NATO should have been a natural vehicle for developing its wider links with Germany and Europe.

Yet, despite the desire of every Canadian government, from that of Mackenzie King to that of Jean Chrétien, for diversified international relations, the search for counterweights has never really been translated into a coherent strategy. Instead, it has been only a vague goal, and no attempt has been made to create a co-ordinated policy approach and plan for its implementation. The unco-ordinated way in which the country's defence and foreign policies were conducted for most of the Cold War era provides an excellent demonstration. The erratic nature of defence policy making in Canada, resulting either from indifference, from competing foreign policy perspectives, or from the impact of a changed external or domestic environment, consistently undermined the ability to utilize the country's defence policy to serve wider foreign policy objectives and goals. This failure arose in part from the question of relevance which overshadowed the making of Canadian defence policy after the collapse of the liberal-internationalist consensus. Likewise, the absence of any independent Canadian strategic culture retarded the development of a Canadian security policy.

In terms of Canadian-German relations there were three important repercussions. First, as will become apparent in the examination of the historical record, the country's defence and alliance policies have been unco-ordinated with, or have worked at cross-purposes to, some of Canada's other foreign policy objectives. Second, the limited scope of long-term policy planning has contributed to a highly reactive approach to defence and alliance policy-making. Because of the importance German decision-makers attached to security policy issues, these two repercussions seriously undermined the development of the bilateral relationship.

Most significantly, however, the absence of a viable security policy and the consequent failure fully to develop its relations with Germany and Europe has contributed to the increasing drift towards "continentalism" in Canada's external relations. This incremental movement towards an ever closer relationship with the United States has been very evident in the area of defence policy,[53] but it has been matched by ever closer links with the United States in other areas as well – most especially in the economic sphere. Indeed, despite the Third Option strategy of the 1970s, an effective diversification of Canadian trade never took place. Instead, trade with the United States continued to grow. By the end of the 1980s, some 73 per cent of Canada's exports went to the United States and 65 per cent of its imports came from that country.[54] The Canada-United States Free Trade Agreement, which came into force in 1989, simply formalized, confirmed, and accelerated a trend which had begun long before.

The reality today is that Canada has finally resolved its counterweight conundrum by embracing a closer economic, political, and military relationship with the United States. Prior to these developments which closed out the Cold War era, Germany was central to any counterweight strategy in Europe. In this sense, the Federal Republic formally held a prominent place in the hierarchy of Canada's external relationships. The analysis in the chapters which follow looks at the forty years of the German-Canadian relationship in detail, examining the important initiatives taken by each country towards the other, identifying opportunities which existed for enhancing bilateral relations, discussing the reasons why many opportunities were not exploited, and evaluating the long-term implications of this legacy for Canada today.

PART TWO

The Canadian-German Political Relationship in the Era of Ostpolitik, 1963–1984

3 Trials, Transition, and Change: The Development of Bilateral Relations to the Early 1970s

Until the formal restoration of West Germany's sovereignty and its entry into NATO in 1955, Canada's relationship with the Federal Republic was a limited one. Although Canada established a diplomatic mission in Bonn soon after the founding of the Federal Republic in 1949 and upgraded its emissary there to the rank of ambassador in 1951 (after formally ending its state of war with Germany), the Bonn government's international legal status as an occupied country placed certain practical limits on its relations with foreign states like Canada. In practice, most of Bonn's international diplomacy continued to be conducted with and through the three occupying Western powers.

Two factors, however, provided Canada with a substantive relationship with Germany, even before 1955. First, as a member of the North Atlantic alliance, Canada had a voice (and in the late 1940s and early 1950s that voice was a relatively active and important one) in the formulation of allied political and military policy in central Europe. And the Germans generally regarded the positions Canada took in a positive light. By the late 1940s Canadian policy already favoured the "controlled integration" of Germany into the political and economic life of Europe.[1] Then, in September 1950, Canada officially came out in favour of the rearmament of Germany with Lester Pearson's statement in the NATO Council supporting the American idea of forming German military units as part of an integrated European force.[2] Within a year a DEA policy paper on Western Europe and the North Atlantic community concluded that the ultimate goal of Western policy should be a "political commonwealth of the Atlantic." "The development of the Atlantic Community," the paper noted, "would have to include current moves toward a united Europe and the place of Germany in that unity." As Lester Pearson elaborated in his memoirs:

My own view was that Canada should support in every practicable way the unification of Western Europe. I could think of no more important step in removing the major cause of the great wars of the last hundred years than to end the feud, and the fears, between Gaul and Teuton, which had killed one hundred thousand Canadians in this century. I saw no reason why European integration and a closer cohesion of an Atlantic community need be mutually exclusive. I saw every reason why West Germany, and one day perhaps a united Germany, should be a part of both.[3]

A second factor linking Canada and West Germany was the deployment of Canadian forces to the Federal Republic and Western Europe from 1951. Their presence gave Canada an immediate and direct stake in the evolution of NATO's political and military policy in central Europe. In essence, it made Canada part of the alliance's "core group." It gave Canadian diplomatic interventions on the salient political and military questions of the day a weight and credibility they would never otherwise have had. Thus, even before the full restoration of German sovereignty in 1955, the role being played by Canada in central Europe was fairly widely recognized and appreciated in governing circles in Bonn.

After 1955, when Canada established a direct political relationship with the Federal Republic, links and contacts with the country's new ally intensified. Even in these early years, however, the two countries held divergent perceptions on some issues. With the end of the Stalin era in the Soviet Union, for example, Canada's expressed interest in an improved relationship between East and West intensified – and was reflected in Pearson's visit to Moscow in 1955. The Germans, in contrast, feared that their interests (particularly with respect to unification) might be lost in the shuffle if détente was pursued too vigorously.

As a result, many of the diplomatic positions adopted by Canada at this time were starkly at odds with German interests. These included Canada's generally positive response to new arms control ideas for central Europe (such as the Rapacki plan of 1958–9) and Ottawa's very sympathetic response to British initiatives for a Berlin settlement. Both the content of Canadian policy and (in the view of Herbert Siegfried, the German ambassador in Ottawa) the amateurish style of its implementation aroused German anxieties. Indeed, in the late autumn of 1959 the ambassador warned Bonn that certain aspects of Canadian policy were, in his view, "remarkably naive" and heavily influenced by London. "The pro-British inclination of the present Canadian government," he stated, "which I cannot emphasize enough, has for us the consequence that every diminution ... of relations between Bonn and London ... has its repercussions in Ottawa."[4]

These concerns were echoed elsewhere in the German diplomatic community, with the German embassy in Paris reporting to Bonn soon after a visit by Canada's secretary of state for external affairs, Howard Green, to Paris that in the French view Canada, of all the NATO states, was now "promoting the softest line."[5] Similarly, Dr Hasso von Etzdorf, the head of the German Foreign Ministry's division responsible for Commonwealth, NATO, and American affairs, noted in a letter to the ambassador in Ottawa that concerns over the tendencies in Canadian policy had recently been expressed by the German defence minister, Franz-Josef Strauss. In fact, von Etzdorf informed Siegfried that German concern over the policy directions being taken by Canada was acute enough to ensure that reports from the embassy in Ottawa were now being forwarded regularly to the foreign minister, Heinrich von Brentano, and on occasion to Chancellor Adenauer as well.[6]

German concern was primarily related to the possible influence that Canadian policy might have on the policies of other NATO member-states. The truth of this assessment is supported by German briefing notes prepared for Prime Minister Diefenbaker's state visit to Germany in 1958. They suggested that Canada's ability, through its membership in NATO, the Commonwealth, and the United Nations, to bring influence to bear on a wide variety of issues was one reason for Germany's interest in close relations with Canada.[7]

While Bonn may have perceived Canadian policy as principally the product of the new government's leadership which was idealistically naive, reactively pro-British, instinctively more isolationist, or all three, it seems nevertheless to have had the support of Canada's own diplomatic community. All indications are that by 1959 both Canadian government and diplomatic circles had come to regard German policy, and particularly Adenauer's own leadership,[8] as counterproductive to the collective interests of the alliance and certainly as an obstacle to the goal of constructive negotiations with the Soviet bloc.[9]

By the early 1960s, it was apparent that the policies of Canada and Germany had drifted to opposite poles within the alliance. The signs were on the wall that it would be increasingly difficult to sustain Germany's hardline policy towards the East in an alliance composed of states desiring a more constructive relationship with the Soviet bloc. Similarly, in Canada the Diefenbaker government's approach to foreign and defence policy decision-making had not inspired the confidence of either Germany or the country's other allies. Even the British (whose political positions within the alliance were often closely analogous to Canada's) harboured some suspicions of their own with respect to the Diefenbaker government. As early in 1959, the British high commission in Ottawa had described Diefenbaker himself as "temperamental and emotional" and warned that London would "have to watch taking him into confidence."[10]

The country's hesitation over endorsing aspects of NATO's political and military policies in the early 1960s only magnified these concerns. Indeed, by 1962–3 Canada was in engaged in an open dispute with its allies over its failure to implement nuclear commitments it had previously undertaken. Thus by this time both Canada and the Federal Republic were in danger of being marginalized or singularized within the alliance – Germany because of its hard-line Eastern policy and Canada because of its schizophrenic foreign and defence policy. Over the coming years, both countries therefore sought to move their political and diplomatic policies into the alliance mainstream.

THE ATTEMPTED REVIVAL OF LIBERAL INTERNATIONALISM

When Lester Pearson became prime minister in 1963, the goal of improving East-West relations received an important boost. Indeed, in May 1963, only one month after assuming office, he stressed its importance to NATO ministers in their meeting in Ottawa when he argued that the alliance needed to "keep on trying to solve problems [in East-West relations], one by one, stage by stage."[11] He expanded on this theme in an address to the NATO Council in Paris the following January: "I am sure it is your view that the chances for reaching a more civilized relationship with the Soviet bloc are likely to be better in the next decade than they have been in the past decade. Provided, however, that we realize that there has been no basic change in Soviet attitudes and provided that we maintain during this period adequate and necessary defensive strength." Pearson, in essence, asserted that the alliance had to adopt a dual strategy of deterrence on the one hand and new political initiatives on the other "to achieve a peaceful relationship with the Soviet world, and for a settlement of the problems of a divided Europe."[12]

These ideas were repeated at a meeting in The Hague in May 1964, when Canada reiterated the importance it attached to tackling NATO's most serious problems directly and to re-emphasizing the fundamentals which held the alliance together. These included: the importance of transatlanticism and the resistance of continentalism in both Europe and North America; the need for concrete proposals which would allow a stronger Europe to play a greater role within the alliance; closer interaction and co-ordination between the civil and military sides of NATO; and improved consultation within the alliance in all spheres.[13]

However, aspects of this approach still made the German government uneasy. For instance, Canada's diplomatic position on NATO's multilateral nuclear force had been largely unsupportive of German desires to see such a force established. Indeed, at the Geneva Disarmament Conference, Canada had often showed too great an understanding, for Germany's liking, of Soviet claims that German involvement in such a force would be damaging to the legitimate security interests of the USSR in Europe.[14] Because some recognition of the Soviet Union's legitimate security interests in Europe would be an important prerequisite for the success of any détente process, the Germans had a degree of anxiety about the extent to which some of their own political and security interests might have to be sacrificed. These German concerns had to be faced by the Canadian ambassador in Bonn, John Starnes.[15]

At the same time, however, the importance of avoiding the singularization of the Federal Republic gradually moved the Bonn government in the direction of a new Eastern policy. Indeed, as early as 1964, and in contrast to the more tense and conflictual Canadian-German relationship of the late 1950s and early 1960s, a growing convergence of Canadian and German interests in areas outside the nuclear realm was increasingly evident. In the course of Chancellor Ludwig Erhard's state visit to Canada in June 1964, Prime Minister Pearson confirmed his government's support for reunification, for the freedom of Berlin, and for the principle that neither of these could be sacrificed in any détente process.[16] For his part, Erhard noted that the Federal Republic was moving to expand trading and other contacts with the countries in Eastern Europe and that although still holding to the Hallstein doctrine, the Germans acknowledged that time was "working against them on this issue."[17] The thrust of the Erhard government's policy was to nudge German policy back gradually into the NATO mainstream. Thus, at the NATO meeting at The Hague one month earlier the German foreign minister, Gerhard Schröder, had "commended" Canada for seeking to emphasize the North Atlantic alliance's positive side. Indeed, Schröder had also argued that the erosion of alliance solidarity on key political and military questions had to be halted.[18]

Therefore the Pearson-Erhard joint communiqué "affirmed that the principal cause of tension in Europe was the persisting division of Germany." The support of both governments for the peaceful reunification of Germany was reiterated, and both leaders declared that while it was essential for the West to maintain its defensive military strength, it was also important to utilize every opportunity to widen the possible areas of common agreement with the communist world. In this sense, "both heads of government agreed that a solution to the German Question would create real opportunities to improve the international situation."[19]

The presence of Canadian forces in Germany had given Canada a direct and, potentially, politically important relationship with the Federal Republic. However, that relationship remained underdeveloped even after some ten years of German membership in the North Atlantic alliance. On the Canadian side, this "underdeveloped relationship" was at least partly a product of residual suspicion of Germany and German political objectives, a distrust which had been enhanced by the problematic relations of the early 1960s.

Political consultations were infrequent and not generally close or intimate. Canada's political relations in NATO Europe were instead concentrated on alliance headquarters in Paris, on Britain, and to a lesser extent on France. Once Prime Minister Pearson sought to emphasize allied unity and the desirability of opening a new dialogue with the Soviet Union, Canada's diplomatic contacts within the alliance had to be both broadened and deepened. Relations with Germany were obviously central in this respect. In the autumn of 1965, for instance, reports from both the Canadian ambassador in France, Jules Léger, and the ambassador to NATO, George Ignatieff, emphasized the growing political and military importance of the Federal Republic within both NATO and Europe. Léger, in particular, asserted that many of the problems in Europe and in Canada's relationships with both the East and the allies touched in some respect on the German Question. He noted that German power and influence was growing so significantly that while the Federal Republic had hitherto accepted a second-class status in Europe, this acceptance would likely not last. He argued that since second-class status was implicit in the division of Germany, it was important for all the allies "to face the problem directly and to try to persuade the Germans that the only real way of attaining first class status is by means of a general settlement which would establish genuine equality through disarmament and a European security system."[20] If Canada was to play any role in such a change, an expanded and closer political relationship with Germany was essential.

This was also the view of John Halstead, who became director of the European Division of the Department of External Affairs in 1966. Halstead believed that Canada's European policy had for too long been "carried" by relations focused on the multilateral NATO setting. He recalled later that when he became director, he believed it was important that the country's bilateral European relationships be expanded, most especially that with Germany, a country he believed to be artificially divided and eventually likely to become unified and emerge as a regional great power.[21]

In March 1966 the West German government issued its peace note, calling for an agreement with Warsaw pact states on the renunciation of force in the settlement of disputes. Then in July, the Soviet bloc announced its seven-point Bucharest programme which, among other things, called for an all-European security conference "to discuss security and promote European cooperation."[22] These were among the diplomatic initiatives which would eventually lead to the Conference on Security and Co-operation in Europe (CSCE) in 1972. Robert Spencer records that the Bucharest declaration fully activated Canada's own efforts to promote and facilitate a dialogue between East and West.[23]

After the coming to power of the grand coalition in Germany in November 1966, officials sought to arrange a meeting between Canada's secretary of state for external affairs, Paul Martin, and the new German foreign minister, Willy Brandt. The new Canadian ambassador to Germany, Richard Bower, noted that such a meeting would be valuable in "underscoring the identity of Canadian and German interests ... [at a] time when Germany is in need of some reassurance that she has understanding and support of her NATO partners." Bower remarked that the Germans remained suspicious of Western efforts to move towards détente with the USSR "without seeking to exact any compensatory concessions on the issue of reunification." He therefore believed that at this juncture:

when a broad spectrum of German policies are under review it is particularly important for Germany's Allies to stress their continuing allegiance to NATO, confidence in Germany and support for her legitimate aspirations ... [A meeting with Brandt] might provide [a] propitious occasion to express understanding for Germany's special problems and to reiterate Canada's desire as a NATO Ally to assist in support of legitimate German interests.[24]

While a meeting between Martin and Brandt had been arranged for December in Paris during a NATO conference, it had to be cancelled because of Brandt's need to attend an important session of the Bundestag. The two men were, however, able to meet informally in Paris and later a letter to Brandt was drafted by John Halstead and the European division for Martin's signature.[25] In it, Canada's strong support for Germany's newly emerging Ostpolitik and for its efforts to reaffirm the Federal Republic's firm commitment to the Atlantic alliance was expressed. (Martin made a similar public declaration in support of German policy in the House of Commons on 19 December.[26]) Then, after noting the alliance's recent decision to establish the Nuclear Planning Group which would permit Germany to partake fully in NATO's nuclear policy-making, the German foreign minister was encouraged to throw the full support of the Federal Republic behind a Nuclear Non-Proliferation Treaty (NPT). In Canada's view this would be essential to address the Soviet Union's legitimate security interests in Europe and would also be a key prerequisite for a genuine détente process in Europe.

Brandt's response emphasized that the NATO meeting in December had been "among the more significant events since the foundation of the Atlantic Alliance." At that meeting, the Council had decided, pursuant to the Harmel Report, and in the light of changes in the international system, to re-evaluate the alliance's political policies and to try to identify new objectives and means for achieving them. Brandt asserted that the proposed NATO study "made it clear that the alliance is a robust organism which is able to adapt itself to changing requirements without abandoning its basic principles and objectives." He also thanked Martin for a statement in support of the Federal Republic's Ostpolitik which Martin had made to the Polish foreign minister during a visit to Warsaw earlier in 1966. On the nuclear issue, Brandt noted that the FRG still had certain reservations about the NPT (particularly in terms of the adequacy of the treaty's provision for nuclear disarmament by nuclear-weapons states) but nevertheless expressed his hope for an eventual agreement which would receive universal acceptance.[27]

The Germans were sufficiently interested in Canada's political positions to suggest that the two countries engage in some form of regular consultation "at the official level" in order to "coordinate policy on East/West relations." This discussion was later expanded to cover a wider spectrum of issues, and the first of these consultations took place on 25 October 1967, when Gunter Diehl, head of the German Foreign Office's policy planning section, met with DEA officials in Montebello, Quebec.[28] Then, in December John Halstead travelled to the NATO ministerial meetings to meet with the deputy state secretary in the German Foreign Office. East-West policy issues and bilateral questions were discussed on both occasions.[29]

Such consultations, even if intermittent and not yet institutionalized, were the first such high-level contacts between Canadian and German officials. They indicated that diplomatic circles in both countries were coming to perceive a convergence of interests between the two states. In consequence, both the FRG and Canada viewed it as desirable to improve consultative arrangements so as to co-ordinate and garner support for policy initiatives and positions.

In the period after 1967, the North Atlantic allies agreed to approach all negotiations with the Soviet bloc on the basis of the alliance's Harmel Report, released in December of that year. This report had enunciated three important principles.

1 Maintenance of adequate military strength and political solidarity to deter aggression and other forms of pressure and to defend the territory of member-states, should aggression occur;
2 In the climate of security created by the maintenance of suitable military capability, to pursue the search for progress towards a more stable relationship with the Soviet bloc in which the underlying political issues could be resolved.
3 To resolve the most critical questions, "particularly the German Question," which lay at the heart of tensions in Europe. In particular, the "unnatural" barriers between Eastern and Western Europe, "most clearly and cruelly manifested in the division of Germany," had to be ended.[30]

Each of these principles was vitally important to the emerging negotiating strategy of the Federal Republic. For Canada, too, the Harmel Report represented the fulfilment of the political approach long advocated by Pearson both as secretary of state for external affairs in the 1950s and as prime minister in the 1960s. Therefore by 1966–7, the common political and diplomatic interests of the two countries had become manifest to senior diplomats in both countries. This new collegiality was soon to be undermined, however, and Germany would develop serious doubts about the continued political solidarity of Canada with this collective allied approach.

THE TRUDEAU DOCTRINE
AND CANADIAN-GERMAN RELATIONS

The minister of national defence, Léo Cadieux, was on a visit to Europe when Pierre Trudeau assumed the office of prime minister in April 1968. Trudeau's statements during his run for the Liberal party leadership had raised questions about the direction that Canada's policies might take if he became leader. His scepticism about many aspects of Canadian foreign and defence policies, particularly those involving NATO and nuclear weapons, was well known.

Not surprisingly, therefore, the questions asked of Cadieux at a press conference in Germany on 23 April focused on the future of Canada's foreign and defence policy in general and of the Canadian military commitment in particular. With Canada's NATO allies clearly in mind, Cadieux stated that he did not anticipate any changes in policy in the near future which would affect Canada's forces in Europe. He also asserted that he did not anticipate any reductions in those forces within the coming year and in fact suggested that any reassessment planned by the new government would not necessarily involve a review of the validity of the Canadian commitments but might instead focus on improving them.[31]

Cadieux's hopes were ones the Germans shared. Indeed, the Canadian embassy in Bonn reported that at NATO meetings in Brussels in May 1968 Gerhard Schröder, the defence minister, again emphasized the need for all the allies to reduce their forces only in the context of balanced force reductions negotiated with the Warsaw pact. Likewise, the embassy noted that the permanent German representative at NATO, Wilhelm Grewe, had proposed that the forthcoming NATO meeting in Iceland formally adopt a resolution which would pledge member-states "not [to] reduce their forces except as part of a pattern of mutual force reductions." In this respect the embassy asserted that Cadieux's comments had served "to quieten, if not remove entirely," German fears about the ultimate direction of Canadian policy under Trudeau.[32]

It was soon confirmed, however, that the prime minister had in mind a much more thorough review which would reconsider some of the basic assumptions of Canada's postwar foreign, defence, and alliance policies. On 29 May, in the course of the federal election campaign, Trudeau delivered an important speech on Canadian foreign policy. "We are going to begin with a thorough and comprehensive review of our foreign policy which embraces defence, economic and aid policies," he stated. He also left no room for doubt that Canada's alliance role was under review: "we will take a hard look, in consultation with our allies, at our military role in NATO and determine whether our present military commitment is still appropriate to the present situation in Europe."[33]

The next week the German ambassador in Ottawa, Joachim Friedrich Ritter von Schwerin, called on the Department of External Affairs to express his government's strong concerns. In a discussion with Basil Robinson, a senior official, he emphasized that the Federal Republic attached great importance to the continued presence of Canadian forces in Europe. He stated that for the past two weeks he had been receiving telegrams from Bonn expressing concern about developments in Canada. He also noted that he would be discussing events in Canada with both Chancellor Kurt Kiesinger and Willy Brandt on a visit he was making to Bonn in a few days. Von Schwerin predicted that Brandt would certainly seek to speak to Canada's new secretary of state for external affairs, Mitchell Sharp, at the NATO meeting in Reykjavik in June. When Robinson informed him that Sharp would likely not attend the meeting, because of the election campaign, the ambassador asserted that he would advise his government to find other ways of drawing its concerns to Canada's attention.[34]

At the Reykjavik meeting the allies agreed on the importance of maintaining the alliance's political and military solidarity. In keeping with German wishes, it was decided that no NATO member would undertake any unilateral action which might have the effect of reducing the overall military capability of the alliance. The allies would remain collectively committed to an insistence that any force reductions be mutual and balanced with similar force draw-downs on the Soviet side.[35]

The Soviet invasion of Czechoslovakia in August enhanced the perceived need for alliance solidarity. Discussions at that time between the chief of the defence staff, General Jean Allard, and the supreme allied commander in Europe (SACEUR), General Lyman Lemnitzer, as well as with other NATO chiefs of staff, made it apparent that there was a widespread consensus in NATO on the need to take measures to strengthen national military contributions. The first priority would be to enhance conventional land forces and the second to improve conventional air support capability while maintaining adequate nuclear air strike resources.[36]

At a meeting of the Defence Council of the Department of National Defence on 7 October, General Allard stated that the SACEUR would expect Canada to put forward some constructive proposals for strengthening its military forces at the NATO Council meeting in November. Options for such a strengthening were considered by the Defence Council on 21 October. These included: enhancing the Canadian brigade in Germany by adding additional armoured and infantry elements which would increase its complement by 750–850 men; tasking additional army units with the job of reinforcing Europe including the option of tasking the Canadian Air-Sea Transportable (CAST) brigade to move to the central front to form a division there in a crisis; and deferring a previously planned reduction in Canada's air division in Germany. The army was clearly pushing for an enhancement of its capability in Europe and in this respect its presentation to the Defence Council even included a proposal to pre-position equipment for the CAST brigade group, which had only recently been tasked to reinforce the alliance's northern flank, at the Canadian air base in Lahr. This would allow the army in Germany to build up its forces there to divisional strength quickly in a crisis. The proposal might have meant acquiring duplicate sets of equipment for that brigade (an extremely expensive prospect).

As logical as these plans may have been as a response to the new challenges confronting the alliance in Europe, the attitudes of the prime minister meant that any enhancement of the Canadian commitment in Europe was out of the question. Even so, the defence minister directed that a submission be made to the cabinet's external affairs and defence committee which was to meet on 28 October, complete with cost estimates of the various options.[37]

The only option which apparently survived the cabinet committee meeting to be considered by the cabinet as a whole was a proposal to retain the air division in Germany at a strength of 108 CF-104 aircraft rather than to reduce it as planned (prior to Czechoslovakia) to 88 aircraft. External Affairs was quick to support the maintenance of the air division at its current strength on the grounds that Canada had to demonstrate some solidarity with its Atlantic allies. In a DEA policy memorandum, which Mitchell Sharp reportedly supported, it was argued: "Canada should join appropriately in [the] collective [allied] response ... [and] accept the desirability of improving the military preparedness of the Alliance ... [it should support] a reappraisal of plans and policies ... [and indicate] the measures it proposes to take concerning its military contribution, it being understood that such measures would not prejudice the defence policy review."[38]

The prime minister was, however, of a different mind. During a cabinet meeting on 7 November, Trudeau made it clear that he opposed any, even a symbolic, strengthening of the Canadian military effort in response to events in Czechoslovakia. Specifically, he believed that Canada should go ahead with its planned reduction of the air division in Germany. He made only one concession: that the Canadian delegation at the NATO meeting should be given "some leeway to report back to the government on the situation." While their initial position should be that Canada would maintain the decision to reduce the air division, "this could be reconsidered if Canada was the only one breaking a united front."[39]

As one American commentator later confirmed, Canada did indeed prove to be "the one hold out" in Brussels to measures designed to improve the alliance's defensive posture in response to the crisis in Czechoslovakia. To avoid breaking completely with its allies, Canada deferred the reduction of the air division.[40] Despite this decision, which "averted undue difficulties for the time being," according to Ross Campbell, Canada's permanent representative to NATO, Canada's defence review and its planned force reductions were causing the delegation "serious embarrassment."[41]

As Bruce Thordarson records, many of the allies made their concerns with the direction of Canadian policy apparent to Canadian officials, including the prime minister (in his January 1969 visit to Europe and the Commonwealth Conference in London),[42] during and after the NATO ministerial meeting. On 13 November 1968, when, on a German initiative, Willy Brandt and Mitchell Sharp met during the NATO meeting in Brussels, Brandt described the discussion in the German cabinet during which it had been decided "that it was right to make it clear to the Russians that we intended to maintain a proper balance of power in Europe." Brandt urged Canada not to reduce its contribution to the effort in central Europe which, although small in overall numbers, was nevertheless important in terms of quality and important in terms of the solidarity of the alliance. "Canadian withdrawal," he argued, "if it were to come, following the French withdrawal [of 1966], could cause great damage to the unity and effectiveness of NATO." He also argued that "if the Russians thought NATO was going to fall apart, the chances of resuming … détente on conditions acceptable to the West would be slim indeed."

Sharp, however, contended that the defence review in Canada was at least partly a response to the fact that Canada's resources were limited and that the government was attempting to determine how best to allocate those scarce resources. Canada's position in NATO was a unique one. It was not a great power and not a European country and as a result "Canadians in general felt their contribution was not vital to NATO." Moreover, Canada had slightly different views "about the significance of events in Czechoslovakia in terms of future Soviet intentions."

These statements appeared to heighten Brandt's own concerns since he then inquired what Canada's views were towards the usefulness of continuing the alliance at all. Sharp tried to respond emphatically that Canada had no intention of withdrawing from NATO and the only issue was the choice of an appropriate contribution. In response, the German foreign minister stressed the important role that Canada had played in the past and asserted that the maintenance of such a role was "both possible and necessary in the future."[43]

Brandt's statements probably reflected genuine concern over the possible implications of Canadian actions for the Federal Republic's developing Ostpolitik. In German eyes, Canadian policy was at risk of becoming a hindrance to NATO and German policy. This view was shared by most other Europeans, and even the French prime minister, Maurice Couve de Murville, had reportedly counselled caution, when Trudeau had asked him about the consequences if Canada withdrew its forces from the integrated military structure of the alliance, as France had done.[44] A new policy direction for Canada was already set, however, given the orientation of both the prime minister and most of the ministers in the government.

After a stormy debate within the cabinet, which has been well chronicled by Robert Bothwell and J.L. Granatstein as well as others, the results of the defence review were announced in April 1969. Contrary to the advice in both the interdepartmental task force (STAFFEUR) report and the recommendation of the House of Commons Standing Committee on External Affairs and National Defence (SCEAND),[45] the government had decided to undertake a phased reduction of Canadian forces in Europe and to reduce the importance of NATO in Canada's defence and foreign policy. The decision also ran counter to the strong advice given by Canada's permanent representative to NATO. In his submission for the STAFFEUR report Campbell had argued that allied defence efforts in Germany should also be viewed in terms of the confidence they gave to Germany, and asserted that "if there is to be any forward movement on East/West issues it will be necessary to retain [the] confidence of Germany."[46]

The decision, announced on 3 April, was made after a stormy series of debates within the cabinet and the cabinet defence committee, and it had nearly caused the minister of defence, Léo Cadieux, to resign. In the course of these debates, the cabinet in fact considered a report prepared in the Prime Minister's Office, which called on Canada to reduce its armed forces to 50,000 men within ten years and commit only an 1800-man Canada-based "task force" to the alliance. Even this proposal was a moderate one in that several members of the cabinet had argued for Canada's complete withdrawal from the alliance. In the end, Cadieux only agreed to remain after Canada's alliance membership had been confirmed and after Trudeau agreed only to announce a "planned and phased reduction" in the forces in Europe and not a complete withdrawal. Many, particularly in DND, apparently thought that a complete withdrawal was nevertheless the ultimate goal, and it was not until the cabinet meeting of 20 May that the maintenance of at least some troops in Europe was confirmed. Given the far-reaching and revolutionary nature of the changes to Canada's defence and alliance policy being discussed, the decision to keep some troops in Europe was actually a sort of victory for the pro-NATO members of cabinet.[47]

Contrary to the account of Granatstein and Bothwell which describes the allied reaction to the Canadian decision as "relatively restrained," the response of its allies to Canada's decision was extremely negative.[48] At both the NATO foreign ministers meeting of 10–11 April in Washington and the May NATO ministerial meeting in Brussels (at which the details of Canada's force reductions were spelled out), Canada was severely and emotionally criticized. One American apparently described the May meeting as "the toughest talk I have ever heard in an international meeting." The Europeans, as Granatstein and Bothwell admit, feared that Canada's cuts might serve as a "stalking horse" for American withdrawal.[49]

This was certainly one of the German worries. In the course of the review, German concerns had been set forth both in a letter from Brandt to Sharp on 14 February 1969[50] and in personal meetings with SCEAND members when they visited Bonn in March. The Canadian members of parliament met with both Helmut Schmidt (chairman of the Social Democrat caucus in the Bundestag) and Karl Monmer (the SPD's defence expert). In their meetings in Bonn and through earlier testimony given in Ottawa by Theo Sommer (deputy chief editor of the liberal newspaper, *Die Zeit*), the parliamentarians were appraised of German fears that a Canadian withdrawal from its military commitments could lead to a "chain reaction" among other alliance members which could put NATO in a difficult and weakened political position. Most importantly, the Canadian decision, in German eyes, "poured water on the millstones" and encouraged the efforts of some members of the United States Congress, like Senator Mike Mansfield, who wanted to reduce the American troop presence in Germany.[51]

In the aftermath of the Canadian government's announcement, German government officials began to voice these views publicly. The defence minister, Gerhard Schröder, "regretted" the Canadian decision on "political, military and psychological grounds," while Chancellor Kiesinger, in an interview with *Welt am Sonntag*, confirmed the long-standing allied view that 10,000 Canadian troops, while not large in absolute numbers, had a significant political weight. "Without doubt," he stated, "considerable reduction or complete withdrawal of these troops could psychologically weaken the alliance. Aside from this, such a decision immediately preceding the start of possible new negotiations with the Soviet Union is not favourable. It is my view that a reduction in the strength of NATO must be accompanied by a balanced reduction [of forces] on the Eastern side."[52]

It was clearly the German view that Canada had reneged on the pledge made in Reykjavik less than a year before to abstain from any unilateral reductions in the military strength of the alliance. Many in the alliance judged the Canadian decision in the same light as France's decision three years before to withdraw from the integrated military structure. Such was the importance to its allies of the transatlantic dimension of NATO embodied in Canada's commitment.

Although a decision had been made, many important aspects of its implementation had still to be considered: most specifically the size, composition, and configuration of the Canadian forces which were to remain in Europe. As part of their effort to influence this process, the Germans were able to utilize the pre-scheduled 8–10 April visit of Willy Brandt to Ottawa. "We all need Canada," Brandt remarked on his arrival to Ottawa. As the *Osnabrücker Zeitung* reported, he deemed it essential to declare clearly how vital continued Canadian engagement in NATO was to the European allies and to warn against underestimating the consequences for the whole alliance of the Trudeau government's decision.[53]

The usually well-informed *Frankfurter Allgemeine Zeitung* reported that Brandt was hoping for an "arrangement" with Canada. The core of his argument in meetings with both Sharp and Cadieux was the political implications which the German government saw arising from the Trudeau government's decision. German officials were to make the case, for instance, that Bonn viewed every weakening of the alliance's conventional forces at this time as an undermining of NATO's strategy of flexible response. Similarly, the Canadians were to be reminded that they could be forced to give up influential NATO staff positions, depending on the size and nature of their final force reductions.[54]

Following his talks with the minister of industry, trade and commerce, Jean-Luc Pepin, Brandt noted to a German reporter that he had also raised the issue of other negative implications for Canada inherent in the defence policy decision.

Foreign Trade Minister Pepin complained ... that Canada feels itself neglected in many of the decisions made by the European Economic Community. Canada, as a large supplier of food as well as raw materials, feels itself insufficiently recognized. [But] I want to state openly that more than one of the participants in these talks ... has drawn attention to the connection between this adequate recognition and the Canadian inclination, or the inclination of certain circles in Canada, not to engage themselves politically as strongly as they have in the past. We have to reflect quite seriously on this fact.[55]

In alluding to this linkage of economic and defence matters, the Germans may have been hoping to induce Canada to modify its plans. Indeed, the *Frankfurter Allgemeine Zeitung* had reported that Canada had already indicated its willingness to take fully into account the views of its allies at the forthcoming meeting of NATO defence ministers in Brussels.[56] This might give the Germans and other allies another opportunity to modify the Canadian decision.

If the Germans hoped to use the Brandt visit to influence Canadian policy, they had only a limited effect in the short term. Trudeau had already departed Ottawa for a short vacation prior to Brandt's visit, making it impossible for Brandt to speak directly with the prime minister. Likewise, cabinet unity had already been stretched to the limit in coming to the decision. However, when cabinet decided on 20 May to reduce the forces in Europe by two-thirds of their 1969 strength, it was also agreed – in anticipation of possibly strong

NATO opposition – that modifications might be made, should they be strongly desired by the alliance.[57] German protestations may at least have helped to alert the government to European concerns, and after the May NATO meeting the reductions were modified to only a 50-per-cent cut. (For further discussion, see pp. 127–32.)

Even though the final Canadian force commitment made to the alliance in September was not as small as it might otherwise have been, the country's relations with both NATO as a whole and with the Federal Republic had suffered a serious political setback. For the second time in a decade, Canadian policy was out of step with the alliance mainstream.

First, in the perception of its allies, Canada had broken NATO unity at a particularly critical time. On the one hand, in the aftermath of the Soviet invasion of Czechoslovakia, the Canadian decision to reduce its forces in Germany while the other allies were emphasizing the importance of a united stand was perceived in Europe as a break with both the principles of the Harmel Report and the allied declaration at Reykjavik. On the other hand, Canadian actions were seen as undermining the credibility of any allied approach to the Soviet Union on the question of mutual balanced force reductions. For the Germans most especially, the Canadian moves were viewed as most unhelpful in terms of supporting the credibility of the German negotiating position with the USSR in its evolving Ostpolitik. If the Canadian decision were to lead to a sense that the security and defence structure which protected the Federal Republic was unravelling, then Soviet concessions would become unnecessary.

Second, the Trudeau government's new approach to defence policy was perceived as having certain possible implications for the transatlantic relationship. There was some concern that the Canadian decision was an indication of rising "neo-isolationism" in North America as a whole.[58] And, indeed, the Trudeau government had justified its decision to scale back its forces in Europe on the grounds that it might have to provide additional resources for the protection of Canadian sovereignty and North American defence. The review had elevated both these tasks to a greater priority than that assigned to NATO tasks. Sharp had even used this "limited resources argument" to justify a possible cutback of forces in Europe in his talks with Brandt in November 1968. In light of the political debate then under way in the United States Congress over cuts to American forces, it is not surprising if the Germans saw the Canadian decision as foreshadowing a shift in North American attitudes towards Europe.

Finally, the specifics of the Canadian decision had certain implications for allied strategy which the Germans found worrying. The Canadian brigade with its Honest John rockets was an integral component of both the NATO forward defence and flexible response strategies. In the perceptions of both Germany and alliance headquarters (SHAPE), allied deployments in central Europe had, first and foremost, to support a forward deterrent posture based on posing "incalculable risks" to any aggressor.[59] The movement of the Canadian brigade off the NATO front line to a reserve role was thus a most unwelcome development for both the German Ministry of Defence and SHAPE. Similarly, the simultaneous decision of the Trudeau government to abandon all nuclear roles for the Canadian forces in Europe by 1972 (a role essential to both flexible response and forward defence) would make Canada the only NATO ally (besides tiny Luxembourg) with forces on the central front to have rejected the nuclear role.

The long-term implications of the defence announcement of 1969 for Canada's wider political and economic interests were far reaching indeed. As Sharp records in his memoirs:

The mishandling of the NATO decision had unfortunate repercussions for years on relations between Canada and our allies in Europe and the United States. The Prime Minister himself discovered this when he sought to establish a contractual link with the European Economic Community (EEC) for economic purposes and eventually became one of the staunchist defenders of our continuing participation in NATO. From what I heard from contacts in Europe and the United States, the mishandling of the NATO decision in the early 1970s [sic] was one of the things that affected adversely the reception in the western world of Trudeau's peace initiative in the early 1980s, ten years later.[60]

In examining the Trudeau decision and its implications, it was not surprising that the general allied impression was that Canada was interested in scaling back its relationship with Europe. Indeed, in German eyes, this trend in Canadian policy was confirmed in the decision, announced by Canada on 3 November 1969, to close its military mission in Berlin. The Germans were apparently not entirely satisfied that the decision to close the mission was taken solely for economic reasons. However, in its public reaction, the German government simply expressed its regret at the move, noting that the presence of friendly nations in Berlin was regarded as a "precious contribution to the viability of the city."[61]

It was clear, that as the former lord mayor of Berlin, Willy Brandt, moved from the foreign ministry to the chancellor's office in the autumn of 1969, Germany's relationship with Canada was not on the best terms that it could have been. In the years that followed, both Canadian and German officials would seek to build on what were generally very similar political perceptions and to repair some of the damage done in the early Trudeau years.

THE SCHMIDT INITIATIVE

When Willy Brandt became chancellor, Helmut Schmidt became Germany's minister of defence. Since its creation in 1955, the Defence Ministry had been under the guidance of conservative politicians, and Schmidt, as the first

Social Democrat to hold the post, brought some new ideas to the office. Schmidt had initially been an opponent of equipping the Bundeswehr with nuclear weapons. By the late 1960s, however, he had become an avid supporter of the NATO strategy of flexible response which had been formally adopted by the alliance in 1967. In contrast to his conservative predecessors, he was most interested in improving the alliance's conventional military capability on the central front, which he regarded as essential both to maintain a proper military balance with the growing capability of the Warsaw pact and to pursue a credible negotiating strategy on balanced force reductions with the Soviet bloc.[62]

In consequence, Schmidt viewed the reduction in Canada's forces with particular concern. Indeed, soon after taking office, he apparently strongly criticized the Canadian decision at the December 1969 NATO meeting in Brussels.[63] During 1970, however, Schmidt seems to have become convinced of the need for a more positive approach towards Canada. This approach came to be centred on measures which would have some impact on righting the deficit in military expenditures which Canada currently faced.

Since the early 1950s, Canadian military expenditures in Germany in support of the brigade and air division had directly benefited the German economy. Although the FRG had concluded offset agreements with both the United States and Britain to cover their costs of stationing forces in the Federal Republic, no such agreement had been concluded with Canada which had always paid for the upkeep of its forces on its own. The only reciprocal procurement arrangement between Canada and the FRG was the Research, Development and Production Agreement signed in 1964. This had been designed to facilitate German military procurement in Canada and to help balance Canadian military expenditures in the Federal Republic. However, Canadian military spending in the FRG, even after the reduction in strength which occurred after 1969, still totalled over $60 million per annum. At the same time, German procurement in Canada amounted to only $26.5 million in 1971 and $9.1 million in 1972. Canadian procurement in Germany was even lower – a mere $4.5 million in 1971 and $1 million in 1972. This deficit in the military balance of payments was matched by a growing overall deficit for Canada in its total trade with the FRG – which had amounted to over $300 million for the 1965–9 period and which continued into the 1970s.[64]

In looking at the options for rectifying this imbalance, Bonn determined that because the German army was in need of enhanced training space, the option of training German troops in Canada should be examined. Since the formation of the Bundeswehr in 1955, it had been necessary to conduct much of its training outside the Federal Republic. Most was done in the United States; for instance, all primary flight training and much of the advanced training of Luftwaffe pilots. Some training had also been carried out elsewhere, including in Canada. In the late 1950s several hundred German flight crew had been trained in Canada as part of the sale by Canada to the Federal Republic of 225 F-86 fighter jets, and, more recently, in the 1960s, the Bundeswehr had conducted numerous cold-weather trials of military equipment in Canada.

A plan was formulated in the German Defence Ministry under which the German army would seek to train some of its forces in Canada. This plan would enable the army to take advantage of facilities and opportunities which might exist in Canada but which were in short supply in the Federal Republic. In the course of the 1960s, the German army had acquired heavy armoured and artillery equipment and with both German and allied units needing training space in the Federal Republic, there was a requirement for additional facilities where the new heavy forces would have greater freedom of manoeuvre as well as "live fire" opportunities. A decision was made to approach Canada about acquiring facilities for advanced training of armoured and artillery units at the platoon and company level.[65]

In early December 1970, when Canada's new minister of national defence, Donald Macdonald, visited Bonn, the plan was formally presented by Schmidt for the Canadian government's consideration. Schmidt frankly asserted to Macdonald that "his motives in putting forward these ideas were political." He thought it would be desirable, on the one hand, to help Canadians to understand the German role in the alliance and, on the other hand, to educate Germans on Canada's own place in NATO. In his view it was important for both the FRG and Canada to facilitate contacts so as to avoid the polarization of the alliance into European and American camps. To help right the balance in defence trade, Schmidt also offered to send Ernst Mommsen, his state secretary in charge of research, development, and procurement, to Canada to look at expanding armaments co-operation. He noted that he was so interested in closer co-operation with Canada that he was willing to pay "some higher costs," if it was clear that advantages would accrue.[66]

In response to Schmidt's initiative, it was agreed that the two defence ministries would exchange questionnaires to deal with specific aspects of both German requirements and Canadian facilities. Schmidt had noted that the Germans preferred to move ahead with training, beginning in 1971, and the Canadian ambassador in Bonn indicated on 11 December that the Germans might have their questionnaire ready within two weeks. However, on the Canadian side, movement was considerably slower, because talks already under way with the British on a similar proposal were occupying personnel and because the decision-making process was more cumbersome.[67]

This drawn-out negotiating process ensured that it would take another three years before the first German troops arrived for training at the Canadian Forces base in Shilo, Manitoba. Despite the long delay and the clear option

of seeking training facilities elsewhere, the Germans were sufficiently committed to developing the relationship with Canada to refrain from abandoning the discussions. When it finally proceeded, training involved two
battalions at a time for three weeks of intensive exercises from the spring
through the summer and into the fall (some 5,000 troops per year). Initially,
the Germans opted to train armoured and self-propelled artillery units at
Shilo. Later in the 1970s, they changed the focus of their training by deploying
armoured-infantry formations (in place of the self-propelled artillery)
together with the tank units.

The arrangement proved so satisfactory that the original ten-year agreement was renewed in 1983 and again in 1993. By that time German training
in Canada had been expanded, through a 1981 agreement, to include low-
level flight training by the Luftwaffe at the Canadian Forces base at Goose
Bay in Labrador. In 1986 Germany was a signatory (together with the United
Kingdom and the United States) to a multinational memorandum of understanding for the use of Goose Bay. The agreement, to run initially for ten
years, allowed the Luftwaffe to deploy 400 military personnel and 25 fighter
aircraft at any one time for low-level flight training. The German combat
aircraft most commonly using Goose Bay were the Tornado and the F-4F
Phantom. Air and ground crews were normally deployed to Goose Bay from
the Federal Republic on two-week rotations for intensive flight training.[68]

The number of sorties conducted by the Luftwaffe steadily increased after
1980, when the first training flights were conducted. From some 400 sorties
in 1980 and about 1100 in 1981, the number of German flights had grown to
nearly 4000 a year by the early 1990s. Of all the allies which were party to
the 1981 agreement, the Germans were the biggest users of the Goose Bay
facility, flying about half of all sorties flown from the base. Training at Goose
Bay allowed the Luftwaffe to conduct exercises at altitudes which were simply
not feasible in Germany, often as low as 100–200 feet.[69]

The economic spin-offs for the regions around Shilo and Goose Bay were
considerable. In Goose Bay, for instance, the physical infrastructure of the
base was valued at about $1.3 billion. By the early 1990s, the annual budget
of the base totalled over $200 million. Some 1000 civilians were either
permanently or temporarily employed there in addition to 600 Canadian
and allied military personnel (not including allied airmen on temporary
training deployments). Instead of being run down, and possibly closed, in
the early 1990s – a near certain fate in the absence of allied training there –
the base actually expanded between 1987 and 1992 and the number of permanent employees at CFB Goose Bay increasing by 150 to some 1500.[70]

The direct and indirect impact on the local economy in Labrador was
significant, with some $15.5 million spent in 1991/2 in the region around
Goose Bay as a result of activities at the base. The German share of this
amount was around $6.1 million. Other estimates of the base's wider
economic impact were even greater, with one study suggesting that the base's

operation added some $128.3 million to Newfoundland's gross domestic product in 1992 while Canada's gross domestic product benefited to the tune of about $282.5 million.[71]

Germany has been the most important and significant of the allies using Goose Bay. Its infrastructure investments and annual financial outlays in support of training there have been of crucial economic importance to Goose Bay and Labrador. In the case of Shilo, the German presence was solely responsible for keeping this base afloat following the Canadian defence budget cuts of the early 1990s. Without German training at Shilo, the base (which injected about $6.7 million annually into the economy of the Brandon region and generated some 470 direct and indirect jobs) would surely have been closed.[72]

It appears that political factors played a prominent, if not dominant, role in the German initiative of 1970 to use military training as a vehicle to establish a closer bilateral defence relationship with Canada. Certainly, it would have been possible for the Germans to find sites in other NATO countries if their sole objective was training their ground force units. From a strictly military point of view, and possibly even economically and financially, a site in the southern United States would have been more logical and could have been utilized year round.

Taking Schmidt's comments at face value, however, it seems that Canada was selected both to make a tangible political demonstration of Germany's interest in persuading Canada to continue its military commitment to Europe and to seek some diversification of the Federal Republic's transatlantic links. This action may have had some effect on Canadian policy, and by the spring of 1972, the minister of national defence was assuring Schmidt that Canada would be making no further reductions to its forces in Europe. This promise took no account, however, of the obvious difficulties which Canada faced in proceeding in a time of budgetary restraint to meet the urgent need of those same forces for new equipment. For his part, Schmidt offered to keep Canada "sufficiently informed" about activities of the Euro-Group so that Canada could participate more fully in armament projects as they developed.[73]

While the German Defence Ministry's interest in the continued presence of Canadian forces in Germany was clear, the implications of the Schmidt initiatives were more far reaching. Since the late 1960s there had been indications of a widening general interest among Germans in improving their relations with Canada.

MISSED OPPORTUNITIES? THE RESPONSE TO OTHER GERMAN INITIATIVES

In June 1967 the embassy in Bonn made a report to Ottawa which coincided with the state visit of President Theodore Heuss to Canada. The report noted ten distinct areas in which the Department of External Affairs saw opportunities for expanding relations between Canada and Germany. These included bilateral defence, co-operation in scientific research, parliamentary exchanges, and exchange visits between government leaders.[74] In each of these areas the Germans had in fact initiated efforts to improve the bilateral relationship.

Once again, political rationales appeared to provide the primary reasons for the wider German interest in developing its relationship with Canada. In late 1967, for example, the Germans approached Canada on the possibility of a co-operative endeavour to establish a uranium enrichment plant in Canada. A memorandum from John Halstead of the European Division at External to the Economic Division noted that although German co-operation with the United States was perhaps most attractive from a technical standpoint, "a non-USA source would be politically welcome to the Germans."[75] The motivation for this initiative, among others, was clearly political rather than economic and reflected a German desire to diversify its alliance relationships.

There was also keen German interest in Canada's proposal for European nations to join in the development of a multi-role combat aircraft. The idea for a Canadian multi-role aircraft originated in 1967 with the call from the minister of defence, Paul Hellyer, for the department to explore the possibility of entering into a programme with one or two selected European allies. It had been directed "to work with Industry, Trade and Commerce and the Department of Defence Production to establish an agreement in consort with one or more countries on a common military requirement, a national objective for the Canadian aerospace industry and a consortium business management plan."[76] A six-member NATO consortium including both Canada and the Federal Republic was then created on 17 July 1968 to develop this aircraft.

Initial discussions had taken place in March 1968 in Bonn, and German and European officers had visited National Defence Headquarters in Ottawa for a briefing on the concept.[77] In a briefing for the minister of defence and the minister of industry, trade and commerce in March 1968, Brigadier-General W.K. Carr, director-general air forces, noted that the Europeans "preferred an aircraft program which would not tie them to the United States."[78] The Canadian embassy in Bonn had noted this emphasis, asserting in a message to National Defence Headquarters in February 1968 that in initial discussions both the Germans and the Canadians had placed "a great emphasis" on carrying out this project "with the widest possible independence from the USA."[79]

Canada had envisaged the multi-role aircraft as a replacement for both the CF-101 in North American air defence and the CF-104 in NATO. The total requirement for the Canadian Forces was envisaged to be some 250–275 aircraft and apart from the military need for the aircraft, the minister of industry, trade and commerce warned that "Canada could slip behind in the military industrial field unless it participated in such a program."[80]

Nevertheless, soon after joining the feasibility study portion of the project in July, the government was balking at the costs associated with the first phase of development of the aircraft. In August 1968, the German defence minister, Gerhard Schröder, had visited Canada at his own request and the aircraft project would have certainly been an important topic of conversation. The embassy in Bonn reported in September that the Germans were "pushing hard on this project," and, indeed, in September 1968 a telegram from the German Defence Ministry to the deputy minister of national defence urged Canada to sign the memorandum of understanding on phase I of the project; the telegram noted that "Canadian cooperation in the program [is] ... highly desired."[81] Despite obvious German enthusiasm, Canada opted out of the programme even before the project definition phase began in May 1969. The European partners then went ahead on their own with the development phase of the project which began in July 1970. When procurement commenced in the latter 1970s for the three remaining partners (West Germany, Italy, and Great Britain), the initial production run totalled some 809 aircraft (see also pp. 91–4).

The German interest in enhancing transatlantic links with the other North American member of NATO also extended into the parliamentary sphere. One of the more interesting initiatives came from a group of three German parliamentarians (representing the major German political parties) who expressed interest in creating a parliamentary association between the Bundestag and the House of Commons. One of the parliamentarians was Hans-Dietrich Genscher of the Free Democratic Party.

In May 1969 Genscher had lunch with an official of the Canadian embassy in Bonn following a visit to Canada. He thought it important to destroy some of the myths which existed in both countries about the other. Likewise, while Canada needed German investment to diversify its sources of capital, the Federal Republic was interested both in exporting its growing surpluses of capital and in finding new sources of raw materials. Finally, he believed there to be a large potential for co-operation in other fields and had as a result "come away from Canada feeling that both countries had much they could offer each other."

This was apparently the second approach by the Germans on the matter of a parliamentary exchange, the first having been made in March 1967. That approach had received an unenthusiastic Canadian response and Ottawa was now urged by the embassy in Bonn to avoid rebuffing the German parliamentarians a second time for fear that they would lose interest. The troop reductions had been viewed in many German quarters as a sign of Canada's political disengagement from Europe. It was the view of the embassy that some gesture should be made to offset this unfavourable impression of Canada.[82]

Unfortunately, the response in Ottawa was lukewarm at best. In a reply to Mitchell Sharp's letter inquiring about the possibilities of a parliamentary association, the speaker of the House of Commons, Lucien Lamoureux, argued that the current budget "could not sustain an additional association." Only if the president of the Bundestag made a formal proposal for the establishment of such an association, would he be prepared to look into the matter further.[83]

Despite Canadian coolness, the proposal for a parliamentary association remained on the agenda. Following a visit by Lamoureux to Germany in the autumn of 1969, the Germans again proposed that "a contact group" be set up between the German and Canadian parliamentarians. However, although the Bundestag's president was invited to make a return visit to Canada in 1971, the Speaker's Office reiterated again in January 1971 that there was no chance of an informal parliamentary group being formed in Canada, like the one which existed in Germany.[84] It seemed, in fact, that the Speaker's Office was uninterested in any form of Canadian-German parliamentary association. Budgetary considerations, lack of interest, and/or the "heavy workload" of the Canadian members of parliament appeared to be the primary excuses.

For officials of the European Division at External, the German interest in an improved relationship with Canada had been demonstrated. It seemed clear as well that the goal of better relations with the Federal Republic fit with the government's new desire, formally expressed in the foreign policy white paper of June 1970, to diversify Canada's external relations. Indeed, Germany was Canada's fourth largest trading partner and its seventh most important source of foreign investment. In political terms, the two countries' complementary positions on East-West détente and on the approach to negotiations with the Soviet bloc had been apparent for some time.

Moreover, early in 1971 Werner Uhrenbacher, the commercial counsellor at the German embassy in Ottawa, had informed a senior DEA official that the Schmidt initiative in particular was reflective of a desire not only by Schmidt but by "other leading figures in the FRG" as well to improve relations with Canada. This itself was part of a more general desire "to develop a greater independence from the United States." "Germany," Uhrenbacher argued, "could gain greater freedom of action by strengthening its ties with other Western countries," and Canada was an evident alternative to the United States "in certain areas."[85]

However, DEA's ability to influence Canadian policy could only go so far (as the failure to respond to the German parliamentary initiatives demonstrated). Nevertheless, in some areas the development of Canadian-German relations did make progress. In April 1971, responding to a proposal originally made during Brandt's April 1969 visit to Ottawa, a Canadian delegation headed by the trade minister, Jean-Luc Pepin, visited the Federal Republic. During the visit, Germany and Canada signed a scientific and technological agreement to promote the development of joint projects. This agreement was described as the first such agreement which Germany had signed with a "technologically developed country."[86] On his return to Canada, Pepin stated that an important purpose of the visit had been "to contribute to Canada's trade and industrial development and to the growth of our exports of advanced industrial products and services."[87]

The German interest in developing relations with Canada in the defence sphere provided certain opportunities and possible advantages as Canada sought, particularly after 1972, to develop its economic and trading relationship with Europe. Indeed, in the area of armaments co-operation, there was an immediate upswing in joint ventures between the two countries. In the aftermath of the visit by State Secretary Mommsen to Canada early in 1971, new life was breathed into the 1964 agreement on research, development, and procurement and a steering committee for the discussion of collaborative armaments projects was created. It comprised officials from both countries and met annually. The agendas for these meetings focussed on discussing procurement programmes which were envisaged in both countries in the coming years. If common procurement requirements could be identified, it then sought, where possible, to bring together Canadian and German companies.

As in the 1960s, the most important collaborative project to arise out of this process was the decision to develop and manufacture military reconnaissance drones. In the 1960s the CL-89 drone had been purchased by Germany from Canada. Its successor was to be the CL-289. Its development began on a joint basis between Canada and the FRG in 1976, with France joining the project in 1977. By the time it entered service with the German and French armies in the early 1990s, the programme was valued at some $1 billion, with Canadian industry being a significant beneficiary in the project.[88]

These were tangible benefits for Canadian industry. However, it seems unlikely that even these limited benefits would have been possible without the increased political collaboration on military issues begun between Bonn and Ottawa in the early 1970s at Germany's initiative. In this regard, the experience of the Trudeau defence review may, to a degree, have heightened the Federal Republic's appreciation of Canada. Certainly, Canada assumed a place of greater significance in Helmut Schmidt's world-view than it would otherwise have had. Schmidt's interest in Canada was again exemplified in July 1972 when he came to Canada to discuss the troop training proposal and related bilateral defence questions, even though he had recently moved from the defence portfolio to finance.[89] In the coming years, his personal interest in Canada would prove instrumental in promoting Canada's political and economic interests in the Federal Republic.

Even so, the lack of a co-ordinated policy approach at the highest levels in Canada continued to be the single greatest impediment to the more comprehensive development of bilateral relations. It virtually ensured that different branches of the Canadian foreign policy establishment responded to the various initiatives emanating from Bonn in very different ways. While the Department of External Affairs was almost always enthusiastic, other branches of government had less interest in developing relations with the Federal Republic. Any project which might cost money (such as the multi-role aircraft programme) proved most difficult to justify in the absence of high-level political direction to proceed with an integrated and co-ordinated government strategy, emphasizing the importance of developing the country's relationship with Germany at all levels. In consequence, major joint armaments projects were few in number (see Appendix Three), and military collaboration on the defence industrial side remained starkly underdeveloped.

Ironically, the Trudeau defence review had shown the potential political leverage and utility of Canadian forces in Europe. Defence policy was the most important vehicle for achieving broader political and economic objectives in the country's relationships with the Federal Republic and with Europe. However, as clear as this lesson appeared to be, the events of the years which followed demonstrated that it was a lesson which had largely been lost on Canada's leaders.

4 Canada, Germany, and Security in Europe, 1970–1984

The essence of the Trudeau government's approach to declaratory foreign policy was to attempt to ensure that policy objectives reflected broader national goals. For this government, three national goals were nominally held to be of particular importance: the maintenance and strengthening of Canada's national unity; ensuring the country's economic well-being; and securing Canada's political independence from the United States. In this sense, the white paper of June 1970, *Foreign Policy for Canadians*, noted that "Canada seeks to strengthen its ties with Europe, not as an anti-American measure but to create a more healthy balance within the North Atlantic community and to reinforce Canadian independence."[1]

It was also asserted that it would continue to be in Canada's interest to participate "in efforts to preserve peace in Europe and find satisfactory long-term solutions to the problems of European security." To "project" Canada's own ideas and policies, use would be made of multilateral institutions like NATO and of bilateral relationships developed with Western allies as well as of expanding links between Canada and East European states.[2] However, while the government's approach emphasized the continuing importance of an active Canadian diplomatic role, the white paper lacked a strategy for achieving the objectives it set out; in fact at the time some analysts argued that the white paper was not specific enough to be called a "policy statement" at all.[3] In terms of relations with Europe, or with the Federal Republic of Germany more specifically, there was therefore a considerable void both in policy guidance and in a co-ordinated strategy to implement the government's policy objectives.

For the Department of External Affairs, and most specifically its European Division, NATO remained the key framework for implementing the government's political goals in Europe. As Robert Spencer notes, in the aftermath of the damage caused to Canada's position within the alliance following the April 1969 decision to reduce its troops in Europe, DEA officials believed it was essential for Canada to pursue a more aggressive diplomatic role which would demonstrate that Canada still had a positive contribution to make to the alliance.[4] This stance manifested itself, first and foremost, in Canada's enthusiastic support for the concept of a European security conference, an idea in which the Federal Republic also had a close interest.

The origins of the idea for a European security conference can be traced back to a Soviet proposal made as early as 1954. In the 1960s the Soviet government came to see such a conference as a potential means of securing Western recognition and acceptance of Soviet hegemony over Eastern Europe. As such the proposal was refloated in 1966. Western governments, however – most particularly the Brandt government – saw a European security conference as a possible vehicle for relaxing East-West tensions and for building bridges between the blocs. As Brandt had stated soon after he became foreign minister in 1966, Germans could no longer wait "for automatism to produce German reunification." The Germans thus viewed a security conference as another opportunity, together with expanded bilateral contacts between the Federal Republic and Soviet bloc states, to thaw East-West relations and to begin a gradual process which would eventually lift the Iron Curtain.[5]

In important respects, Canadian officials shared these objectives. John Halstead noted some years later that he had seen an opportunity to develop what was originally a Soviet proposal for a European security conference to suit Western objectives.[6] The most important goal would be to promote the human dimension of East-West interaction and to create opportunities for increasing human contacts across the divide. As Thomas Delworth, head of the Canadian delegation at the preliminary conference negotiations in Geneva, remarked on reflection the question to which Canadian officials and others – most notably Danes, Austrians, and West Germans – sought an answer was whether ideology could be taken out of interstate relations for the benefit of the individual. If it could be, a conference might be a way to promote small incremental and practical measures to facilitate a broad range of human contacts. In this sense, Canadian objectives and goals were very close to those of the Federal Republic.[7]

The years preceding the opening of multilateral East-West preparatory talks in Helsinki in November 1972 were marked by intense diplomatic activity and intra-alliance consultations to determine the objectives, timing, and agenda of a European security conference. It was particularly important to ensure that any such conference supported, and in no way undermined,

Western political, diplomatic, and security objectives. For Canada, four matters were crucial to ensuring that a European security conference met that requirement.

First, the participation of both the United States and Canada was vital. The North American powers had a crucial stake in European security, and most West European states in fact viewed the exclusion of either North American state as unthinkable. Initial Soviet proposals, however, had called for a conference of European states, and some West European states, particularly France, sympathized with this idea. Canadian diplomats were therefore instructed to re-emphasize that security in Europe was an issue in which both Canada and the United States had a vital interest. Canada sought, for example, to make sure that the prospective conference be titled the "Conference on European Security" rather than the "European Security Conference." (In the end its official name was the Conference on Security and Co-operation in Europe – CSCE.) There was some concern therefore when the Dutch foreign minister, Joseph Luns, reportedly stated in June 1969 that because of Canada's "new attitude" towards NATO, it need not be included in discussions in Europe on European security. However, by the time of the autumn 1969 NATO Council meeting, it had become apparent that the alliance would adopt a clear position that both American and Canadian participation was essential.[8]

Second, Canada was committed to ensuring that German interests be fully protected in any conference. The long-standing Canadian view was that any détente process in Europe undertaken without German agreement was doomed to failure before it even began. Thus, a security conference had to support and complement the initiatives which the German government was pursuing on a bilateral basis with the Soviet Union and other East bloc states. Moreover, the option of the peaceful reunification of the two Germanies had to be protected and the status of West Berlin could not be compromised.[9]

Third, the conference should recognize the legitimate security interests of all states in Europe, including the Soviet Union, and promote measures to reinforce mutual confidence. For NATO, the question of Mutual Balanced Force Reductions (MBFR) was a key component of such confidence-building, and Canada, among other NATO states, was determined that MBFR talks should proceed in parallel with a security conference. In fact, the willingness of the Soviet Union to enter MBFR talks and, for example, to sign a mutually satisfactory Berlin agreement would be important Western preconditions for a security conference and were seen as essential demonstrations of Soviet good faith.[10]

Finally, Ottawa came to view humanitarian questions and human rights (what became known as Basket Three issues[11]) as especially important. Canada's enthusiasm and promotion of this aspect of the conference was evident as early as February 1971 when a draft proposal from the NATO secretariat appeared to reflect American scepticism about the real accomplishments which one could expect from a security conference. The Canadian delegation at NATO was promptly reminded of the "concrete results" which Ottawa hoped for from the conference. These concrete results would have to be manifest in the lives of everyday people. Because the West would be making major concessions, including the recognition of the German Democratic Republic, "compensating and positive gains" would also have to accrue to the West.[12]

On all these matters, West German perspectives essentially complemented Canadian views. West Germany viewed the conference on security and particularly Basket Three issues as an important vehicle for building a new relationship between East and West. Moreover it believed that the involvement of both North American states would ensure the success of détente in Europe. As a result, in April 1970, when the secretary of state for external affairs visited Bonn for meetings with both Chancellor Brandt and the new German foreign minister, Walter Scheel, he was assured of the Federal Republic's complete and unreserved support for both American and Canadian participation in any security conference.[13]

From the beginning, therefore, consultations with the Federal Republic were viewed as crucial in promoting Canada's objectives. As Spencer reports, in the aftermath of Willy Brandt's visit to Ottawa in April 1969, the Canadian ambassador in Bonn, Richard Bower, had apparently been instructed to "open a channel of regular liaison" with German officials on the subject of the security conference.[14] In addition to consultations conducted through the embassies in Ottawa and Bonn, meetings held between officials accredited to NATO in Brussels were also key in formulating diplomatic positions. Discussions between political leaders of the two countries, often held on the margins of international meetings, also began to take on a greater political importance.

Despite this convergence of political and diplomatic interests, Canada's decision to reduce its forces in Europe continued to cast a shadow over relations between the two countries, and both Mitchell Sharp in his April 1970 visit and Léo Cadieux in a June 1970 visit to Germany were questioned intently on the future of Canadian NATO policy.[15] Likewise, immediately following Sharp's visit, the new Canadian ambassador in the Federal Republic, G.G. Crean, warned in a cable to Ottawa that Scheel's complimentary remarks on Canada's diplomatic position notwithstanding, "it would be a mistake to imagine that relations with Canada form any essential element in German foreign policy." Canada still had quite a way to go, he argued, "to make up [for] our policy of troop reductions" and the closing of the office in West Berlin.[16] Moreover, not all aspects of Canada's new diplomatic efforts in Europe, which were designed at least partly to help restore Canada's credibility with its European allies, received the unreserved and enthusiastic support of the Prime Minister's Office.

TRUDEAU AND GERMAN UNIFICATION

The diplomatic posture Canada assumed within NATO vis-à-vis East-West détente was very much in the tradition of Pearsonian quiet diplomacy. It was a behind-the-scenes role which sought to make use of both multilateral discussions within the alliance and bilateral diplomatic relationships to advance Canadian views without moving outside the NATO mainstream. This role was, in some ways, out of step with the prime minister's desire to make Canada's foreign policy more broadly reflective of its more diverse national interests and less focused on what some circles regarded as a futile search for influence within NATO. However, it was also possible to look at Canada's diplomatic role as fulfilling government desires to see the alliance place less emphasis on military issues and develop a stronger political dimension as a way of promoting positive change in Europe. Among the individuals uncertain about the future thrust of Canada's European policy was the prime minister himself.

This was true in particular with respect to the country's German policy. In August 1970, an External Affairs memorandum to the prime minister outlined the essential aspects of Canada's German policy, arguing that Canada should not in any way change its official position on the legal status of the regime in East Berlin as that would undercut the Federal Republic's negotiating position in discussions with the Soviet Union and the GDR. Trudeau, however, perceived the non-recognition of the GDR as an untenable policy position. The division of both Germany and Europe was a reality which Trudeau believed to be irreversible, at least in the short term. Non-recognition only perpetuated a Cold War position towards the German Question. Since the Trudeau government had moved to recognize the People's Republic of China and to support its claim to the China seat at the United Nations – an acceptance of what was "real" – Trudeau seemed to be considering whether it might now be the time to explore a more "realistic" policy option on Germany as well.

On the External memorandum, Trudeau wrote that while Canadian policy on the GDR seemed reasonable for the present, "when the time approaches for a change ... let us try to lead rather than follow the pack." Moreover he asked whether Canada's support for the concept of a united Germany was really a well founded one, thus raising questions concerning the impact that German unity might have on Europe's stability and whether it would not be more sensible to move Canadian policy quickly towards the recognition of both German states rather than to continue to recognize only the Federal Republic.[17]

In their response, written in the name of the secretary of state for external affairs in December, DEA officials, most probably from the European Division, repeated their assertion that it was important not to undermine the

West German government's negotiating position. Canada, it was argued, had a strong interest in seeing the FRG's policy towards the East succeed and that policy should therefore be actively supported by Canada. This position would simultaneously "serve to sustain the mutual confidence that exists between West Germany and its NATO allies" and strengthen Canadian-German bilateral relations "which in the current evolution of European affairs we regard as essential."

On the question of German unity, the drafters of the department's response argued that it was doubtful that the division of Germany could be permanently maintained. The boundary between East and West Germany had little cultural or historical significance, and the GDR itself seemed to lack all the "cultural elements necessary for separate nationhood." The feeble sense of national consciousness in the GDR would not "long survive if its inhabitants had a completely free choice." Moreover, the prime minister was reminded that it would be wrong to assume that the policy of normalizing relations with the East which the German government was pursuing in any way represented an acceptance of the division. In these circumstances, any effort by Western states to agree to perpetuate artificially the division of Germany would be a real source of frustration and instability "which sooner or later could produce an explosion." The only credible policy for Canada, it was asserted, was to continue to promote the deepening of German integration in NATO and the European Communities while working to bridge the gap between East and West and overcome the German division in the context of a more united Europe.[18]

The force of the department's arguments apparently impressed the prime minister, who added a comment on the document. "Thanks, this was very helpful." Even though there was no evident change in Canada's policy, concern remained over the ultimate direction that the Trudeau government was likely to take. Thus, a DEA memorandum written for the occasion of Trudeau's spring 1971 visit to Moscow cautioned the prime minister to remember that the Soviet Union hoped that the détente process would weaken the cohesion of the Western alliance.[19] The most dramatic event of this visit was the signing of a draft protocol on Canadian-Soviet consultations on 20 May. The protocol had apparently been proposed by the Soviet Union on short notice. Without informing the cabinet, Trudeau agreed to the protocol and argued later at a press conference that it was "an important step towards the establishment of the most autonomous foreign policy possible." Both the protocol and Trudeau's comments raised concerns among Canada's allies and the officials in External alike. Neither the secretary of state for external affairs nor the minister of national defence had been consulted in advance about the protocol.[20]

However, it was during and after Premier Aleksei Kosygin's return visit to Canada six months later that allied, and particularly German, concerns over the drift of Canadian policy were especially aroused. In a private conversation with the Soviet premier, Trudeau did re-emphasize Canadian determination to support Brandt's Eastern policy. However he also noted that Canada maintained the freedom to recognize the GDR when it considered it appropriate. If the FRG and the GDR were unable to reach an accommodation, then his government would have to decide on new policy options at that time.[21]

Whatever private encouragement these comments may have given the Soviet government in terms of a more "balanced" Canadian policy on the German Question, it was the subsequent public pronouncements of both Trudeau and Sharp which raised new concerns in the FRG. In a television interview in November 1971, Trudeau noted that Kosygin had asked him about Canada's policy on recognizing the GDR and that he had confirmed Canada's support for the principle of recognition, arguing that the present delay in taking this step was governed by the fact that intra-German negotiations were still under way. At the same time, the secretary of state for external affairs was declaring that Canada favoured the membership of both German states in the United Nations.[22] Then, in an interview on the CBC radio programme, "Sunday Magazine," Sharp, in direct contravention of the declared goal of German policy, asserted: "No one nowadays assumes that there will be a united Germany ... that idea whoever had it is more or less abandoning it now [sic] at least any of the principal political factions have."[23]

These comments were picked up by the German and European press and were reported to Bonn by the German embassy in Ottawa. Canada's ambassador in Bonn subsequently reported to Ottawa that the pace of public discussion in Canada had caused some alarm. Indeed, the state secretary in the Chancellor's Office had delivered a speech in which she had urged the Federal Republic's friends and allies to "refrain from initiatives which might disturb inter-German negotiations." This, Ambassador Crean noted, included not just the establishment of relations with the GDR but even trade talks.[24] In a report a few days later, Crean emphasized that the whole Eastern policy of the FRG government was controversial enough in West Germany's domestic politics without the allies causing additional problems for the Brandt government.

On 29 November, the German ambassador to Canada, Baron von Mirbach, called on Sharp, ostensibly to thank the government for its official support of Germany's Ostpolitik initiatives and to report that progress was being made. Sharp reassured the ambassador of Canada's continued support and von Mirbach expressed his relief that press reports concerning Canadian policy had been "inaccurate."[25]

While Canada's official policy remained on track, this episode probably confirmed German suspicions that the potential for some possibly unwelcome change remained. And indeed, even after Trudeau had sent his congratulations to Brandt in May 1972 on the successful conclusion of the first agreements with the GDR, External Affairs told the director general of the West European, North American, and NATO division of the German Foreign Office, Klaus Simon, who was on a visit to Ottawa, that Canada would likely revise its German policy, should the FRG fail to ratify its Eastern treaties.[26] German officials were already fully aware of the serious consequences which would likely result for the Federal Republic's relations with the allies, if it failed to ratify these treaties whose fate now lay with the Bundestag. Given the nature of the Trudeau government's alliance policy, a lecture from Canada about the German need to sustain a consistent foreign policy was out of place.

CANADIAN AND GERMAN APPROACHES TO DÉTENTE

The prime minister's unease with aspects of Canada's policy on the German Question revealed that while Canadian diplomats were content with playing a behind-the-scenes "honest broker" role more suited to Canada's stature and position within the alliance, Trudeau at times found the policy too reactive and insufficiently expressive of Canada's own interests and perspectives on the security problem in Europe. It also revealed that while the Federal Republic and Canada were both committed to détente, the factors motivating that commitment differed. For the Germans, support for détente rested firmly on the issue of the German national question. Through détente and the CSCE process, the goal of German and European reunification could be kept alive. This issue was of vital importance to West German politicians and public alike. In fact, one can argue that the détente process was more important for the Federal Republic than for any other state in the alliance. For Canada, however, détente and the CSCE process were much more amorphous concepts and were certainly not vital concerns of the government or the country.

In consequence, Canadians could, on occasion, afford to be somewhat bolder and more idealistic in making proposals, and Canadian political leaders, particularly the prime minister, felt freer to challenge, from time to time, some basic Western positions. Tied much more closely by its vital national interests, Bonn placed great emphasis on ensuring allied unity in support of Germany's own particular objectives in Europe. The Federal Republic was therefore alarmed by any initiative or proposal which it saw as likely to challenge either the solidarity of the Western security structure or the pattern or stability of relations between East and West, in particular those between East and West Germany. As a result, Germany often displayed what was, from a Canadian perspective, a much more cynical attitude to the prospects of any significant breakthrough in East-West negotiations.

In some areas, such as the MBFR talks, the Germans were in fact reluctant to see any agreement at all out of concern about the possible implications that force reductions would have for the nature of the military relationship among the major powers in NATO. Indeed, this German position led to some significant German and American clashes on MBFR. While the Germans saw the talks as one means to pre-empt unilateral force reductions by the United States (perhaps forced through by congressional opponents of the American troop presence), the Americans viewed the discussions as a possible tool for overcoming German and European resistance to these same force reductions.[27] The Canadian position on this issue was somewhat more optimistic and idealistic than that of either Washington or Bonn. Ottawa placed much greater stress on the value of such reductions and on the ultimate possibility of an agreement. Canada also emphasized the need to restore some "dynamism" to the MBFR process so as to achieve an agreement and preserve the credibility of NATO policies in the public eye while simultaneously strengthening allied unity. Ultimately, the words "dynamism" and "MBFR" did not seem to go together since thirteen years of talks were to yield no agreement.[28]

Within the CSCE, the Federal Republic sought to expand and consolidate the inroads and gains it had begun to make in the opening of relations with the GDR and in the improvement of relations with the Soviet bloc. Through the CSCE, Ostpolitik became a continuous process for the FRG. While the Soviet Union had originally sought a European security conference as a key means of legitimizing its hegemonic position in Eastern Europe and freezing the status quo in Europe, the Federal Republic envisaged the CSCE as a forum through which barriers between East and West could be slowly eroded.

As outlined by the foreign minister, Hans-Dietrich Genscher, in the Bundestag in 1974, both government and opposition were agreed on German goals in the CSCE process:

- The conference should contribute to a lasting understanding between East and West – an understanding insulated from the everyday issues which might still divide East and West.
- Germany should use its freedom of manœuvre to the maximum to promote German national objectives in the conference.
- The conference should be of direct benefit to people and not just states.
- Security and co-operation would best be furthered if human rights, self-determination, and basic freedoms were respected everywhere.
- The conference must not hinder any German policy objectives, most particularly any movement towards a political solution in Europe in which the German people, through free self-determination, could regain their unity.
- The conference could not be considered a replacement for the Atlantic alliance.[29]

For the Germans, therefore, the primary importance of the conference was, as Brandt stated in 1969, to prevent any further alienation of the two parts of Germany. By improving the lot of ordinary citizens living in Eastern Europe and particularly in the GDR, the CSCE was also perceived in Germany as a tool of gradual liberalization. The Federal Republic's diplomatic efforts within the context of the CSCE were thus a complement to its evolving "Deutschlandpolitik" of the mid- to late 1970s which was seeking, through the lever of economic aid and deeper political and cultural contacts, to bring the two German states and peoples closer together. As Genscher stated in 1976: "No one can have a greater interest than we Germans that the [CSCE] achieves its objectives to improve the relations and contacts between states and peoples throughout Europe. No one has a greater reason than we to facilitate détente and co-operation over borders and between blocs."[30]

Even while the CSCE and its complementary forum, the MBFR talks, were seen as institutions through which the Western states could promote their collective objectives in direct talks with the Soviet bloc, they were also used to promote the often unique and sometimes differing political objectives of particular states. This is why the CSCE process gave birth to a plethora of overlapping caucuses and informal bilateral contacts through which states with similar interests and outlooks sought to develop common positions and approaches. Many of these still exist in the post–Cold War Organization for Security and Co-operation in Europe.

On a diplomatic level, despite occasional divergences in perspective, the political understanding between the Canadian and German foreign ministries remained good. Canada regarded the CSCE talks as extremely important. The mutual commitment of both Canada and the Federal Republic to the success of multilateral European security negotiations was evident from the outset. The emphasis both countries placed on humanitarian and human rights issues led to close co-operation, both in the period leading up to the Helsinki and Geneva talks and in the Belgrade and Madrid follow-up talks of the late 1970s and early 1980s. Both the Federal Republic and, to a much lesser extent, Canada had vested domestic political interests in seeing greater opportunities for contact and movement across the Iron Curtain. Both countries, however, saw such a development as an incremental process and thus, while tangible achievements from a particular round of negotiations were important, patience and a long-term perspective were an intrinsic part of their strategies.

During the first meeting between Sharp and Genscher in the spring of 1974, these elements were underscored in discussions concerning the CSCE. Sharp stated that "the importance of achieving results" meant that the Western side had to "patiently continue negotiations and not ... accept a closing off of the current CSCE phase." Genscher was in complete agreement with this position.[31]

The general approach of Canada and Germany to the CSCE differed from that taken by the United States, at least in the Helsinki and Geneva rounds. The Americans judged, quite correctly, that their bilateral relationship with the USSR was of much greater importance. The American interest in and impact on the multilateral talks was limited at best. The American secretary of state, Henry Kissinger, thought many of the issues discussed were obtuse, esoteric, and of limited relevance.[32] John Halstead recalled that in his own conversations with Kissinger, the secretary of state admitted that he expected discussions with the Soviet Union to yield little. Kissinger recalled that as a boy living in Nazi Germany, he could remember that even though Western newspapers and magazines were freely available in Berlin, this in fact changed nothing in Germany. The same, he believed, would be true in the Soviet bloc, even if more contact with things Western was permitted.[33] The lack of interest among the Americans was easily apparent in the discussions and meetings of contact groups on the Basket Three: the American delegation submitted only one of 209 contributing documents.[34] Later, during the Belgrade talks, while Bonn and Ottawa sought to prevent the conference from degenerating into an ideological shouting match, the United States created another problem when the newly elected Carter administration saw the talks merely as an opportunity to indict the Soviet Union for its human rights violations.[35]

For the Canadians and Germans, by way of contrast, lower profile discussion with the East and the incremental but positive progress that this yielded was seen to be of greater benefit. As Peyton Lyon records, so close were the Canadian and German positions on some of these questions that in the Geneva talks the Germans suggested that the Canadian delegation "manage" the NATO text on family reunification, an issue of vital importance to the Federal Republic and of immense importance domestically in Germany. Co-operation on this issue proved so successful that virtually every feature of the draft found its way into the Final Act.[36] Later, in his opening statement to the Belgrade meeting, Klaus Goldschlag, the Canadian representative, eloquently emphasized that an atmosphere and climate of trust between the peoples of Europe was dependent on breaking down the artificial barriers between East and West. Major excerpts from this speech were printed by the *Frankfurter Allgemeine Zeitung*, which described the statement as the clearest explanation of the connection between national interest and the détente and security process in Europe.[37]

CANADIAN-GERMAN POLITICAL CONSULTATIONS

Closer co-operation between the two countries may have contributed to the enthusiasm with which the German Foreign Ministry took up the onset of direct and regular political consultations with Canada in the autumn of 1978. The regular consultations which emerged as a result of an agreement concluded in the course of Prime Minister Trudeau's August 1978 state visit to Germany provided for working out a system for regular political discussions between high officials and diplomats from the two countries. These would help facilitate closer and more meaningful political and diplomatic co-operation and policy co-ordination between the two countries.

The membership of both the FRG and Canada in extra-NATO forums such as the CSCE, the United Nations Security Council in 1977 and 1978, and G-7 summits seemed to underscore the need for more regular consultative procedures. Thus, in discussions through the German ambassador in Ottawa soon after the August state visit, the German preference for a system of political consultations which would occur before or after major international gatherings was revealed. These would, it was determined, perhaps be more meaningful and useful than regularly scheduled or ad hoc meetings unconnected to multilateral discussions.[38] The German interest in these talks was confirmed in the regular and high-level consultations which began later that autumn. Among the German visitors to Ottawa in late 1978 and in 1979, were Hans-Jürgen Wischnewski, the state secretary in the Chancellor's Office, Günter van Well, the state secretary in the Foreign Office, and Klaus Kinkel, director of the Planning Bureau in the Foreign Office and senior adviser to Genscher. Also making the trip to Ottawa for consultations in the same period were the Foreign Office's director of arms control and disarmament, the political director, and the director of the North American division (twice). The issues discussed covered a wide range: regional issues, East-West relations, terrorism, arms control questions, Namibia, the CSCE negotiations, and a host of others. In general, the results proved considerably more useful than had been envisaged in the Trudeau-Schmidt communiqué of August.[39]

While co-operative relations were generally close, some areas of difference were nevertheless evident: for instance, about the exact emphasis to be placed on points in the CSCE talks. From the beginning the German government placed significant weight on the principle of self-determination and had sought Canadian support on this matter. Some in Canada, however, seemed to have reservations about a declaration of principle on this point, primarily because of the precedent it might provide for Quebec. In the end, the Final Act referred both to the right of peoples to self-determination and to the need to respect the territorial integrity of all states.[40]

By the time of the Belgrade follow-up conference, the Germans were most anxious that gains made thus far would not be upset by the break-up of the conference and CSCE process. These gains included a considerable increase, in a short period, in the number of ethnic Germans allowed to leave the Eastern bloc and in the number of Germans allowed to leave the GDR to settle or visit the Federal Republic. The government attributed these gains in part to the CSCE process.[41] As a result, a Canadian proposal which sought to tighten up provisions of the concluding document at Belgrade so as to give a greater "automaticity" to procedures for family reunification and family visits was, in the words of one DEA memorandum on the subject, opposed by the West Germans "almost as much as [by] the East, largely because the East Germans had told them that the concept was frightening and could endanger other activities."[42]

Despite its limitations, which at Belgrade and thereafter included a German emphasis on consultations within the EC caucus over those within the NATO caucus,[43] Canada's bilateral relationship with Germany in the CSCE context was an important one, both in advancing Canada's diplomatic initiatives and in developing its political relations with the Federal Republic. The multitude of issues and the number of actors with whom the German delegation at the CSCE conferences was dealing meant that interaction with Canada was not very high in the hierarchy of German concerns, notwithstanding its relative importance on some selected issues.[44] However, the increasing political importance of the CSCE to the Federal Republic in the 1980s, as well as Canada's consistent enthusiasm for the process, supported the continuance of a good Canadian-German relationship in the multilateral discussions.

THE TRUDEAU PEACE INITIATIVE AND RELATIONS WITH GERMANY

From the mid-1970s on, Canada had by and large stayed in the Western mainstream in terms of policy towards the Soviet bloc. Even after the onset of the "new" Cold War towards the end of the decade, the Trudeau government had maintained this policy, increasing its defence spending by the agreed NATO minimum of 3 per cent annually in real terms, taking symbolic steps such as boycotting the Moscow Olympics, and agreeing, by the summer of 1983, to allow the testing of American cruise missiles over Canadian territory (a step which, given his long-standing negative attitude towards direct involvement with nuclear weapons, was particularly difficult for the prime minister). However, towards the end of 1983, with NATO on the verge of deploying its new medium-range missiles in Europe, with the Soviet Union threatening to break off all arms control talks, with the Madrid round of the CSCE coming to a largely inconclusive end, and with the East-West shouting match having reached a fever pitch as a result of the Soviet downing of a Korean passenger aircraft which had strayed over its territory in the Far East, Trudeau again prepared to break ranks and try to inject new life into the East-West dialogue.

Trudeau's motivation was most probably the product of a genuine concern over the sharp downturn in East-West relations and the feeling that he could not wait until he was out of office to act.[45] His belief was that political leaders in the two camps were talking past each other and that rigid political positions on both sides had emerged because of a bureaucratization of East-West relations. He likely thought the CSCE negotiations and other traditional diplomatic approaches had been exhausted and would almost certainly be unable to break through the East-West divide. Despite nearly fifteen years in power, his scepticism towards traditional diplomacy and about the nature of inter-state relations had changed little.

In September 1983, despite the reluctance and even anger of some Canadian officials and diplomats, a working group was set up directly under the Prime Minister's Office to formulate a peace initiative which Trudeau could present to Canada's allies, to the Soviet bloc, and to Japan and China. In a speech delivered in Guelph, Ontario, on 27 October, Trudeau presented his strategy for rebuilding confidence in East-West relations and for re-establishing a high-level dialogue between the United States and the Soviet Union. Five specific proposals were advanced: a conference of the five nuclear powers; enhancing the Non-Proliferation Treaty; turning the forth-coming CSCE conference in Stockholm into a foreign ministers meeting; accelerating the pace of MBFR discussions; and a ban on high-altitude anti-satellite weapons.[46] In a series of visits to the United States, Western Europe, and China, Trudeau outlined his ideas to a host of world leaders and Geoffrey Pearson, the former Canadian ambassador in Moscow, travelled to the USSR to present Soviet leaders with Trudeau's ideas. However, the peace initiative secured little in the way of positive support from Canada's allies, and it was given hardly any coverage in the European press. The coverage it did receive was largely sceptical.[47] Canada simply did not have the stature to be taken seriously on such an initiative, particularly by the superpowers.[48]

In Europe, however, the goals of Trudeau's initiative, if not the means chosen to advance those goals, found some degree of sympathy among European leaders. For the Germans, in particular, there was a desire to construct a "safety net" around the negotiations on intermediate-range nuclear forces (INF), should the Soviet Union walk out.[49] Thus, following their meeting early in November, Chancellor Helmut Kohl wrote to Trudeau, agreeing that "direct contact between President Reagan and General Secretary Andropov is important for East-West relations" and support-ing the idea of an East-West summit, a proposal which Kohl noted he had "repeatedly advocated" in Washington.[50]

German interest in the Trudeau initiative was again evident later in November when the Germans notified both the Canadian mission to NATO and the embassy in Bonn that Foreign Minister Genscher requested a meet-ing with Canada's secretary of state for external affairs, Allan MacEachen, to discuss the peace initiative at the forthcoming NATO ministerial meeting. The embassy in Bonn recommended to Ottawa that Canada take advantage of the opportunity because "it has never been easy to get Genscher to focus on things Canadian."[51]

At the meeting in Brussels on 8 December, Genscher insisted the alliance had to retain the political initiative and that while it had to demonstrate its political solidarity by proceeding with the INF deployments (for the purpose of thwarting Soviet attempts to decouple Europe and the United States), it also had to indicate its willingness to co-operate with the East. It was for this reason that the Federal Republic had proposed that the North Atlantic Council issue a political declaration that stressed its desire to foster arms control and disarmament efforts in all possible areas. In this regard, German thinking closely corresponded with that which underlay Trudeau's initiative. Genscher went on to note that while the INF deployment was necessary to demonstrate the political cohesion of the alliance, he was worried by the schism it had created in East-West relations.[52]

The German perspective, one which echoed that of Kohl in his letter to the prime minister, was certainly a product of German anxiety over the prospect of a complete breakdown in the East-West dialogue and, possibly, in intra-German relations as well. Indeed, in the autumn of 1982 when Trudeau had visited Germany and met Kohl just shortly after he became chancellor, Kohl had reportedly told the prime minister that every downturn in East-West relations had a negative impact on Germany. Both German states therefore had "a special responsibility" in the maintenance of peace.[53] The German desire to protect the country's Deutschlandpolitik against any collapse in East-West relations was apparent.

It was therefore not surprising that both Kohl and Genscher put their support behind the idea that NATO foreign ministers attend the opening of the forthcoming Stockholm CSCE conference, which was the last forum for East-West negotiation left since the Soviet Union had abandoned all bilateral talks with the Americans as well as the MBFR discussions.[54] This would be the only one of the proposals in the Trudeau peace initiative which was ultimately adopted by the alliance.[55]

While sharing many of the same concerns of Trudeau, most Germans appear to have regarded his initiative as "well meant but ineffective." As Colonel Roland Foerster, the German defence attaché posted in Ottawa at the time, commented: "Canada liked to see itself as a big peacemaker" on the international stage, but the "notion that one could solve the East-West divide by simply sitting around a table and talking was naive."[56] Trudeau's decision to include East Berlin in the capitals visited in Eastern Europe also raised some eyebrows in the alliance and especially with the Germans. Visits by Western statesmen to the GDR were rare and, as a result, this part of Trudeau's European trip got fairly large play in the West German media, but not out of any enthusiasm for the peace initiative's ideas.[57]

In general, Bonn's views on the peace initiative were based on the belief that, unlike Trudeau, the Germans had a full appreciation and understanding of the realities of the East-West balance of power, of Soviet policy, and of the limitations on the German ability to influence and alter either. As a result, Genscher was consistent, both in his December 1983 meeting with MacEachen and in an a November 1982 with Trudeau, in emphasizing the slow, small, and gradual change which could be brought through forums such as the CSCE. Indeed, in attempting to reassure MacEachen in 1983, Genscher expressed his confidence that the Soviet Union would "eventually choose cooperation as a route to follow, since it was in their long term interest to do so."[58]

The prime minister's peace initiative had demonstrated both the advantages and disadvantages of public rather than private Canadian diplomacy. On the one hand, a public approach had the advantage of focusing attention at the highest levels on Canadian ideas. Even if they had only a limited chance of having any influence, their presentation in a public fashion drew attention to the depth of Canadian concerns and thus made allies more anxious to address those concerns, if only to maintain alliance unity. A public approach, if used skilfully, can sometimes serve as a bargaining tool to effect more substantial gains. However, there is nothing to indicate that the Trudeau initiative was intended in this way; in fact, all indications are that it was a serious and genuine effort to shake up the leaders in both East and West in the hope that they could commit themselves to a more effective dialogue.

In this respect the initiative was, for the most part, a failure.[59] It is no exaggeration to state that in the eyes of many world leaders, Canada looked foolish. Certainly the lack of coverage in the European press bears witness to this fact. The failure of the initiative demonstrated once again that Canada's best hope for having real, if modest, influence on the international stage is in a limited behind-the-scenes role in a multilateral forum. After 1983, the CSCE became one of the more important forums in which to pursue this objective. In the aftermath of INF missile deployments in the late autumn of 1983, the Soviet walk-out from all East-West arms control discussions meant that the talks in Stockholm on confidence- and security-building measures did in fact become the only forum for inter-bloc discussions. They therefore became vitally important in maintaining an East-West dialogue.[60]

Then, after the revolutionary changes in Soviet policy initiated by Mikhail Gorbachev in the mid- to late 1980s, the CSCE began to realize some of the spectacular goals that German and Canadian diplomats had originally set out to achieve when the process had first begun some two decades before. Indeed, early sceptics of the whole process, such as Kissinger, have since come to view the Helsinki agreements and the CSCE as having been instrumental in contributing to the collapse of the Soviet system. Kissinger has even gone so far as to describe the human rights elements in the Helsinki process as "the most significant provision" of the whole agreement which "was destined to play a major role in the disintegration of the Soviet satellite orbit."[61] The CSCE, originally pursued so enthusiastically by Canadian officials at least in part as a means through which Canada could demonstrate its continued interest in Europe, had become one of the more successful, if least publicized, aspects of German-Canadian political co-operation.

5 Canadian-German Economic Relations: A Lost Chance?

The Trudeau government's initial motivation for intensifying its efforts to improve relations with the Federal Republic was of course an economic one. The Nixon economic shocks of August 1971 had shown how vulnerable Canada was to fluctuations in American economic policy. The government's Third Option trade strategy, announced in the autumn of 1972, ostensibly sought to move more earnestly in the direction of diversifying the country's trade and economic relations. From the end of 1973, the government's effort in this respect was focused on Europe, and within Europe on the Federal Republic of Germany. At the same time, however, and in spite of the higher weight accorded by Canada to NATO after the Defence Structure Review in 1974–5, the country's defence policy remained insufficiently supportive of Ottawa's new trade and economic policy objectives.

By the early 1970s, the FRG was Canada's fourth largest trading partner and its seventh most important source of foreign investment. Moreover, Germany was the number one destination of Canadian investment in continental Europe. While in overall numbers and percentages, trade with Germany made up only a small percentage of Canada's total world trade (about 1.8 per cent of exports and 2.63 per cent of imports), there was, as an internal DEA memorandum noted, considerable room for expansion and improvement.

GERMANY AND THE THIRD OPTION

In 1970 an internal DEA memorandum had noted that Germany already possessed the most powerful economy in Western Europe and that its political voice was "beginning to rise to match its economic strength." "Its voice," it was asserted, would be central "in determining the EEC's political and economic relations with other countries." "The development of closer relations with the FRG" was thus an essential aspect "of the government's policy towards Europe."[1] Nevertheless, from the outset the ability of External Affairs officials to get this point across to the government was often an uphill fight. Even their own minister stated in retrospect that in 1970 there was "no hint then of the coming rapid ascendancy of West Germany in the European Community."[2] The failure of Canada's political leaders to appreciate the central role of Germany in Europe made it difficult initially to bring the necessary momentum to Canadian-German relations. Only in 1971–2 did the Trudeau government finally "rediscover" Europe.

In the late spring of 1972, just as Canada was beginning to develop its Third Option policy, a senior German Foreign Office official, Klaus Simon, visited Ottawa. Canadian officials took this opportunity to convey the importance which Canada attached to its relationship with the Federal Republic. In a meeting with the heads of DEA's key divisions, Gilles Mathieu informed Simon that Germany was very important in the envisaged Canadian strategy for expanding its trading relations with Europe. With the entry of the United Kingdom (Canada's second largest trading partner in 1972) into the European Community (EC), Ottawa was anxious both to protect its trading relationship with the United Kingdom and to develop its links with other EC members. Asked whether or not Europe was interested in an expanded relationship with Canada, Simon replied that European countries had already devoted considerable time to considering the Canadian position and that a more outward-looking EC policy was desired. He also quoted from an internal German memorandum which noted the importance of developing relations between the EC and other industrialized countries.[3]

Although some Canadian officials hoped for a quick contractual agreement with the Community in 1972, it was soon apparent that notwithstanding Simon's comments, the Community was, by and large, uninterested. It was only after hard lobbying by Ottawa in 1972–3 that the Community invited Canada, in November 1973, to submit its ideas for improving relations.[4] Even in getting this far, German support seems to have been crucial. At the October 1972 EC heads of state and government meeting in Paris, Chancellor Willy Brandt had spoken of the need for a "dialogue" between the EC and its principal industrial partners and he had specifically mentioned Canada.[5]

German support for Canada was matched by increasing Canadian diplomatic support for Germany within NATO. Specifically, Canada had strongly backed the inclusion of a statement in the NATO final communiqué of December 1972 underscoring the alliance's support for the efforts of the German people to regain their unity. This assistance prompted a letter of thanks to A.E. Ritchie, DEA's under-secretary from the German ambassador, Rupprecht von Keller.[6] Ottawa also improved its standing in Bonn through its decision to reopen its mission in Berlin. The Canadian ambassador to the Federal Republic, G.G. Crean, had lobbied hard for this decision, arguing that it was important that Canada, the only one of the larger NATO states not represented in Berlin, restore its diplomatic presence there, particularly prior to opening any mission in the German Democratic Republic.[7]

Canada's closer diplomatic relationship with Germany seemed to have borne fruit when the foreign minister, Walter Scheel, reportedly pledged to represent Canada's interests in Europe after a September 1973 visit to Canada during which he met with the prime minister at Harrington Lake as well as with Mitchell Sharp and senior DEA officials.[8] The EC's call to Canada for an aide-mémoire, which would outline ideas on improving the economic and trading relationship between Europe and Canada, followed in November. These Canadian proposals for a contractual link were presented to the Community in April 1974.

However, these first proposals were not well received, and in its report to the Council of Ministers in September, the European Commission expressed its strong reservations about the Canadian ideas. In essence, the Commission questioned the precedent that such an agreement would set. It also argued that the proposals were too vague about how to proceed to create an improved trading relationship. Perhaps most crucially, it was widely perceived (though this remained officially unstated) that Canada's relationship with the United States was simply too close and all-encompassing. There was a fear that any agreement between Canada and the EC might serve to bring the Americans in through the back door. The EC was very reluctant to extend to Canada any concessions which it was not also prepared to make to the United States. This was certainly the position of France; a fact which the prime minister found out for himself when he paid his first official visit to continental Europe by travelling to France and Belgium in October 1974.[9]

Late in 1974 reports emerged that some officials in the German Foreign Office shared these apprehensions about aspects of the Canadian initiative to the EC.[10] Perhaps reflecting the view of some in the German Foreign Office or Economics Ministry, a story in *Time* on 4 November 1974 referred to West Germany as "unenthusiastic" about a special accord with Canada. However, this view was strongly refuted by the German ambassador in Ottawa. In a visit to the department soon after the prime minister's trip to Europe, von Keller re-emphasized that Germany fully supported the Canadian démarche. In fact, he likened Germany's strongly supportive and leading position to that of the "prow of a ship" and pledged to take up the issues raised in the *Time* story with the magazine's Canadian bureau and correct their "ill-informed thinking."[11]

The primary German rationale for supporting and sustaining the Canadian initiative was almost certainly political and strategic. In 1975 only about 0.8 per cent of West Germany's total world trade was with Canada.[12] However, by backing the contractual link, the Germans deferred any Canadian defence review which might lead to a further reduction in or even a withdrawal of Canadian forces; and the threat of such a decision remained a reality at least until after the results of the Defence Structure Review were announced in the autumn of 1975. Indeed, both the defence minister, at the December 1973 NATO ministers meeting, and Trudeau, in his October 1974 visit to Brussels, had again spoken of a possible review of the continued presence of Canada's forces in Europe or of general defence spending cuts.

In addition to staving off this possibility, German support for Canada's objectives also underscored Bonn's emphasis on a multilateral transatlantic relationship. This German policy emphasis had become even stronger in reaction to American leanings towards bilateralism in transatlantic relations in this period.[13]

Likewise, by the 1970s the Federal Republic had become interested in diversifying its sources of raw materials to avoid over-dependency on the Soviet Union for such supplies, particularly in gas and oil. Investigation of a possible Canadian alternative was of interest to German officials. Additionally, an expanded economic relationship with Canada might provide opportunities for exporting some of Germany's surplus capital to an industrial country where skilled labour was available.[14]

In the autumn of 1974, Canada took the most important decision that it could to demonstrate its political interest in Europe; it began a review of its defence policy. An important goal of this review was to look at ways of improving Canada's force posture in Europe.[15] The maintenance of a main battle tank capability by this force was viewed as the most tangible indication of Canada's determination to remain committed to the defence of central Europe, and a host of allied and German officials had made apparent their desire to see Canada re-equip its brigade in Europe with a new tank.[16] Indeed, during the May 1975 NATO meetings, Trudeau had agreed to Chancellor Schmidt's request that discussions take place between Canada and the Federal Republic on the question of Canada's contribution to the defence of Europe.

Then during a June visit to Canada, the German defence minister, Georg Leber, reiterated to the prime minister his view that Canadian troops based in Germany be properly equipped. Leber remarked that Canada must not only make a "commensurate and effective" military contribution, but it must also "be seen to be doing so." This should "involve the continual presence of Canadian ground forces in Europe and in order to ensure that these forces could adequately protect themselves ... they would logically require tanks." In response, the Germans were told that the defence review would confirm the Canadian presence in Germany.[17]

This assurance created a good atmosphere for Trudeau's two visits to Europe in 1975 during which he sought to promote the contractual link. During his March 1975 state visit to Germany, he met Schmidt for the first time. The reputations of both the German chancellor and the Canadian prime minister had preceded them. Schmidt was somewhat of "a young star" in Germany and had a reputation for arrogance which apparently made Trudeau slightly sceptical of him. Trudeau had a reputation as somewhat of a playboy but also as an intellectual willing and anxious to challenge traditional ways of thinking. In fact, a lengthy story in the *Frankfurter Allgemeine Zeitung* prior to his arrival had played up this reputation.[18] Some six years earlier, Schmidt's initial experience with the results of a Trudeau defence policy had not been positive, and Trudeau's failure to meet with Schmidt during the latter's visit to Canada in 1972 may have enhanced this negative impression. Thus, each man approached the other with some misgiving.[19]

Schmidt was ill at the time of Trudeau's visit, and the prime minister was received by the foreign minister, Hans-Dietrich Genscher. There was only time for a brief courtesy call on the chancellor, but the two men reportedly established an "instant rapport" and both came to respect the other's intellectual ability. Trudeau came out of his Bonn meetings "most satisfied" with the result, since both Schmidt and Genscher had pledged to provide continued support for Canada's trade initiatives with the EC.[20] After Trudeau's subsequent visit to Brussels in May, negotiations on the contractual link began in earnest. These lasted over a year, mostly because of the requirement for endless consultations within the Community. However an agreement with the Community was finally signed in July 1976 and came into effect on 1 October of the same year. The agreement called for the development and diversification of trade through commercial co-operation, for the facilitation of inter-corporate links by various means, and for the creation of a joint co-operation committee responsible for promoting and reviewing progress.[21] A diplomatic post had already been opened by the European Commission in Ottawa back in February.

The events of 1975–6 brought an end to the slide in Canadian-German relations which had begun with the defence decision of 1969. The purchase of the German Leopard I tank in May 1976 was evidence of Canada's decision to re-emphasize the importance of NATO within its defence priorities, while the achievement of a contractual trade link with the EC symbolized Germany's support for Canada's trade strategy towards Europe.

The linkage between defence and trade cannot be overstated. During their first real business meeting in Helsinki in July 1975, Trudeau thanked Schmidt for German support on the contractual link, to which Schmidt simply replied "we have to" and then immediately turned the conversation to the subject of Canada's defence review and to the future of its Europe-based forces.[22] Contrary to the impression given by Trudeau and Ivan Head, his foreign policy adviser, in a 1995 book, an implicit, if not explicit, link was drawn by both Schmidt and other German officials between German support for Canada's trade initiative and a revision of Canadian defence policy.[23] Indeed, in September 1975, Trudeau had written Schmidt personally, confirming that Canada would remain "committed to maintaining a NATO force level which is accepted by our allies as being adequate in size and effective in character."[24] (See also, pp. 139–42.)

Although the issues remained difficult ones, exchanges on them were now occurring relatively frequently and at the highest possible levels, reflecting the extent to which the bilateral relationship had developed. Indeed, the evolution of relations in the late 1970s and early 1980s came, in large measure, to be driven by the close personal relationship between the prime minister and the chancellor.

BILATERAL RELATIONS PEAK

Between 1968 and 1973, Prime Minister Trudeau had made several official visits abroad, including trips to China and the Soviet Union. However, despite the nominal emphasis the government's 1970 white paper placed on the improvement of relations with Europe, no official visits were made to continental Europe, aside from a January 1969 trip to Rome. As far as relations with Germany were concerned, no Canadian prime minister had made a state visit to the Federal Republic since Diefenbaker's trip in 1958. Likewise, Chancellor Brandt never visited Canada during his term in office, nor did he and his Canadian counterpart ever meet on the margins of an international gathering.

This changed dramatically after 1974. Between 1975 and 1982, Trudeau made a minimum of five official or unofficial visits to Germany during which he met with the chancellor, Schmidt visited Canada on six occasions, and the two met at least eight times while attending international gatherings.[25] This dramatic increase was attributed to the very close personal friendship which developed between the two men and also to the mutual desire, particularly on the part of Canada, to improve the bilateral political relationship.

In July 1976, Schmidt paid his first visit to Canada for discussions with Trudeau. The private stop, which followed a trip to the United States, allowed the two leaders to discuss a wide variety of issues including a deepening of the relations between the two countries.[26] During an official visit to Germany in May 1976, Allan MacEachen, the secretary of state for external affairs, had emphasized the "high priority" which Canada attached to improving relations, not only with the Community but also with the Federal Republic.[27]

Within the Department of External Affairs, these personal links opened up an opportunity to accelerate the development of political and economic relations. In 1975, John Halstead became Canada's new ambassador in Bonn. The appointment of a senior DEA official, who had for years advocated a much closer bilateral relationship, symbolized the desire for closer ties. During his time as ambassador, Halstead tried to increase the frequency of contacts between senior political officials, parliamentarians, and businessmen from the two countries, and to put them on a more systematic foundation.[28]

To facilitate this evolution, DEA sought a framework agreement which would set up more regular political, economic, and financial consultations between Canadian and German diplomats and officials. Such consultations, in the political realm, had already been initiated in the late 1960s and had been widened in an exchange of letters between Mitchell Sharp and Walter Scheel in 1971. However, as Halstead told Günter van Well, the state secretary in the Foreign Office in May 1977, they still did not, in his opinion, "correspond to [the] growing importance of [the] relationship" between the FRG and Canada.[29] Ultimately, it was the personal relationship between Trudeau and Schmidt which would ensure that these discussions developed into the meaningful consultations they would later become (see above, pp. 75–7).

Schmidt's 1977 State Visit

The state visit of Schmidt to Canada in July 1977 was the first by a German chancellor since the trip of Erhard in 1964. For the Canadians, the visit offered a crucial opportunity to provide the spark which might truly ignite the two countries' economic relationship. In a meeting in December of 1976 with the heads of Canada's missions in Europe, the new secretary of state for external affairs, Don Jamieson, had reportedly stated that the next twelve to eighteen months would be the "testing time" for the contractual link. Either Canadian and European businesses would take advantage of the opportunities it offered or they would not.[30] The chancellor's visit was thus crucially important in beginning to foster such Canadian and German contacts. Meetings were planned for the chancellor with provincial premiers, government officials, and businessmen in Ontario, Alberta, and British Columbia.

For the Germans, the visit to Canada and the simultaneous one to the United States would afford an opportunity to address bilateral problems which had emerged with both North American states. German nuclear sales to Brazil was the most important of these issues because the Carter administration opposed the sale of a German uranium enrichment plant to that country. Canada was also upset with the Community's nuclear export policy and had suspended its uranium sales to Europe. This suspension, according to statements made to DEA officials by the German ambassador in Ottawa, Count Max Samlich, was causing Schmidt considerable domestic difficulties. Similarly, in a meeting early in 1977, the head of the European Commission delegation in Ottawa, Curt Heidenreich, told Trudeau's chief foreign policy adviser, Ivan Head, that the Canadian position on nuclear exports was making his job of promoting economic co-operation between Canada and the community more difficult.[31]

When Schmidt's visit began in Vancouver on 7 July, the tricky issue of Canada's uranium export policy was put off for a later discussion. Initial discussions between the prime minister and the chancellor focused instead on a range of other bilateral and multilateral issues.[32] On the broad aspects of key political issues confronting the alliance, there was a convergence of views between both leaders.

Both leaders shared concerns over the American administration's public efforts to indict the Soviet Union for its human rights record. Schmidt's impression of the position of President Carter was an especially sceptical one. Indeed, Schmidt later described Carter as a man "ignorant" of the basic realities of power and of the political situation in Europe.[33] Both Trudeau and Schmidt believed it was important to avoid a public shouting match with the Russians and, instead, to protect the gains which had been made in the Helsinki process. Under this accord, tens of thousands of people had already been able to come to the Federal Republic from East Germany and Eastern Europe. If this progress was to be maintained, both the prime minister and the chancellor realized it was vital that the Soviet Union's attitude towards the CSCE process remain favourable.

Both Trudeau and Schmidt believed that the strength of the Euro-communist parties in Western Europe was growing. Trudeau thought that their success might inspire dissident elements in Eastern Europe to press for liberalization, which might in turn lead to another Soviet crackdown and a lowering of the Iron Curtain once again. Schmidt, however, feared that communist participation in government in France or Italy would lead to a rightward policy shift in both West Germany and the United States. He apparently feared that the right in France might even resort to "extra-legal means" in response to such a development. The implications of such developments for East-West relations worried the Germans, and the chancellor again emphasized that the Federal Republic was totally committed to détente since without it, the division of Germany "could become a bleeding wound." It was in this context that Schmidt re-emphasized that American leadership was vital "but within the NATO framework."

He then expressed his "concern about the tendency of NATO allies other than the United States and Germany to reduce their military contribution because of economic difficulties." Trudeau seemed to agree in general terms but again argued that for Canada NATO was primarily a political rather than a military organization. In response, Schmidt underscored the position that for the Federal Republic the military side of NATO remained "extremely important."

While sharing generally similar views on a variety of important East-West issues, especially the primary importance of continuing an uninterrupted East-West dialogue regardless of human rights abuses in the Soviet bloc, there remained an underlying, even if now reduced, divergence of opinion on the military role of NATO. For West Germany, the military dimension was by far and away the most important aspect of its relationship with Canada. Yet Canada's response to this reality was always inadequate. For instance, although Canada had announced an increase in defence spending early in 1977, the government still believed it to be unnecessary to address more seriously the commitment-capability gap which confronted the Canadian Forces and their military commitments in Europe. Even though the government had moved to re-equip its NATO-assigned forces, it never accepted the notion that it could utilize defence policy to support its diplomatic and economic policy objectives. Indeed, although in many ways he came to accept the utility of NATO and the value of a continued Canadian contribution, the prime minister seems never to have changed his basic view that NATO's military role was anachronistic. In this most important respect, the perceptions of the German and Canadian leaders were and remained sharply different.

In terms of that aspect of the bilateral relationship which mattered the most to Canada – the fostering of trade links with Europe – the Schmidt visit also demonstrated that there were some important obstacles in the way of government efforts to give life to the contractual link and to spark an upswing in Canadian-European economic relations. Both Canada's uranium export policy and its foreign investment screening process were causing problems.

The issue of uranium exports had caused friction as early as 1975 during the meeting between Schmidt and Trudeau in Helsinki. At that time the chancellor had reportedly argued that stringent nuclear export controls would not prevent those states that really wanted nuclear weapons from acquiring them. He apparently predicted that Brazil would have nuclear weapons in a few years anyway, whether they were a result of German exports or equipment provided by Westinghouse. Trudeau, however, stated his belief that this view was too "fatalistic" and that more stringent nuclear export controls were still worth the effort.[34]

In the subsequent 1977 meeting in Ottawa, the prime minister asserted that Canada would consider resuming these exports on an interim basis, pending the outcome of an international study on the nuclear fuel cycle and on the peaceful uses of uranium.[35] This outcome seemed to satisfy the Germans. By October 1977 an interim agreement for lifting the uranium export ban had still not been concluded, however, and an internal DEA memorandum acknowledged the consequent German irritation. The ban was finally lifted in December.[36]

The other problem discussed in the chancellor's conversations with Canada's provincial premiers between 7 and 12 July 1977 was the role of the Foreign Investment Review Agency (FIRA). Schmidt reportedly stated his belief on several occasions that the federal government's agency was seriously deterring German business from investing in Canada. Interestingly, all provincial premiers, whatever difficulties they may have had with the agency, nevertheless reportedly defended FIRA in their discussions with Schmidt. Even Premier Peter Lougheed of Alberta stated that his government was "happy" with the way FIRA was working.[37] Despite repeated Canadian assurances that FIRA would not constitute a serious impediment to the vast majority of German and other foreign investments, the agency nevertheless remained a continuing irritant in Canadian-German trading relations until its abolition by the Mulroney government soon after it took office in 1984.

As numerous analysts have pointed out in assessing the implementation of the Third Option, the most significant problem was the difficulty of getting European and Canadian businesses to test the waters of a new market. Nor, apparently, was there much enthusiasm among senior bureaucrats in the Department of Industry, Trade and Commerce and the Finance Department. This reality, when combined with the undermining effects of the policies on uranium exports and on foreign investment, meant that the Third Option and its child, the contractual link, soon proved to be a failure.

The Multi-Role Combat Aircraft Project

Although a nominal strategy to promote a diversification of the country's trading relationships, the Third Option effectively lacked a co-ordinated industrial and trade policy plan to secure its implementation. This failing was particularly manifest with respect to the federal government's unwillingness to become directly involved in fostering closer economic ties with Europe. Such opportunities certainly did exist, in particular with respect to the federal government's own spending power. Indeed, as one German analyst argued at the time, the federal government's spending power was the primary vehicle for developing Canadian-European trade as well as broader industrial co-operation. In the late 1970s the most promising area in which the federal government could develop these trading and industrial links was aircraft procurement.[38]

A few months after the contractual link came in to being in 1976, an opportunity arose for Canada to rejoin the Multi-Role Combat Aircraft project which it had abandoned in 1968. In November, Canada's ambassador in Bonn met with officials of Messerschmitt-Bolkow-Blohm, the prime German contractor in the project. At that time Canada was invited to become a partner in the project. The Panavia consortium which had been formed in March 1969 was then comprised of three countries: the United

Kingdom and West Germany each with a 42.5-per-cent share, and Italy with a 15-per-cent share. German officials emphasized that they were prepared to give Canada a fair set of industrial benefits, but that a decision would be required within six months.[39]

The project was now a multibillion-dollar endeavour. The production programme, which had been initiated in July 1976, envisaged an initial production run of 809 aircraft for the three participating countries (eventually some 1000 aircraft were built). The aircraft's primary role was to be low-level interdiction (attack) and in this capacity it would replace the Federal Republic's F-104 Starfighter. In addition, a special air-defence version was to be procured by the Royal Air Force for long-range interception over the North Atlantic. In this latter capacity, the twin-engined aircraft (designated Tornado) had an endurance time of some two hours when conducting combat air patrols three hundred to four hundred nautical miles from base; this flying time could of course be extended with in-flight refuelling. Its intercept radius was some 300 nautical miles at supersonic speed and more than 1000 nautical miles at subsonic speed.[40]

The air defence Tornado was designed not as a "dog-fighting" fighter aircraft but rather as a long-range interceptor. It thus seemed to be particularly well suited for North American air defence against bombers unaccompanied by fighters. It could also fulfil all the peacetime interception/ sovereignty-protection duties required both over the North and off Canada's Atlantic and Pacific coasts. In central Europe, procurement of the ground-attack version of the Tornado would allow Canada's air forces to carry out the conventional interdiction mission in a modern combat environment while providing commonality and inter-operability with both the Luftwaffe and the Royal Air Force.

Despite these potential benefits, the offer to enter the consortium as a fourth partner was not taken up by Canada. However, discussions continued into 1977 and 1978 about a possible Canadian purchase of the Tornado. Early in 1977 Lieutenant-General W.K. Carr (who had been involved with the project in the late 1960s and who was now head of Air Command in the Canadian Forces) paid a visit to Germany to meet with German aviation industry officials. According to press reports, the Panavia group was offering Canada the opportunity to undertake final assembly of any Tornados procured for the Canadian Forces. In addition, Canada was offered a share in the production of Tornados for Britain, Italy, and the Federal Republic. Likewise, offers of European-Canadian industrial co-operation outside the air industry sphere were reportedly on the table. From a political standpoint, as the German newspaper *Süddeutsche Zeitung* noted, purchase of the Tornado by Canada would significantly raise Canada's profile in Europe and also prove to be a major economic and political coup for European industry.[41]

Despite the obvious boost that participation in such a project would give to Canadian-European industrial co-operation and to advancing the Third Option strategy, the Tornado was soon rated last in the New Fighter Aircraft competition launched by Ottawa in 1977. Besides the Tornado, this competition included four American aircraft (F-15 Eagle, F-14 Tomcat, F-16 Falcon, and F/A-18 Hornet) and the French Mirage 2000. In both the ground-attack and long-range interception roles, the two versions of the Tornado were equal or superior to the other aircraft in the competition.[42] Nevertheless, the Canadian Forces wanted a multi-role aircraft capable of operating in both an attack and an air-defence capacity; it also wanted an agile "dog-fighting" aircraft not the long-range interceptor that the air-defence version of the Tornado was. Essentially, it sought to retain maximum aircraft flexibility in all possible combat environments while satisfying both fighter communities in the air force: the pilots of the 1st Canadian Air Group in Germany (who flew the CF-104 in an attack role) and those flying the CF-101 under the North American Air Defence (NORAD) regime. In the end, the primary reason for the elimination of the Tornado was a financial one. The diverse requirements of Air Command would have to be met in a single aircraft type because cabinet had set a firm and inflexible ceiling of just $2.34 billion for the entire NFA project.[43]

Whether or not the military requirements set by the air force and the budgetary contraints imposed by the cabinet really fit with Canada's actual strategic and military needs, let alone supported the country's political and economic objectives vis-à-vis NATO Europe, the decision was made late in 1978 to eliminate the Tornado (as well as three other expensive aircraft – the F-15, the F-14, and the Mirage) from the competition. In April 1980, after much delay, the American F/A-18 Hornet was purchased by Canada. The Hornet was an extremely capable multi-role aircraft whose cost fit Canada's budget. However, in the ground-attack role in central Europe, Canada was the only NATO country to deploy this aircraft. It thus lost the chance to retain aircraft commonality with the Luftwaffe and the Royal Air Force. Likewise, in the air-defence role in North America, the Hornet was also capable, but it lacked the range of the air-defence version of the Tornado.[44]

Before this decision was made the Germans had continued to lobby hard for the Tornado. The chancellor raised the subject himself with both the prime minister and Ambassador Halstead in the context of discussions on the Third Option. However, the Canadian air force itself was uninterested.[45] In the decision to eliminate the Tornado from the competition, the Canadian military received some measure of support from an unlikely source – the German defence attaché in Ottawa. Colonel Rolf Klages, an air force officer, agreed with Canadian air force officers that the Tornado was unsuited for Air Command. Indeed, during the September 1978 visit of the new German defence minister, Hans Apel, to Canada, Klages urged him not to proceed with his plan to argue strongly in favour of the Tornado purchase. Instead, Klages asserted that if he urged the Canadian defence minister to purchase the Tornado, he would "look foolish" because the Canadians "would never buy the aircraft." Brigadier-General Paul Manson, the Canadian project officer, later thanked Klages for his intervention.[46]

The Impact of Trudeau's 1978 State Visit

In the absence of big projects, DEA had to concentrate on improving the numbers and quality of contacts and consultations between the two countries. The establishment, in 1978, of regular political meetings to co-ordinate increasingly similar approaches to a variety of international issues was complemented by the initiation of wider discussions to implement consultations in the areas of financial and economic policy as well. Thus, in the autumn of 1978, Hans-Jürgen Wischnewski, the state secretary in the Chancellor's Office, visited Canada to co-ordinate the terms for these high-level political contacts.

In his meeting with the clerk of the Privy Council, Michael Pitfield, Wischnewski explained that he had been directly instructed by Chancellor Schmidt to co-ordinate the development of consultative arrangements with Canada.[47] Schmidt's personal interest in these talks was thus absolutely key in ensuring a successful beginning to both the political and the financial talks.

The financial consultations began in September 1978, when Bill Hood, assistant deputy minister in the Finance Department, along with Robert Johnstone, assistant under-secretary at DEA for economic affairs, met in Washington with Manfred Lahnstein, under-secretary in the German Finance Ministry. It was decided that the consultations on the margins of international meetings would discuss financial issues of mutual interest. There would be three participants from each side; on the German side they would include one senior official from the Finance Ministry and another from the Bundesbank (normally its president, Karl-Otto Pöhl). Procedures were also discussed for annual economic consultations which would seek to promote communication and contacts between the business communities of the two countries.[48] In addition to these consultations in the political and financial realms, annual staff talks between senior military officers from both countries had begun in 1977.[49]

Despite these positive developments, it was widely recognized by many officials that as long as government refused to put its money where its mouth was, the bilateral relationship would be unlikely to progress to the level of quality or intensity desired by the Canadian government. This was evidently alluded to during the visit of Wischnewski, when Pitfield stressed the continuing need for a "joint venture which would capture [the] imagination of [the populations of both countries]." In response, Wischnewski noted that Canada's best opportunity for developing a closer relationship with the Federal Republic lay in the NATO sphere. The alliance was essential for the FRG's survival, and Canada should thus seek to "cash in more through this contact."[50] However, with both a defence policy review and the commitment of additional resources to defence or collaborative armament projects seemingly out of the question, it was necessary to concentrate on efforts to improve the bilateral economic relationship more or less in isolation.

Canadian officials therefore put the emphasis on initiating meaningful economic consultations along the lines of those already begun in the financial and political spheres. In a letter from the DEA's under-secretary, Allan Gotlieb, to Pitfield in October, three purposes in economic consultations with the Germans were outlined: to open lines of communication to senior German officials; to facilitate frank discussion of specific issues and policies which inhibited closer relations; and to consult on wider political and economic issues outside the bilateral sphere. It was recommended that an interdepartmental management team of deputy ministers be convened to formulate an agenda for the first such consultation.[51] The interdepartmental meeting itself was held late in November and was chaired by Don McPhail, an assistant under-secretary at DEA.

An ambitious agenda was formulated to bring German and Canadian businessmen together for joint ventures in Germany, Canada, or third markets. Another goal was to create a better climate of business confidence by addressing more forthrightly problematic issues such as FIRA and Canadian concern over the Community's agriculture policies. Finally, it was seen as desirable to create an advisory group of Canadian businessmen which might eventually be expanded into a series of advisory committees with representatives from various associations and chambers of commerce. To explore German interest in these ideas, it was decided to send a group of Canadian officials to Bonn in 1979.[52]

Even before this group left for Bonn, DEA received indications that the Germans were less than fully enthusiastic about the Canadian plans, which one official of the German Economics Ministry apparently described as "very ambitious," implying that they were in fact "too ambitious." During the visit of the German economics minister, Count Otto Lambsdorff, to Canada in February 1979, these German perceptions became quite apparent to Canadian officials, and a DEA memorandum prepared for a follow-up meeting of the interdepartmental committee noted that "the Germans seem primarily interested in going through the motions by keeping the discussions broad and general."[53]

The truth seemed to be that officials of the German Economics Ministry saw little in the way of tangible benefits accruing to Germany through a closer economic relationship with Canada. Even the annual economic consultations appeared to have been accepted reluctantly, and in the absence of firm instructions from Germany's political leaders that the Canadian initiatives should be facilitated, German economic officials seemed intent on stonewalling. It seemed just as likely that such instructions would not be issued as long as the Canadians failed to provide clear indications of a desire to accommodate German interests and invest in building a closer relationship.

During the short-lived Clark government in 1979–80, DEA officials apparently sought to convince the new government of the need to ensure that Canada's defence and economic policies were more closely synchronized. However, some close advisers of Clark's new secretary of state for external affairs, Flora MacDonald, were apparently sceptical of the real benefits for Canada in a continuation of its military presence in Europe. Certainly by this time it was apparent that the Third Option strategy and the contractual link had not yielded the benefits that had been hoped for. As a result, many believed that the Europeans (despite what were regarded as Canada's positive signals on the defence policy side in the mid-1970s) had themselves shown insufficient interest in Canada's economic and trade initiatives to warrant a great investment of resources in Canada's military commitments in central Europe.[54]

In the process leading to the preparation of a new foreign policy paper, the need for greater consistency and policy co-ordination was nevertheless recognized. Thus, in a speech delivered in Toronto on 6 December 1979, MacDonald argued for "continuity" in the search for closer relations with both the EC as a whole and individual member-states of the Community. "I think, three broad questions ... should engage our attention in the months ahead," she stated.

First how do we make the Community aware of our views and interests at a time when the energies of the members focus on the internal harmonization of their policies. Second, what steps can we take to enhance our joint benefit in the areas of trade, investment and the exchange of technology. Third, how can we draw together our security and economic interests in Europe so that they are mutually supportive or at least so that the major components of our policy are not in conflict with each other.

She went on to note that the security and economic fields were "intertwined" and that while Canada fulfilled its responsibilities in one area, "we must be sure that our European allies are fully sensitive to our needs in the other [area]."[55] Whether these views would have resulted in a new emphasis on the importance of Canada's military commitments in Europe or whether they were the precursor of a new attempt to withdraw those forces will never be known, since the Clark government collapsed only one week after the minister's speech.

A FINAL EFFORT TO GIVE MOMENTUM
TO THE RELATIONSHIP

During the 1979–80 election campaign, Pierre Trudeau again confirmed that despite the Soviet invasion of Afghanistan in December 1979, his perception of defence policy and military spending had not significantly changed. "We think there are more useful things to do than to fight wars and put a lot of dough into armaments."[56] Thus, with the reinstatement of a Trudeau government in February 1980 election, defence policy returned to where it had been a few months before. There were no new attempts to bring it into line with other government policy objectives; the only compensation to offset this development was a resumption of the close Trudeau-Schmidt relationship.[57]

This high-level political relationship would continue to be of vital importance, since the West German profile in international affairs seemed to have been on a continuous rise in the 1970s while Canada's standing in both Germany and Europe remained low. Indeed, in a memorandum prepared to brief the new secretary of state for external affairs, Mark MacGuigan, for his meeting with Hans-Dietrich Genscher, the frustration of some in the department was very evident. It was admitted that Canada did not rank very prominently among German foreign policy priorities and the organization of the German Foreign Office was cited as evidence: only one junior officer looked after Canadian affairs. Moreover, the German embassy in Ottawa was much smaller than the Canadian embassy in Bonn.[58]

By 1980 the interest of the German foreign minister in Canada also appeared to have waned considerably since Genscher's enthusiastic approach to the Canadian embassy in 1969 on the subject of parliamentary exchanges. A visit by Genscher to Canada had been scheduled for nearly three years but had been postponed on several different occasions because of events in Canada or Germany. When MacGuigan again issued the invitation during a meeting with the German foreign minister in New York in September 1980, Genscher appeared barely interested. Likewise MacGuigan's comment that there was a need to bring "momentum" to the Canadian-German economic relationship received no direct response from Genscher. The Canadians were compelled to reissue their invitation later in the year.[59]

Again, it was the relationship between the two heads of government which provided some additional momentum for the relationship. In October 1980, Trudeau had written Schmidt congratulating him on his recent election victory and inviting him to visit Canada once again. It was decided to take advantage of the economic summit, to be hosted by Canada in July 1981, and to combine it with a visit by the chancellor which would be focused on bilateral economic issues. In the lead-up to this visit, both the German embassy in Ottawa and the Canadian embassy in Bonn were instructed to submit ideas for closer economic consultation and areas of possible joint projects. In this respect, the stop of the prime minister in Bonn in November 1980 and his pre-summit trip to Bonn in June 1981 helped to lay the groundwork for Schmidt's visit to Canada in July.[60]

By the early 1980s, the Germans were beginning to think of ways of counterbalancing the Federal Republic's existing energy relationship with the Soviet Union. According to some estimates, the FRG would be importing some 20 per cent of its natural gas from the Soviet Union by the year 2000. In addition to potential strategic problems, Western Europe's energy dependence on and technology transfer to the Soviet Union had become a major political issue between European governments and the newly elected administration of Ronald Reagan in the United States.[61] While any Canadian sources of energy would only come on line in the long term, the Germans were interested in exploring options.

An important focus of the discussions between the prime minister, the chancellor, and key ministers in their July meetings was therefore collaborative energy projects and wider German investment opportunities. Under terms of the National Energy Program (NEP), which had been initiated by the Trudeau government in November 1980, the federal government had begun a policy designed both to Canadianize the energy sector and to generate greater revenues for the federal government as it sought to curb the growing power of the oil-producing provinces (principally Alberta).[62] Towards this end, the government envisaged the construction of huge energy megaprojects which would provide large-scale industrial benefits to the manufacturing sectors of the Canadian economy. The prime minister reportedly told Chancellor Schmidt in their meeting on 17 July that the total investment required had been estimated at up to one trillion dollars by the mid-1990s. Canada, Trudeau apparently asserted, could not provide such sums on its own and thus required foreign investment. Schmidt confirmed his sympathy with the NEP's goals and even offered his congratulations, should the NEP permit Canada to get the upper hand with the multinationals.[63] The chancellor also was said to have advanced the case of the German oil company, Faber, which had just applied to FIRA for a joint venture in the oil sands. This was made "special note" of by the Minister of Industry, Trade and Commerce, Herb Gray.

The chancellor, in outlining the energy vulnerability of the Federal Republic, expressed his hope that Germany's energy imports could be diversified. In response to Schmidt's query about the prospects of natural gas exports, both Finance Minister MacEachen and Trudeau assured him that there were such prospects for the 1980s and 1990s, despite Canada's policy of exporting only energy surplus to its own needs, because it was hoped to bring on line the considerable potential in both the Arctic and off the east coast. Trudeau, in fact, encouraged German investment in this sphere, arguing that one or two megaprojects "would do a lot to solidify our economic relations."[64]

Ultimately, of course, these hopes fell victim to the rapid collapse of world oil prices and with them the multibillion-dollar megaprojects. Canada had to be content with the smaller gains which accrued from the July discussions. As a "jump start" for a significantly enhanced economic partnership, it was agreed that both leaders would designate a senior official to come up with two or three "hard initiatives" and a proposed calendar for implementing them. In a veiled reference to the probable reluctance of some German officials, the prime minister noted in a letter to Schmidt that the purpose was to "give high profile evidence of our determination as leaders to advance our economic relationship."[65]

For the task, Canada appointed Gordon Osbaldeston, secretary of the Ministry of State for Economic Development (described by Trudeau in his letter to Schmidt as "the most senior official dealing with economic policy in our government structure"), while the Germans appointed Per Fischer, ministerial director for economic affairs in the German Foreign Office. After his visit to Germany in September, Osbaldeston reported to the prime minister and recommended the formation of a management team composed of senior officials from key government departments with a mandate to "strengthen the economic component" of the bilateral relationship. Several other recommendations were also made for intensifying the economic relationship, including the provision for the cabinet of an overall strategy for managing the bilateral relationship.[66]

Canada had long been seeking to increase its manufactured exports to the Federal Republic because raw material exports still amounted to some 70 per cent of total sales abroad. Thus an important focus for the management team, which was chaired by Derek Burney, assistant secretary responsible for the Bureau on Trade, Development and General Economic Relations within DEA, was on improving trade in finished goods. In contrast, German expectations were found to be focused primarily on the opportunities for energy development projects and energy exports. During the Fischer visit to Ottawa in March, the dominant issues discussed related to possible opportunities in the energy sector. This left the Canadians somewhat dissatisfied, and while seeking to encourage German interest in this area, a memorandum prepared for a June 1982 meeting between Trudeau and Schmidt in Bonn nevertheless suggested that the prime minister ask the chancellor what sectors other than energy held promise in German eyes.[67]

In terms of the development of wider trade and industrial links, the Foreign Investment Review Agency continued to crop up as an irritant in the economic relationship. Although Schmidt had told Trudeau privately that he saw the necessity of FIRA,[68] other German officials and German business did not share this view. The Germans had hoped that the presence of a representative from FIRA on the interdepartmental management team would mean that German investment applications would receive special treatment, and the embassy in Bonn reported early in 1982 that this view was becoming common currency.[69] However the Canadians informed the Germans, including Count Lambsdorff during a visit by the economics minister to Canada in August, that all the requirements for investment remained in force. Even so, the government did move to institute new procedures so that investments by small and medium-sized businesses could be processed more quickly.

Although Trudeau had promised to strengthen FIRA during the 1979–80 election campaign, the response of one Canadian official to Per Fischer's inquiry about this government promise, was to reassure Fischer that the government's actions might not follow its rhetoric.[70] And Canadian actions did in fact go some way to overcoming German business concerns: between 1974 and 30 September 1983, FIRA rendered decisions on 293 investment proposals from the FRG. Of these, 282 (96 per cent) were allowed and 11 disallowed. Ten of these 11 proposals were resubmitted and 6 were allowed in their revised form. This acceptance rate was even better than the overall FIRA approval average (91 per cent). Even so, in a DEA memorandum which discussed this issue in 1983, it was admitted that the primary difficulty which FIRA created was the perception among foreign investors that Canada was creating bureaucratic impediments to investment by requiring companies to engage in complex and time-consuming application procedures.[71]

By the summer of 1982, there had been some gains in the development of a closer economic relationship. Two-way trade between Germany and Canada had increased to some $3 billion by the early 1980s. Likewise, although only 31 per cent of Canadian exports were in finished products, this was double the percentage of just two years earlier. Moreover, cumulative German investment in Canada since 1952 amounted to well over $4 billion, making Canada the third largest recipient of German investment outside the EC.[72]

The Trudeau-Schmidt initiative provided a further boost to this trend, with several joint industrial projects begun between Canadian and German firms as a result of the economic consultations of 1981–2.[73] A German-Canadian Chamber of Commerce and Industry had been formed and a German-Canadian conference held in August 1982, both of which brought together German and Canadian firms. Finally, Lambsdorff paid an important visit to Alberta and Ottawa in July and August 1982 designed to strengthen economic links.

Despite some positive developments, it continued to be the perception in many circles that the bilateral economic relationship was not being fully exploited and that it certainly had not come close to developing to a point where it could be said that the Third Option strategy was being successfully implemented with respect to Germany and Europe. In fact as indicated in

Table 1
Trends in Canadian and German Trade, 1975, 1979, 1983

I.   Canada's trade with the FRG, the EC, and the United States as a percentage of its total world
     trade (exports and imports)

	1975	1979	1983
FRG	1.9	2.2	1.6
EC	10.3	9.5	7.4
United States	64.0	67.0	69.0

II. FRG's trade with Canada as a percentage of its total world trade (exports and imports)

	1975	1979	1983
Canada	0.81	0.9	0.79

Source: International Monetary Fund, *Direction of Trade Statistics Yearbook,* 1982 and 1985
(Washington 1982 and 1985).

table 1 the percentage of Canada's trade with the European Community had
actually declined from 1975 to 1983 while the percentage of its trade with the
United States had markedly increased! Even though the dollar value of
Canadian trade with the EC and West Germany continued to expand (with
the EC from US$7.1 billion in 1975 to US$10.3 billion in 1983; and with
Germany from US$1.3 billion in 1975 to US$2.2 billion in 1983), overall trade
with the United States was simply growing that much faster.

   Certainly some of the reasons for this outcome were structural and
involved the problems of fostering Canadian-European trade links in the
difficult climate prevailing in the world economy during the late 1970s and
early 1980s.[74] However, Ottawa's efforts to overcome these obstacles and
encourage the development of Canadian-European trade ties were also
totally inadequate in the context of the goals which had been enunciated in
the Third Option.

   In the area of defence procurement, for instance, the federal government
in fact contributed significantly to the growth of Canadian-American trade
at the expense of other regions. This was done principally through its decision to acquire some $3.5-billion worth of military equipment (in the form
of the Aurora maritime patrol aircraft and the F/A-18 Hornet fighter) in the
United States. Both the Aurora and the Hornet deals also spawned additional
industrial offset spending with, for instance, McDonnell-Douglas (the
builder of the Hornet) committed to invest some $2.453 billion in Canada
by 1995. Despite the high quality of these weapon systems and aside from
the beneficial economic dimensions of these agreements, these procurement
decisions nevertheless worked at cross-purposes to the government's

declared economic and trade policy strategies.[75] Had this procurement been focused on Europe instead, the resulting defence and industrial co-operation would have been a major shot in the arm for the Third Option strategy. Some confirmation of this proposition can be found in the Canadian-German trade figures for 1979 which partly reflect an increase in trade resulting from the $187-million purchase of Leopard tanks (then being delivered) and the associated offset agreements.[76]

Thus, despite the enhanced enthusiasm that the Trudeau government had in the early 1980s for expanding Canadian-German economic relations, its policy with respect to trade diversification had been unco-ordinated and only halfheartedly pursued. Indeed, a DEA report from mid-1983, which reviewed the progress in Canada-FRG economic relations, noted that a key recommendation in Osbaldeston's 1981 report – to provide cabinet with a strategy for managing the relationship – remained unimplemented.[77] It was only in October 1983 that a concrete Export Development Plan for Germany was belatedly published. The plan, which was approved by cabinet's committee on economic development, centred on the implementation of various "action plans" to expand and improve Canadian-German trade in ten key sectors.[78] Yet in many ways the plan fell under the adage of "two little too late" since it only emerged in the twilight of the Third Option strategy.

Likewise, despite its positive aspects, the Lambsdorff visit of July/August 1982 was not utilized to its full potential. For one thing, in the planning for the visit which had, after all, been sought by the Canadians for some time, the Germans were reportedly informed that the prime minister and other senior Canadian officials might be unavailable to meet with Lambsdorff. Then, in the Alberta portion of the visit, the German economics minister was prevented from meeting with the Alberta premier because of a federal-provincial dispute over the conditions and terms for such a meeting. In Alberta, cabinet ministers traditionally reserve the right to decide which persons and officials would be present at their meetings. On the occasion of Lambsdorff's visit, it was decided that Alberta cabinet ministers should meet with the German minister alone. However, Ottawa insisted on having an official from External Affairs present during any such meetings. The dispute emerged at the last minute and the resulting federal-provincial impasse proved most embarrassing for the Canadian government. Even the attempted intervention of the German ambassador, Erich Strätling, who telephoned Alberta officials in an effort to put the planned meetings back on the agenda, could not break the deadlock. As a result, while Lambsdorff did meet with Alberta's minister of international trade, Horst Schmid, the planned meeting with Premier Lougheed did not take place.[79] Incidents such as this, which could have been avoided through more thorough advance federal-provincial consultation and planning, in their own small way undermined the development of the bilateral relationship.

The high-water mark in the Canadian-German bilateral relationship was reached in the summer of 1982 when Helmut Schmidt visited Canada for the last time as chancellor for a private trip with Trudeau in the Arctic.[80] Likewise, toward the mid-1980s, the trade and economic priorities of the Canadian government shifted and a marked policy evolution began – away from the idea of trade diversification towards an emphasis on the importance of ensuring guaranteed access to the United States market. The shift to continentalism would ultimately have profound implications for Canada's relationship with Europe and would also prove to be another small contribution to a widening of the transatlantic relationship between Europe and North America in the 1980s.

CANADIAN-GERMAN POLITICAL RELATIONS: SOME CONCLUSIONS

From the late 1960s on, there were enhanced opportunities to develop the Canadian-German bilateral relationship. Certainly many government officials in Canada recognized the deepening of bilateral relations as an important policy objective. Moreover, the FRG was seen to be Europe's most important rising economic and political power. However, throughout the period in question, bilateral relations were consistently described in Canadian memoranda as either underdeveloped or as not developed to their full potential. There were several reasons for this assessment.

First, the decisions of the Trudeau defence review of 1968–9 meant that relations with the Social Democrat–led government which took office in Germany in 1969 got off to a bad start. Thereafter, for the better part of the 1970s, a great deal of effort was spent both by Germans (principally in the Defence Ministry) and Canadians (particularly in DEA) to repair the damage and develop a reasonably stable defence and security policy relationship. In this sense, Canadian political leaders never really understood the central importance that strategic and military questions played in the German security policy framework and the vital place that the North American commitment had within that framework.

Second, even after it became apparent to Canadian political leaders in the mid-1970s that Canada's search for an improved trading relationship with Europe was linked to the question of Canada's military commitments, there was no serious effort to use those commitments as a political and diplomatic lever in the pursuit of economic objectives. Beyond the halfhearted re-equipment of the forces in Europe to prevent a further erosion of military capability, no serious consideration was given to a defence policy review which would move actually to improve capability or even just restore it to a pre-1969 level. While it seems unlikely that an increased defence effort would, by itself, have made the implementation of the contractual link successful, it might well have focused German political attention at the highest levels on more earnestly facilitating Canadian-European trade links.

This could have been done most especially in the area of military procurement. As one Canadian government document belatedly acknowledged in October 1983:

Europeans have especially viewed Canada's decisions on major military and transport purchases as a measure of the federal government's support of the Third Option diversification policy. In 1976 Canada purchased 128 German Leopard Tanks from the f.r.g. at a cost of DM 360 million. The prime contractor, Krauss-Maffei, agreed to offsets in Canada equal to 40 per cent of the purchase price over 10 years. Notwithstanding this transaction, some concern has been expressed in Germany over the failure to receive other large contracts in Canada.[81]

The Defence Structure Review of 1974–5 had identified certain basic areas of the Canadian Forces which had to be re-equipped. However, even this limited re-equipment effort proceeded more or less independently of the government's economic and trade policy objectives. If a more comprehensive, and *long-term* re-equipment programme focused on Germany and Europe had been launched, it would not only have significantly boosted Canadian-European trade but also have spawned wider and more permanent industrial co-operation. Such a programme could have been designed especially for the air and land forces though the preliminary steps involved in a naval acquisition programme could also have been begun (including perhaps the nuclear submarine project eventually proposed in the 1987 defence white paper). Cabinet's spending ceilings for individual projects would need to have been more flexible to facilitate the acquisition of particular weapon systems (such as the Tornado aircraft). However, had such acquisitions been closely co-ordinated with industrial policy objectives, the total economic, political, and military benefits associated with such a defence build-up would have far outweighed the costs. The impact would have been that much greater when one considers that Canada already ranked at the bottom of the NATO alliance in defence spending as a percentage of gross national product (see Appendix Five).

In general terms, the failure of Canada's political leaders to make effective use of the country's alliance and defence policies to facilitate wider political and economic objectives is at least partly attributable to the country's vacuous strategic culture and the apparent inability of decision-makers to think in terms of using military power to support political objectives. This would also be evident during the prime minister's peace initiative in 1983–4, when Canadian policy seemed to be insufficiently cognizant of the realities of the East-West balance of power and Canada's position in that balance.

Third, the pursuit of the Third Option with respect to Germany was halfhearted at best. While the government, and the prime minister himself, made great efforts to see that a contractual link was actually signed, there was no subsequent co-ordinated approach to encourage firms and business to take advantage of the opportunities available. Certainly the fact that by mid-1983 no cabinet-level strategy had yet been formulated with regard to Canadian-German relations is a prime example of this lack of action.[82] Trudeau has not usually been described as a vehement economic nationalist and although in the aftermath of the Nixon shocks he came to accept the desirability of encouraging a move by Canadian business away from over-reliance on the American market, he was not prepared to move towards major government intervention or expenditure to facilitate such a policy objective. In short, in the absence of a co-ordinated industrial and trade strategy, the Third Option's goals never had much of a chance.

The broader security policy objectives of the FRG in the period after 1969 (centred, as noted in chapter 2, on strengthening multilateral Atlantic links) meant that the Germans were interested in improving and deepening their relationship with Canada. Such a policy objective fit with a German desire to build counterbalances to the American relationship within the alliance. Indeed, this interest was demonstrated in the various political, military, economic, and parliamentary initiatives launched in the late 1960s and early 1970s. Moreover, toward the end of the 1970s, the closeness of German and Canadian positions on a wide variety of issues, and of the countries' leaders, had also drawn the FRG towards Canada.

Nevertheless, there was also a tendency in West Germany to take Canada for granted and, until 1969 and even thereafter, this limited the attention that most German officials paid to Canada. In this sense the Trudeau defence review may have had the effect of awakening an interest in Canada within the German defence policy making community. Indeed, it was the principal reason for the Schmidt initiatives of 1970 with respect to German training and defence procurement in Canada. Cutting the forces in the Federal Republic got Bonn's attention, but given the centrality of strategic and military factors in Germany's security policy framework, Canada's desire for greater reciprocity in the transatlantic relationship could have been demonstrated in other more subtle ways. Both the United States and the United Kingdom had extracted substantial economic and financial concessions from the Germans as compensation for their existing military presence or for an increase in that presence. There is no reason to suppose that Canada could not have done likewise.

After 1975, the Germans were "content" with their relationship with Canada, since they had in large measure succeeded in stabilizing the Canadian military commitment. While the Germans were likely satisfied with the state of bilateral relations, Canadian memoranda, by way of contrast, consistently emphasized the wider potential of the relationship which was not being realized. This, in part, reflected the growing differences in power and status between Canada and the Federal Republic. Canada's profile in Europe had always been low, while Germany's status both within the North Atlantic community and internationally rose considerably in the 1970s. The gap in the expectations that both countries had of their bilateral relationship is therefore understandable.

German political support was instrumental in securing Canada's contractual link with the EC in the first place, and this support was largely motivated by political and strategic factors, principally a desire to tie the Canadian military commitment more securely to Europe. Had Canada invested the necessary policy attention at the highest political levels, as well as additional resources, in building a stronger political and economic relationship, it probably would have been able to do so. Certainly the prominence of Helmut Schmidt, first as defence minister, then as finance minister, and finally as chancellor, and his close relationship with Trudeau would have proved invaluable in this respect.

Schmidt's personal interest in the Federal Republic's relations with Canada was demonstrated on several occasions and often his personal intervention as chancellor seemed crucial in moving the German bureaucracy to facilitate Canadian initiatives with respect to the development of the bilateral economic and political relationship. Likewise, during his tenure as defence minister, his initiatives with respect to the training of German forces in Canada and German procurement in Canada were very important in the wider development of the military and political relationship. However, there was often a lack of interest at the highest levels within Canada, and as a result the development of a more comprehensive bilateral relationship was not pursued with vigour and insight. The failure to utilize Canada's military presence in Germany to its full political and strategic advantage, and to co-ordinate the country's defence policy closely with its wider economic and political objectives in Europe, is the most glaring example of this weakness.

PART THREE

The Canadian-German Military Relationship

6 Canadian Forces in Europe: The First Twenty Years

In 1946, in keeping with the desire of Prime Minister Mackenzie King to limit any future overseas involvements by Canada, the government had hastily withdrawn its military forces from Europe. By the late 1940s, however, Mackenzie King had retired, to be replaced as prime minister by Louis St. Laurent. As well, there had been a substantive change in the international climate, and in 1949 Canada was one of the founding members of the North Atlantic Treaty Organization. Nevertheless, the government still did not believe that it was necessary to consider deploying Canadian troops in Europe.

There were two important reasons for the decision of the Canadian government to return Canadian forces to Europe in 1951. First of all, the deployment was prompted by the emergency conditions prevailing in Europe in the early 1950s and by the concomitant perception that the Soviet Union might well be tempted to use force (or authorize the use of force by its satellites as it had done in Korea) to achieve its objectives in Europe. The atmosphere in Europe in 1950–1 was one in which war was considered potentially imminent, necessitating immediate and decisive action by the Atlantic alliance.[1] While Canada's forces might remain in Europe for some time, once Europe was in a position to provide for its own defence (within say five to ten years), it was envisaged that they would be withdrawn. This remained the general view for some time; Canada (unlike the United Kingdom or the United States) refused to make any public statement only during the 1954 London Conference that its forces would remain in Europe.[2]

The second reason for the Canadian decision to deploy forces in Europe in 1951 arose from the sense of international obligation felt by the St. Laurent government because of its perception that the current international climate required absolute solidarity within the alliance. For this reason, the costs associated with Canada's deployment were accepted as a necessary expenditure, and from the beginning Canada therefore assumed responsibility for nearly all expenses associated with its military presence in central Europe.[3]

Because the decision to deploy forces to Europe was seen, first and foremost, as a necessary demonstration of Canada's political commitment to the defence of Europe, the larger and long-term strategic, political, and even legal implications of that decision were really only considered as an afterthought. For instance, the question of where specifically to base the Canadian brigade in Germany was not debated until the summer of 1951, barely two to three months before the brigade's departure. Yet the political consequences of such a decision were important. So, too, was the question of the specific legal framework under which the Canadian forces were to be based in Germany. However, since the decision to base forces in Europe had been made in a highly reactive fashion in response to events in Korea, questions about the specific Canadian political and military interests involved in the deployment of these forces were not foremost in the minds of decision-makers.[4]

Although the larger strategic and political implications of Canada's presence had been discussed only on the margins, certain political dimensions inherent in that deployment soon became apparent. This was the case in three specific areas in particular:

1   the initial military importance and value of the Canadian commitment to the allied command in Europe;
2   the relationship of the Canadian military commitment to Canada's political and diplomatic influence on European security issues; and
3   the political importance that the Germans came to attach to the Canadian contingent from the very outset of its announced deployment.

In this last area in particular, Germany's direct interest was instrumental in transforming the Canadian commitment from one made to the alliance in general to one made to the Federal Republic most specifically. In later years this German interest would become particularly apparent in the Federal Republic's close attention both to Canada's orientation to NATO strategy and to the reductions and reconfiguration of Canada's forces in Europe at the end of the 1960s.

THE MILITARY VALUE OF
THE COMMITMENT

Beyond its political and symbolic importance, the Canadian presence in Europe was, in the context of the early 1950s, a significant military contribution in its own right. In June 1950, the allies only maintained fairly weak occupation forces in the Federal Republic of Germany.[5] In consequence, even the single 6000-man brigade committed by Canada was immediately appreciated as an important military asset. The qualitative value of the Canadian brigade, which was composed in the early to mid-1950s of a high proportion of World War II and Korean War veterans, was a factor which was noted and reported by the German embassy in Ottawa.[6] The air commitment was of even greater significance militarily. Between 1951 and 1953 the RCAF air division, comprising 12 squadrons of F-86E Sabre fighters, was set up at bases in southwestern Germany and northeastern France. This commitment would eventually rise to 300 operational first-line jet fighters.[7] At a meeting in June 1951 in Paris with chiefs of the NATO air forces, General Eisenhower, the Supreme Allied Commander in Europe (SACEUR), revealed how highly he regarded the Canadian air commitment by pressing for an even greater effort. He argued that "for the next few years Canada, the United Kingdom and the United States should produce air power since other NATO countries were seriously lacking in technically trained personnel and had no chance period of producing the air forces required of them during this period. Thereafter, Canada, the United Kingdom and the United States could consider the further strengthening of their ground forces."[8] The plan for the RCAF, as spelled out later by Air Marshal W.A. Curtis, would have involved a build-up to an overall strength of some 1400 jet combat aircraft. This would have included adding a second Canadian air division of light jet bombers to the fighter commitment already made. In total, a possible build-up in Europe to nearly 500 jet fighters and bombers was envisaged.

The reaction of the minister of national defence, Brooke Claxton, to this plan was a furious one: "Nothing but the unbridled enthusiasm of our airmen could have produced such a result. I was exceedingly annoyed when I heard about it and made our Air Force go right back to the Paris group and say they had acted entirely without instruction and that we would not be adding any aircraft whatever."[9] Although the RCAF's premature response to Eisenhower's plan was reversed by an angry Claxton, the reported views of Eisenhower on the military value of the Canadian air commitment are important. It can be assumed that Canada's subsequent moves in 1955 to replace four of its Sabre squadrons with the more capable CF-100 all-weather fighter, while retaining the eight other F-86 squadrons in Europe, enhanced the military value of the air commitment.

The recognized military value of Canada's air commitment was also reflected in Germany's decision, made in late 1956, to purchase 225 F-86 Mk-6 aircraft from Canada. This sale, in addition to being a major boost for Canada's aviation industry, was instrumental in contributing to a 75-per-cent increase in the dollar value of Canadian-German trade between 1955 and 1957. The purchase was key for the German Luftwaffe because these new F-86 Mk-6s (plus 75 older model Sabres provided as mutual aid) constituted more that 20 per cent of all the combat aircraft which the Luftwaffe planned, as of 1956, to acquire. Undoubtedly, the example set for the Germans through the air-defence mission of the Canadian air division in Europe contributed to the Federal Republic's selection of the Canadian-built F-86 as the Luft-waffe's day fighter.[10]

While the number of combat aircraft deployed in Germnay declined in the 1960s, the quality of the Canadian commitment remained high as the F-86 and the CF-100 were superseded by the CF-104 Starfighter. Likewise, the brigade commitment was reinforced in 1961, and although the overall strategic value of this ground force commitment could have been greater if it had been increased to division-level strength, the tactical military value of even a brigade-sized effort remained important (see Appendix Two). Indeed, from the late 1950s, as the overall strength of the British Army of the Rhine was reduced, the military value of the Canadian brigade (which was a part of that army) was actually enhanced.[11]

The military significance of the Canadian commitment to the Allied Command in Europe certainly enhanced the political relevance of Canada's position in the alliance as a whole. The strength of Canada's presence in central Europe increasingly came to be used (rightly or wrongly) as a measuring stick of the level of Canada's commitment to NATO in general. Indeed, in the future, changes in the composition, configuration, and missions of Canada's forces in Europe would be seen by the allies as important indicators of the strength of Canada's commitment both to the alliance itself and to important aspects of the alliance's military and political strategy.

THE MILITARY PRESENCE AND CANADA'S POLITICAL INFLUENCE: GERMANY'S ADMITTANCE TO NATO

A second dimension of the Canadian presence which soon became apparent was the fact that Canada's military deployment rapidly came to be viewed, particularly in Canadian diplomatic circles, as an essential vehicle for enhancing Canada's influence in European and alliance affairs. Prior to the deployment of Canada's forces to Europe (in fact, just two days before the communist invasion of South Korea), the Canadian minister in Bonn, T.C. Davis, remarked that:

Events here will to a great extent be decided by what the French, the British and the Americans do. Representatives of other countries have no voice in decisions reached, nor is their opinion sought. In the case of Canada, we are signatories of the Atlantic Pact and, under that Pact, whenever by reason of events our obligations thereunder become due, then we must act, to all intents and purposes automatically. Still, as I have said, we seem to have no direct say in the formulation of policy which may affect the due date of such obligations.[12]

The deployment of forces in central Europe did, however, give Canada a direct stake in the political events occurring there. Although its voice was obviously still a modest one, its diplomatic interventions in a multilateral organization such as NATO had a greater credibility after 1951. Certainly, in some cases, such as the London Conference on the rearmament of Germany in the NATO context in 1954, it is likely that Canada would not even have been at the table, had it not been for its military presence in Germany.

In the aftermath of the failure of the French National Assembly to ratify the treaty on the European Defence Community (EDC) in August 1954, Canada was anxious to participate in any subsequent discussions on German rearmament in the NATO context. Indeed, since July, Canadian diplomats had been working on drafts of concepts and ideas whose objective was to use NATO as the context in which Germany could be rearmed but still integrated in a multilateral framework. These ideas and concepts had been discussed with British officials, and in early September the main elements of the Canadian plan were presented to both the American State Department and the British Foreign Office.[13] While the ultimate solution proposed by the British foreign secretary, Anthony Eden, saw NATO and the Brussels Treaty play complementary roles in achieving Germany's military integration, Canada's position nevertheless represented an important voice for the continuation of a strong and even a strengthened NATO. Its position was in close congruence with that of Britain and welcomed as important support especially in light of the Eisenhower administration's long-standing scepticism about the viability of a NATO solution.[14]

In the days and weeks following the rejection of the EDC, the backing of the United Kingdom became crucial in securing Canada a voice in the negotiations and in making that voice a meaningful one. Early in September, after Chancellor Konrad Adenauer had agreed in principle to a "NATO solution," Eden began to plan a nine-power conference under NATO auspices. At the NATO Council meeting of 9 September, the British permanent representative argued that the conference would explore various possibilities for German rearmament with the powers most immediately involved. Participants in this conference would therefore logically include countries that would have forces in Germany after the conclusion of a rearmament agreement and the restoration of German sovereignty, and those neighbours of Germany which were prepared to make sacrifices to ensure that German rearmament was subject to effective control.[15]

There were therefore two significant reasons why Canada secured a seat at the London Conference. First, its diplomatic contributions and interest had been evident since July, especially to the British, and it seems likely that the British Foreign Office thought the Canadian contribution would be a positive one. Second, and more importantly, Canada maintained forces in Germany, which gave it a direct stake in the outcome of the talks on German rearmament. That this way the key to the invitation for Canada to participate in the London talks seems to be proven by the absence of Denmark. The Danes, although still maintaining forces in Germany in 1954, had stated their intention to withdraw those forces once German rearmament began. Whether or not the Danes, given their geographical proximity to Germany, could have been participants in London, had they insisted, it is clear that the presence of Canada's forces in Germany gave it a voice which it would not otherwise have had on a matter of critical importance to European and NATO security. As Canada's ambassador to NATO, Dana Wilgress, noted to Lester Pearson on 10 September, such participation was significant: "Any country not a member of the working group would have very little scope to suggest modifications at the time that the plan was put forward to a NATO ministerial meeting for fear of upsetting a delicately balanced applecart."[16]

Canada's role at the conference was a modest one, described by the secretary of state for external affairs, Lester Pearson, as that of an "honest broker," but it was apparently important to the British as a supportive voice arguing for the continuance of a strong NATO and for enhanced powers for SACEUR to consolidate the alliance's central role (powers which SACEUR ultimately received).[17]

THE POLITICAL VALUE OF THE MILITARY COMMITMENT TO THE FRG

The third political implication of Canada's commitment of forces to central Europe became clear even before the first units arrived in Germany, namely, that the commitment to NATO was a simultaneous commitment to the Federal Republic. This became evident in a legal and political conflict which erupted over whether the Canadian forces being deployed in Germany were to be regarded as "occupation forces" or solely as defence forces. The use of Canadian troops for occupation duties was something which the minister of national defence was reportedly anxious to avoid.[18]

First, Claxton was a "strong believer in asserting Canadian organizational control over Canadian troops."[19] This principle had evolved as a result of the experiences of the two world wars and was one which Canadian governments, and especially the country's defence ministers, were expected to defend. It was perceived that the participation of Canadian troops in occupation duties under British command would seriously lesson that control. Second, there were diplomatic and political reasons for not assigning the 27th Brigade to occupation duties. On 4 October 1951, the under-secretary of state for external affairs, A.D.P. Heeney, and other senior officials from DEA met with the chief of the general staff, Lieutenant-General Guy Simonds, and other Army officers. It was suggested to Simonds that any directive or supplementary instructions issued to the commanding officer of the Canadian brigade take note of

Canada's political view of Germany.[20] Drafted in the Department of External Affairs, discussed in the Chiefs of Staff Committee, and apparently submitted to both Pearson and Claxton, the supplementary instructions were clearly the product of a political desire to see the Federal Republic become a fully integrated participant in the Western political, military, and economic system. Indeed, as mentioned in chapter 3, in September of 1951 a DEA policy paper on "Western Europe and the North Atlantic Community" had concluded that Western policy should seek to create a Western community of states of which German would be a part. Early on, therefore, Canadian decision-makers were committed to a political policy which sought to encourage Germany's equal treatment by the Western allies.

Thus, the supplementary instructions issued to Brigadier Geoffrey Walsh, the commander of the brigade, on 6 November stated:

The deployment of the Brigade in the U.K. Zone of Germany under command of Commander-in-Chief, British Army of the Rhine, may give rise to political misunderstanding among many people – Germans, British and even Canadians. It is hoped that you, and the officers and men under your command, will be able to reduce such misunderstanding without injury to anyone's feelings ...

You will receive separate advice on the legal status of the Brigade under the laws now in force in Germany. Whatever the technical legal position may prove to be under the Occupation Statute, the important fact is that politically the Brigade is not part of the occupation.

The instructions went on to note that the objective of allied policy was to move towards the full and equal integration of the Federal Republic into the wider European and Atlantic community. This development was "inconsistent" with the maintenance of the occupation or with powers which interfered in German domestic affairs. Thus, Canada had an obligation to pursue policies which advanced this allied objective and encouraged West Germany to integrate completely into the Western community of states.

In the past, the West German Government and people have shown some reluctance to re-arm because of the obvious fear of seeing their country overrun and demolished in the event of war. More recently the West Germans have gone a long way to overcome this defeatist attitude and the presence of your troops along with others under the Supreme Commander will further strengthen their national spirit and morale. Although any people is inclined to resent the presence of large numbers of foreign troops stationed on their soil in time of peace, the Germans have become adjusted to the presence of such forces and appreciate the need for them from the point of view of their own security.

... the German government has made clear that its participation in the Western defence effort would be on the principle of complete equality and this has now become a domestic political issue of prime importance. It follows that any actions on the part of our troops at this stage giving the German people the impression that they are being treated as a defeated or subordinate people will not only be bitterly resented but will do harm to the Allied cause.[21]

By assigning the Canadian forces the sole mission of defending Germany, and avoiding occupation duties, Canada also assumed all the financial costs associated with the stationing of its forces in Europe. Despite this burden, the policy secured strong support from within the cabinet. Even the minister of finance, D.C. Abbott, stated in a meeting of cabinet in February 1952 that, "in the interests of retaining the good will of the German people towards the Canadian troops and of maintaining this country's traditional policy of paying its own way, Canada should assume the maintenance costs of the 27th Brigade [including] in the post-occupation period."[22]

This Canadian decision, and the way it was implemented, did, however, cause some friction between Canada and its alliance partners. When Ambassador Davis delivered a note to Chancellor Adenauer announcing the impending arrival of the 27th Brigade in the Federal Republic, the note did not mention that the forces were being deployed under the authority of the allied occupation statute. Instead, it stated that the Canadian forces would "form part of the North Atlantic forces designed to preserve the peace by preventing aggression against Western Europe." It went on to state that it was the hope of the Canadian government that "the presence of the Canadian force in Germany will be an important factor in the development of close and friendly relations between our countries."[23]

Adenauer made immediate use of the Canadian note in the negotiations with the three allied powers which were then under way to hammer out a new relationship between the FRG and the occupying powers, to end the occupation regime, and to restore a large measure of the FRG's sovereignty. After quoting the note in a meeting with allied high commissioners on 3 October, Adenauer stated his view that in future all allied forces in Germany should be based there by contractual agreement and not by virtue of their status as former occupying powers. "Germany," he added "would never feel she had a real partnership" under circumstances which saw the allied powers continue to exercise supreme authority in defence matters.[24]

The dispute which raged for several weeks thereafter put Canada in an embarrassing position. Press leaks, likely orchestrated by the German government, made Canada appear to be out of step with its allies. The crisis finally subsided after Davis and the British high commissioner, Sir Ivone Kirkpatrick, drew up a statement which clarified the situation and which Claxton could use in the House of Commons to announce the brigade's dispatch. Then, in a meeting with Adenauer on 15 October, Kirkpatrick asserted that under an amendment to the occupation statute made in March, the allies could bring troops from other states into the FRG to participate in the defence of Western Europe. Thus, in legal terms, there was nothing new in either the Canadian note of 2 October or in the deployment of Canadian troops to the Federal Republic.[25]

The Canadian position had been used by the Germans to try to acquire additional leverage in their negotiations with the Western allies. In subsequent months, therefore, Canadian officials were especially anxious to avoid any repetition of these events. These concerns were reflected in the supplementary instructions to Brigadier Walsh. Walsh was urged to remember the delicacy of his situation and maintain a "proper balance" in his relations with the Germans and the other allied forces: "The status of the Canadian Forces and of those actually in occupation duty should not be used by the Germans to embarrass the Occupying Powers ... It is expected that the Germans will do everything they can do to improve their bargaining power (in the negotiations for a new contractual relationship), and there are already indications ... that the Germans are not above seizing any opportunity to suggest that their authority in this matter is considerably greater than is in fact the case."[26]

These events demonstrated that "the mere presence" of the Canadian brigade in Germany was "a political fact of considerable importance."[27] From the beginning the Canadian presence made an important political impression. Canada's decision to take financial responsibility for its forces in Germany was widely reported in the German press in 1951 and continued to receive coverage into 1953 as the air division commitment was fully activated.[28] The much larger forces of the occupying powers were financially supported by the German government and until the German defence forces, envisaged under the European Defence Community treaty (signed in 1952), were built up, the Germans would continue to provide substantial resources for the former allies. The unique Canadian position thus received considerable attention. Moreover, it was recognized that the Canadian effort was a considerable strain on Canada's peacetime resources and this knowledge increased the value of the action. The German minister in Ottawa, Werner Dankwort, reported in May 1951, for instance, that Canada was spending $138 per capita on its defence effort which was more than either the United Kingdom or France.[29] Canada's allies were somewhat put out by this publicity. Indeed, the Canadian ambassador in Paris noted that the embassy had been informed by French officials in February 1952 that the Canadian decision to pay the cost of its forces in Germany was "embarrassing" for France in its own discussions with the Federal Republic.[30]

The political importance of the Canadian military commitment in central Europe thus went far beyond its symbolic strengthening of the allied deterrence posture – though its significance in this respect must not be underrated. The military commitment provided Canada with a profile in Europe many times larger than before. As a result, Canada had greater diplomatic weight, both in NATO councils and in its bilateral discussions with other allied powers and with Germany.

Dankwort also reported to Bonn in April 1952 that since Canadian troops had been sent to Germany some six months before, "an accented interest" in the integration of Europe and in the "German problem" had developed in Canadian élite circles – government, parliament, and the media.[31] Indeed, in a report in January 1953, he concluded that Canada's political and diplomatic policy towards the FRG was supportive of German interests, and he argued that Germany would do well "to secure, in all international forums, the voice of Canada as a spokesman for the middle powers."[32]

The positive impression of the German mission in Ottawa was matched by a generally positive view at the highest levels in Bonn. In his letter to the ambassador welcoming the Canadian brigade deployment, Adenauer stated: "I consider the move of the Canadian Infantry Brigade Group as Defence troops to Germany as a sign of joint desire for peace and join in the hope of your Government that the Canadian contribution to the defence of the West will develop good relations between our two nations."[33]

In a report in August 1952, Davis summarized the contribution made by North America to stabilizing the political climate in Europe. In the aftermath of the outbreak of the Korean War, there was a total absence of confidence in Europe, especially in Germany, about the future: "I have never experienced such a complete acceptance of approaching disaster." Davis believed the American response to have been critical in securing the peace in Europe and urged that the effort be continued: "We must never forget that the major force deterring Russia is the presence here of American and to a lesser degree, Canadian forces from the new world. The presence here of these forces also gives confidence to the European nations. If it was ever suggested that they be withdrawn at the moment even in part, these countries would fold up like an accordion."[34]

In general, Canada's political and financial decisions with respect to the deployment of its troops made a long-lasting impression on governing circles in Bonn. For instance, in the lead-up to the nine-power London Conference in 1954, Canada came out strongly in support of the rearmament of Germany in the NATO context without any discriminatory restrictions.[35] Furthermore, Canada's forces in the Federal Republic developed a generally good relationship with the civilian population wherever they were stationed. The first allied unit in Germany to be accorded the "freedom of the city" was the Royal Canadian Regiment – an honour bestawed by the city of Soest in 1964.

CANADA, THE FRG, AND NATO STRATEGY

NATO strategy for deterrence and for the defence of central Europe after 1954–5 was composed of two particularly important and interdependent elements: first, the emphasis on the early use of nuclear weapons in the event of any Soviet attack on NATO territory and, second, the incremental establishment of a strategy of forward defence (which was in place by 1963) to ensure the defence of West German territory occurred as close to its eastern boundary as possible. Both these elements of NATO strategy had a decisive effect on the composition and make-up of the forces Canada deployed in central Europe and both were also of crucial political and strategic importance to the Federal Republic. The significance attached by the FRG to NATO strategy made Bonn especially anxious to ensure that allied states with forces deployed in central Europe remained committed to the strategy as formulated. Simultaneously, it made the German government extremely wary of any hints of a lessened commitment to that strategy.

In the case of Canada, the Germans were strong supporters of the position of the Supreme Allied Headquarters in Europe (SHAPE) that the Canadian forces in Europe be re-equipped. Canada had accepted the basic premises of this NATO strategy when it had first been adopted in 1954–5, and planning had begun in the Department of National Defence immediately thereafter for the reconfiguration of the Canadian brigade in Germany as a mechanized formation. Then in 1958–9 decisions were taken to give both Canada's ground and air forces in Europe nuclear roles. From this point on, Canada was committed to a strategy which emphasized the importance of the alliance's "forces-in-being" – that is, those forces immediately available on the outbreak of hostilities. In presenting this revised role for Canadian forces, the chairman of the Chiefs of Staff Committee, General Charles Foulkes, had informed his colleagues in July 1959 that the possibility of a limited war was now thought to be extremely remote and that "all forces" were therefore being built up around nuclear weapons.[36]

In hindsight, there should probably have been some type of consolidation of Canada's defence commitments in central Europe at this time. By the late 1950s the political and military importance of the Canadian deployments in central Europe had certainly been demonstrated. However, it was also clear by this time that the resources which had been provided for defence in the "emergency conditions" which had prevailed in the first half of the decade would no longer be available. With both the Army brigade and the RCAF division facing major re-equipment requirements, there was an inherent logic to proceeding with some form of consolidation. The land commitment might have been the better one to retain given the nature of the re-equipment being demanded by SHAPE for the air division. That role would require the country to purchase nuclear strike aircraft solely to equip the air division in Europe. This made the role of the RCAF in Europe completely distinct from its role in Canada. Despite the questionable nature of the nuclear strike role for the RCAF in Europe, once the commitment to this mission was made, it could only be unilaterally abandoned at great political cost.

Both the Army and the RCAF, supported by SHAPE, were pressing for a re-equipment of both land and air forces in Europe. The Diefenbaker government, possessing little expertise in this area, yielded to military advice and opted for a "limited" re-equipment of both contingents. Limited re-equipment on a limited budget meant that the brigade could not be expanded into a more formidable and viable division-sized force as some of NATO's military authorities wanted while the RCAF would only be able to replace its combat aircraft in Europe with the new nuclear strike jets on a one-for-two basis.

Canada thus embarked on a course that was to continue for some three more decades: to muddling along with respect to the equipping and configuration of its European military commitments while trying to avoid the harder political and military decisions associated with consolidation. In the late 1950s, this policy approach remained viable because budgetary resources were still relatively substantial. However, as the years passed, and the shrinking defence budget caused the commitment-capability gap to grow wider, the shortcomings and limitations of this approach would become more and more evident – as each major defence review made clear. Even before 1960, there were three points with regard to the military roles that Canada was performing in central Europe which worried both Liberal and Conservative governments. These were the financial costs associated with the commitments, the relevance of the commitments in a military sense, and the general "appropriateness" of the missions assigned to the forces in central Europe.

The cost and relevance issues associated with the deployment in Europe had been raised as early as 1957 when the Liberal defence minister, Ralph Campney, envisaged the withdrawal of Canadian forces from Europe in the not-too-distant future. Quite simply, for many Canadians it made little sense to maintain forces in Europe at the cost of some $150 million per year (or about 10 per cent of the defence budget) when European and German rearmament seemed to be reducing the strategic relevance of these forces. However, this thinking was premised on the belief that the air defence of North America would become the priority mission of Canada's forces in the years to come. When the credibility of the bomber threat evaporated in the late 1950s, the Diefenbaker government decided that Canada's most useful contribution to the alliance would be in central Europe through the limited re-equipment of both its land brigade and air division – in keeping with NATO strategy.

Even though the questions of cost and relevance were thus temporarily resolved, the issue of the "appropriateness" of the Canadian commitments in central Europe soon arose because of the nuclear element of the roles envisaged for the forces in Europe, most especially for the air division. Even though the policy decisions related to the acquisition of nuclear strike aircraft and nuclear-tipped surface-to-surface rockets had been made in cabinet, many ministers (especially the secretary of state for external affairs, Howard Green) began to question the wisdom and desirability of going ahead with the acquisition of the nuclear warheads for Canadian ground and air forces in Europe. As the influence of this policy perspective in cabinet increased in the early 1960s, so to did Canada's vacillation about whether to carry through with the earlier decisions. The result was that the country's military policies slowly began to drift in the opposite direction from those of its allies and, in particular, away from those favoured by the Germans and SHAPE.

Under the terms of the NATO agreements to which Canada had acceded in 1954, all the allies had pledged to deploy their forces in Europe only in accordance with alliance strategy.[37] Canada, having agreed to re-equip its forces now clearly stood in violation of its agreements.[38] This retreat from earlier commitments quite naturally precipitated a crisis with the alliance which ultimately resulted in the defeat of the government in 1963. This crisis, more than any other, demonstrated the extent to which Canada's "temporary" military role in Europe had become the most important symbol of its commitment to the alliance and to NATO strategy.

The events of 1963, and the election of the Liberals under Lester Pearson, confirmed that Canada would remain committed to the basic elements of NATO's forward defence and nuclear strategy. However this commitment was never an enthusiastic one. Rather it was accepted out of the need to maintain the solidarity of the alliance and the credibility of Canada's position within it. While Canada sought to fulfil its existing nuclear commitments to the alliance, it would, over the long term, seek to phase its forces out of most of these roles and undertake to make a largely conventional force commitment to NATO.

The defence policy of the new government, as revealed in its white paper of March 1964, was to provide a more flexible and lighter force to the alliance to meet a scale of possible contingencies from a mere political demonstration of resolve through, for instance, the commitment of a battalion group to the largely political Allied Mobile Force (AMF), to the provision of larger brigade-sized units with tactical air support in the event of an outbreak of general hostilities with the USSR. This policy represented a clear break from the previous emphasis in favour of forces-in-being stationed in Europe. While, previously, mechanized army units in Canada had been equipped at only training levels which enabled them to provide rotation replacements for the brigade in Europe, the whole army was now to be re-equipped and provided with sufficient air and sea transport for its rapid deployment in a crisis.

There was widespread agreement in informed circles in Canada on the desirability of moving to this mobile force concept which was seen to fit not only Canada's NATO role but also its United Nations tasks and the requirements inherent in a viable defence of Canadian territory. Indeed, even General Foulkes, who had strongly supported the concentration of resources on forces-in-being in Europe, now publicly advocated a change to focus

Canada's defence resources on the build-up of a mobile "ready reserve" which would ultimately be based exclusively in Canada and available for operations in Europe or elsewhere.[39]

There were, however, certain implications in Canada's new defence concept for the country's position in NATO's evolving strategic debate and therefore also for its political relationship with Germany. While the defence white paper of 1964 confirmed the retention of the brigade and air division in Europe, it was apparent that the heavy mechanized and nuclear strike roles designated for these forces were not entirely congruent with the lighter mobile forces that the government seemed to envisage for the Canadian Armed Forces as a whole. Nevertheless, the political priority of maintaining existing commitments was sufficient to carry the day and leave these forces in their front-line roles in central Europe.

The costs of fulfilling the forward defence and nuclear strike missions on the alliance's central front were certainly increasing; and they were ones which the Canadian government would have to meet, especially if the country's forces were to remain militarily relevant. Since the late 1950s there had been continuous pressure from SHAPE, German General Hans Speidel (the commander-in-chief of allied land forces in central Europe), and the British (to whose Army of the Rhine Canadian land forces in Europe were still assigned) to raise the strength and readiness of the Canadian brigade in central Europe. Despite the long-standing efforts of the government to maintain the brigade within its 5500-man ceiling, the Berlin crisis of 1961 finally provoked an increase in that ceiling to 6600 men, making it one of the strongest units of "brigade" size in Germany.[40]

Despite the value of the Canadian brigade, the military mission on the central front really required Canada to deploy a more strongly reinforced brigade or small division. Each of the other NATO stationing powers in Germany in fact envisaged the deployment of corps-sized formations in central Europe. In Canada's case, however, budgetary restrictions driven by the growing strength of the "question of relevance" associated with the country's military commitments in Europe ensured that such a strengthening of ground forces in central Europe would not be seriously considered for another twenty years. Budgetary restrictions also affected Canada's air commitment in Europe. Higher than anticipated attrition losses among the new CF-104s of the air division meant that additional aircraft orders were required to maintain the division's authorized strength of 144 aircraft. However, in keeping with Canada's subtle shift away from the previous emphasis on its forces in Europe, the 1964 defence white paper confirmed that attrition replacements for the air division would not be procured and that as a result the strength of the air division would gradually decline.

This subtle change in Canada's orientation to NATO strategy had a wider potential political importance. Differences among the allies on the formulation, implementation, and interpretation of the evolving flexible response concept existed throughout the 1960s and indeed into the 1970s and 1980s. In the mid-1960s, allied strategic views were particularly divided. As a result, in December 1964, NATO defence ministers instructed the Defence Planning Working Group to proceed as "quickly as possible" with an examination of the main strategic issues confronting the alliance for the purpose of reaching some common understanding among the allies on these issues.[41] The working group produced a report for the May 1965 NATO ministerial meeting which noted that three distinct viewpoints were held by the allies on alliance strategy and the role of nuclear weapons in that strategy.

The first view (in varying degrees subscribed to by most of the allies including the United Kingdom, the United States, and Canada) held that it was "neither appropriate nor realistic" to strengthen the capability of the Allied Command in Europe for fighting nuclear war. Instead, two important propositions were advocated:

1 That existing nuclear forces, mainly external (that is, principally the strategic capability of the United States), were sufficient to maintain stable deterrence or to wage general war; and
2 That the greatest practical danger to NATO was war developing out of a local hostile action or conflict. NATO's flexible capability should therefore be strengthened to contain any limited aggression and prevent escalation.[42]

The second view was that there has "hardly ever, if at all, been an unpremeditated military conflict." Such a conflict was even less likely now that there were nuclear weapons. The nature of the Soviet military build-up and the integration of tactical nuclear weapons with conventional forces suggested that any Soviet attack could involve a general offensive with limited use of nuclear weapons "which could not with certainty be described either as general war or local hostile action." Too much reliance on external (principally American) strategic nuclear forces was therefore not as credible as tactical nuclear forces directly under SACEUR's command. Similarly, instead of emphasizing more flexible mobile forces, NATO states should continue to build up conventional forces capable of meeting and defeating a general Soviet offensive. This was the view of Germany, Italy, and SHAPE.[43]

Finally, there was the view held by France, which, simply summarized, argued that "ground forces available in Europe were not an essential factor." What was important were "nuclear weapons and the will to use them."[44]

SACEUR's request with respect to Canadian force goals for 1970 had been for a continuation of the mechanized division commitment (with one-third deployed in Germany and two-thirds in Canada available on mobilization – M-Day – plus shipping time), an increase in nuclear delivery support units, and an increase in the nuclear strike contribution in Europe. Acceptance of these goals would, a summation for the Defence Council in May 1965 noted, mean a shift in Canadian support from the "first viewpoint" to the "second viewpoint." However, Canada, the DND memorandum argued, had already "charted its course." The concepts outlined in the 1964 white paper were closely in step with both the first viewpoint and with American thinking on the main strategic issues facing the alliance. These concepts were premised on the view that, in particular, NATO required "quick reaction, airportable, non-nuclear strategic reserves with tactical air support" to respond to unanticipated crises as they occurred. The memorandum for the Defence Council thus concluded:

Canada's force planning and budgeting is committed to strategic assumptions generally along the lines of the "first viewpoint." Acceptance of the second or third viewpoint would mean a repudiation of the White Paper.

The Canadian real interest in the NATO force planning exercise is, after all, to rationalize and reconcile, as far as possible, allied force planning with our own.

Happily, the consensus of the exercise, "the first viewpoint," seems to be proceeding generally in harmony with our own objectives. The exercise deserves continuing Canadian support in this direction.[45]

In a sense, however, Canada still had one foot in each camp. By maintaining its heavy brigade and nuclear strike air division in central Europe, it made available forces in NATO Europe that both SHAPE and the Germans wanted. This was particularly true of the air division, for which more significant reduction options were presented to the government than were in the end adopted.[46] For this decision, both the Germans and SHAPE were grateful.[47] Nevertheless, it was the German view that the nuclear strike capability assigned to SACEUR should not just be maintained but built up, a view relayed to the defence minister, Paul Hellyer, by the German defence minister, Kai-Uwe von Hassel, during the former's visit to Bonn in June 1964.[48]

Canada's military presence in Germany continued to involve the country in these important strategic debates which persisted into the 1970s and 1980s. The Federal Republic's interest in Canada's basic orientation on NATO strategy remained high, because all questions associated with NATO's political and military strategies were vital ones for the Germans. While Canada retained an interest in these questions, it was not nearly as intense. Canadian decision-makers were, as a result, often slow to recognize both the degree of German interest in these questions and the potential political importance to Germany of Canada's position on such matters.

Canadian ground and air forces in central Europe always had a political and also a tactical military importance which was underrated in Canada. For nearly all of the Cold War era, the strength of the alliance's conventional forces in central Europe was perceived within NATO to be inadequate. In the 1960s, for instance, in central Europe, the alliance only deployed some 25 combat-ready divisions as against the 56 (22 Soviet) deployed by the Warsaw pact. Moreover, the Soviet Union had another 60 divisions of varying capabilities in the USSR itself and these could be moved to reinforce forces on the central front much more easily than NATO troops could be transported across the Atlantic.[49] Likewise, although it was true that German rearmament had doubled the size of the forces available in central Europe by adding 12 divisions to the alliance's peacetime strength, the quality of these forces remained somewhat weak for some years because of the problems involved in building up such a large military force from scratch.

Thus, the ability to hold a forward defence position against even a limited Warsaw pact offensive remained under serious question until the late 1960s and, indeed, into the 1970s and 1980s. In the aftermath of the invasion of Czechoslovakia, for example, the German defence white paper noted that the government viewed the stationing of allied forces in Germany and their integration into the alliance's military structure as the "decisive requirement" for German security. It also noted that allied defence ministers had agreed early in 1969 to raise the strength levels of their existing military units, to modernize and supplement their armament, and to intensify training.[50] The German emphasis on the desirability of improved conventional forces would be maintained by Helmut Schmidt when he became minister of defence and would also be reflected in NATO's emphasis in the 1970s on improving conventional capabilities.[51]

Canada's front-line role in the alliance thus continued to be militarily important. Prior to the reductions of 1969, for instance, the air division held nearly 10 per cent of all the combat aircraft (and 20 per cent of theatre nuclear strike assets) available to SACEUR in central Europe. Similarly, in 1966–7, the 4th Canadian Mechanized Brigade Group (4 CMBG) with its authorized strength of some 6600 men still represented some 10 per cent of the strength of the British Army of the Rhine (BAOR) of which it was a part. With an armoured regiment, three infantry battalions with M-113 armoured personnel carriers, self-propelled 155-mm guns, Honest John surface-to-surface rockets, and other elements, it was, in most respects, the BAOR's strongest and most important brigade.[52] Even though a larger ground force commitment was probably required in central Europe, the brigade was nevertheless highly regarded within the BAOR and within the whole Northern Army Group (NORTHAG) sector. This high reputation when combined with the brigade's front-line role in NATO's strategy of forward defence yielded Canada political and military influence out of proportion to its overall strategic significance to the alliance.

Prior to France's withdrawal from NATO's integrated military structure in 1966, Canada contributed about 1.8 per cent of the staff for the Allied

Command in Europe. Although small in numbers, the 259 Canadians assigned to NATO in Europe[53] (in particular, the 83 officers) held some key positions on the staff of the BAOR, in NORTHAG, in the 4th Allied Tactical Air Force (ATAF), and at SHAPE itself. In addition to these permanent positions, General Jean Allard had been given command of one of the four divisions of the BAOR from 1961 to 1963 (a testament to British appreciation of the Canadian brigade)[54] and in 1966 Major-General Gilles Turcot was given command of NATO's mobile force. Canadians thus had some real influence in the formulation of both alliance strategy and operational plans.

This influence was however a subtle one and, as a result, questions linked with the "appropriateness," the relevance, and the costs associated with the Canadian presence in Europe were never answered to the satisfaction of Canada's political leaders. Their response was already evident in the Pearson government's refusal to allow defence budget increases to keep up with the rate of inflation and in the government's decision in 1967–8 to reduce the strength of the brigade in Europe to pre-1961 levels. However, the "question of relevance" would manifest itself most especially during the Trudeau government, which, as discussed in chapter 3, was by and large totally unconvinced of the military and political importance of Canadian forces in Europe. The ultimate effect of its 1969 decision, which eventually reduced those forces in Europe by 50 per cent, was to remove the brigade from the NATO front line and to withdraw Canada from any involvement in the alliance's nuclear missions. Canada's profile, and thus its influence, within the alliance was correspondingly reduced.

The British were the first to feel the impact of the 1969 decision as they were forced to make up for the reduced combat capability of the BAOR. This at least partly explains the angry reaction of Britain's defence minister, Denis Healey, to the Canadian decision at the May 1969 NATO ministers meeting.[55] The United Kingdom and Germany were deeply concerned with the Canadian withdrawal and collaborated closely in attempting to fill the gap. In December 1969, the British announced that they would be moving the 6th British Infantry Brigade to Germany and West Germany, for its part, agreed to offset 80 per cent of the costs of this move through the purchase of military goods in the United Kingdom.[56]

Over the next twenty years, most of Canada's activity within the alliance was expended in simply trying to restore the Canadian position within NATO to the level of confidence which the country had earlier enjoyed. Much of this effort was in turn centred on trying to ensure that those Canadian forces retained in Europe were assigned military roles and equipped to fulfil missions which both SHAPE and the individual allies, particularly the Germans, considered important and credible. That the military roles, configuration, and missions of Canada's forces in Europe were directly connected with

Canada's political weight in the alliance is something which Canadian decision-makers became aware of only gradually and even then only partially.

LIGHT OR HEAVY FORCES? THE IMPORTANCE OF THE MILITARY CONFIGURATION OF THE CFE

In the aftermath of the Trudeau cabinet's decision to reduce Canada's forces in Europe, the question became what type of force to provide for the alliance in Europe and how to equip it. The cabinet decision of 20 May 1969 had outlined a proposal to maintain a force of approximately 3500 men in Europe with the land element "reconfigured" and "assigned for employment with the Allied Command Europe Mobile Force (land)" and the remaining air element, consisting of two CF-104 reconnaissance squadrons, to be "employed in central Europe with the 4th Allied Tactical Air Force."[57]

This reconfiguration corresponded to the three principles for a Canadian force deployed in Europe which the cabinet could agree on. First, the reduction in strength associated with this reconfiguration would see Canada's forces in Europe drop from a combined strength of some 10,000 men to 3500. While many in the cabinet, including probably the prime minister himself, had wanted a complete withdrawal from Europe, the retention of some forces was the price demanded by the defence minister, Léo Cadieux, for staying in the cabinet.

A second goal of the reconfiguration was to provide the opportunity in future to equip the forces in Europe with systems similar those of the Canadian forces in North America. Especially important to the government in this respect was the decision to end the nuclear roles to which Canada had committed itself in the late 1950s. The assumption of a light ground force role with Allied Command Europe's mobile force and the elimination of the nuclear strike role for the air force in Europe fit into this objective.

The third principle was that this reconstituted force posture was to be in place by 1972 and was not to prejudice any later decision to withdraw completely from Europe. By equipping forces based in Europe and North America in a compatible way, the option of withdrawal would remain militarily viable.

The reconfiguration of Canada's land forces as light, mobile, and highly flexible forces was of course in keeping with a long-standing desire (first officially reflected in the 1964 white paper) both to reduce the costs associated with maintaining both light and heavy forces in the land force posture and to build an army more in keeping with what were seen to be Canada's strategic requirements. Unfortunately for the government, there were basic impediments to achieving the light force reconfiguration now proposed.

First, procurement decisions based on the retention of a heavy force configuration in the army had already been made. As a result of the 1964 decision to retain a heavy brigade in the NATO front line, both the brigade in Europe and another brigade in Canada (which provided rotational replacements for Europe) had been designated "mechanized" formations and equipped accordingly. One thousand M-113 armoured personnel carriers and some 50 M-109 155-mm self-propelled guns had already been acquired. These weapon systems (especially the M-109 howitzers) were largely incompatible with the light rapid deployment role now envisaged for the army.[58]

Likewise, the air division was stuck with two aircraft types whose the capabilities were at either end of the scale of what was now desired. The CF-104 was a strike/interdiction aircraft essentially unsuited for a rapid deployment role in support of mobile ground forces, while the CF-5, which had been purchased to provide close air support for the army's light brigades, was now regarded by the air force as largely inadequate for the European environment where an aircraft with a better air-defence capability was seen as essential.[59] Although the CF-5 was eventually tasked to Europe's northern flank in 1971, it was never based in Europe despite occasional proposals in this direction.

A second impediment to reconfiguring Canada's forces in Europe was the cost. With the defence budget frozen at $1.8 billion, the amount of money available for capital equipment acquisitions was limited: in 1970/1, to $222 million and in 1971/2, to $232 million.[60] By this time the programmes to acquire the CF-5, new naval support ships, and DDH-280 class destroyers were at their spending peaks. Indeed, the latter project had ballooned from an original estimate of $142 million to a total cost by 1970 of $242 million.[61] As a result the cabinet was informed in May 1969 that "because of the capital expenditures involved in the acquisition of ships, a transition to new roles could not easily and quickly be programmed."[62]

This lack of money placed substantial limitations on the army's proposed acquisition of combat, light observation, and utility transport helicopters to equip its mobile forces. In June of 1969, it had been estimated (probably somewhat optimistically) that new helicopters would cost a total of $97 million. With the budget freeze, this level of expenditure could simply not be afforded. Thus, only 50 new utility transport helicopters were purchased in subsequent years, and these were designated for employment with Mobile Command in Canada. Likewise, only 12 of a similar number of new Kiowa observation helicopters were available for deployment with Canada's land forces in Europe. The purchase of the Cobra attack helicopter (originally proposed as a necessary complement to the above acquisitions) did not proceed at all.[63]

The third factor preventing the reconfiguration of Canadian forces in Europe was political. In the period after 1969, both SHAPE and the European allies (the Germans most particularly) made consistently clear their desire that Canada continue to deploy both heavy mechanized land forces and strike/interdiction air forces in central Europe. In the case of the ground forces, the allies were ultimately successful in changing the Canadian decision; in the case of the air forces they were only partially successful.

The proposals put forward by Cadieux at the meeting of NATO defence minsters in May 1969 to reduce the Canadian forces from a combined strength of 10,100 to 3,500 men was very badly received by the allies.[64] The question of light forces on the central front had been addressed by NATO's military committee in 1965, and the committee had concluded that the conversion of existing heavy units to light brigades was "fraught with difficulty." Because of the need to maintain heavy mechanized forces on the central front to match those of the Warsaw pact, it was concluded that it did not make sense to re-equip Canada's forces for a light role either as part of the NORTHAG or for a theatre reserve role on the central front. A memorandum from the chief of defence staff, Air Chief Marshal F.R. Miller, to the Defence Council in January 1966 concluded that "for the foreseeable future, then, the reequipment for heavy weapons and logistic support cannot be abandoned so long as forces are maintained on the Central Front in Germany, or elsewhere, with the possibility of ultimate deployment on this front."[65]

The widespread perception of both SHAPE and the European allies that a light role on the central front had a decidedly lower military utility than a mechanized role meant that the Canadian reduction was perceived as even more substantial and far reaching than the nominal two-thirds proposal indicated. Most importantly of course, the decision, coming as it did only three years after the French decision to withdraw from NATO's military command, was seen as a possible indication of an increasing willingness on the part of some of the allies to formulate their military force postures on a national basis without regard for the collective interests of the alliance. The fear that the United States Congress might thereby be more likely to force the American administration to move in a similar direction was heightened.

While the intensity of the negative allied reaction to the Canadian decision came as somewhat of a shock to Cadieux, the request for modifications from NATO member-states had been anticipated. The cabinet had decided prior to the meeting that, "if after consultation with NATO modifications to the planned posture as agreed to above are strongly desired by NATO, then the suggested modification or modifications will be referred to the Cabinet for further discussion and decision."[66]

In negotiations with the Canadian government over the future configuration of Canada's forces in Europe, General Andrew Goodpaster, sought to salvage as much from the past Canadian deployment as he could. SACEUR's initial proposal was for a Canadian force strength of 8300 – more than double the initial Canadian proposal. After Cadieux rejected this suggestion, SHAPE had instead proposed some 6500 Canadian troops in Europe. It was suggested that Canada re-equip its brigade with "armoured cavalry equipment." If modelled on an American armoured cavalry regiment, this reconfiguration might have required both a new main battle tank and possibly a combat helicopter of the Cobra type. As Cadieux reported to the cabinet, the department could in no way afford such acquisitions in the current budget.[67]

General Goodpaster also had specific problems with the air commitment proposed by Canada. Withdrawal by Canada from the nuclear strike role constituted a loss of nearly 20 per cent of the nuclear-capable air power available to SACEUR in central Europe. Goodpaster thus asked that Canada maintain two squadrons (18 aircraft each) in the nuclear strike role and a third squadron in the reconnaissance role. This configuration would limit the reduction of air assets to some 10 per cent of the total nuclear aircraft available to SHAPE.[68]

This suggestion provoked controversy within the cabinet where there was a consensus against continuing in the nuclear strike role. The prime minister in particular was opposed to the manning of "first-strike" nuclear weapons by Canadians. In response, Cadieux argued that the nuclear strike role would only be continued on an "interim basis" until 1972 because the reconnaissance role alone was regarded as unbalanced and not viable. On this basis the cabinet agreed to retain, until 1972, a commitment of three squadrons (two strike and one reconnaissance) of 54 CF-104 aircraft comprising 3 squadrons of 12 single-seat operational aircraft in Europe, 4 dual-control trainers, and 14 additional aircraft manned as a fly-over commitment from CFB Cold Lake in Alberta.[69]

The government had tried to advance and promote the light force role throughout the summer of 1969. In June it had been proposed that the assignment of Canadian ground forces to a new light mobile role go ahead. That role, as the chief of the defence staff, General Allard, informed Cadieux, would see the Canadian ground forces becoming part of Allied Command Europe's mobile force and held in reserve for deployment in either of the NATO flanks or even in central Europe, although they would not be committed exclusively to the central front as such.[70] In this respect the structure of the German army's airborne brigades was apparently examined as a possible model for the Canadian force.[71]

However, the immediate assumption of this role was not possible because the equipment necessary for the reconfiguration would be unavailable until the early 1970s. Moreover, it would have made nonsense of Canada's procurement of both the M-113 armoured personnel carriers and M-109 self-propelled guns just two to three years earlier. The minister of national defence therefore proposed, and the cabinet agreed, to continue to use the existing equipment until the light force equipment became available, hopefully in two to three years.[72] This decision to delay the implementation of the reconfiguration of Canada's forces ultimately provided the opportunity for both the army and the allies to help ensure that it never took place.

Under an agreement with SACEUR, reached in August/September 1969, a mechanized "battle group" of 2800 men was to be deployed on the existing Canadian air bases at Lahr and Baden-Söllingen. A combined strength level of 5000 men for the land and air commitments was agreed to between Canada and SHAPE. Despite the decision to co-locate the forces, a frozen defence budget and previous equipment procurement decisions meant that any further co-ordination of land and air roles would not be possible.

Economic factors were most important in the decision to redeploy Canada's ground forces to southern Germany, with the option having been considered as early as 1967.[73] Economic considerations were reinforced by a desire on the part of some Canadian officials, most notably the chief of defence staff, to provide Canadian land forces in Europe with a more recognizable and distinctive Canadian identity, apart from British forces.[74] Military or strategic considerations were hardly, if at all, involved.

Be that as it may, the 4th Canadian Mechanized Battle Group (still known as 4 CMBG) took on, from the fall of 1970, an operational role in the Central Army Group (CENTAG) sector. Although the specific role of 4 CMBG was still undefined, its heavy equipment suggested a reserve counterattack role. Despite its small size, 4 CMBG would soon come to be regarded as an important tactical military asset in the CENTAG sector. Indeed, when it moved into that sector, it became the first and only in-theatre reserve formation available to the CENTAG commander since the withdrawal of French forces from allied command in 1966–7. It is scarcely surprising that very soon after arriving in its new sector, both SHAPE and CENTAG sought to ensure that 4 CMBG stayed exactly where it was and acquired the necessary heavy equipment to carry out a credible strategic reserve mission in that region.

In subsequent years this political interest that the allies had in the military roles and configuration of Canada's forces in Europe would become more fully apparent to Canadian leaders. Among Canada's NATO partners, it was of course the Germans who would have the greatest interest in seeing Canada maintain a militarily credible force in central Europe. This German interest had been manifest ever since the country's entry into NATO in 1955 and in the aftermath of the formal adoption of the forward defence strategy by the alliance. In the coming twenty years, the active interest of the Federal Republic in the operational missions being undertaken by Canada's forces would become evident from time to time and would in fact become the decisive factor in ensuring that Canada retained and (towards the end of the Cold War period) even sought, finally, to augment its military capabilities in central Europe.

CONCLUSION

The military contribution made by Canada's forces in Europe to the collective allied deterrent and defence effort in the first two decades of the Cold
War has been an understudied and undervalued dimension of Canada's
initial contribution to European security. Because Canadian troops only
comprised some 1 to 2 per cent of allied ground forces based in central
Europe by the 1960s, few analysts bothered to consider the Canadian military
role very seriously. At the time even many informed observers considered
these forces to be of relatively marginal military utility and their role as
almost exclusively political in nature. In fact, the chief of defence staff from
1966 to 1969, General Allard, remarked in 1967 that nobody "would seriously
argue that one brigade and six squadrons of aircraft could be significant to
the military balance of Europe."[75] Likewise, the secretary of state for external
affairs at the time, Mitchell Sharp, later recorded that "the size of our
contingent in Europe was not particularly important. What mattered was
the strength of our [political] commitment to the Alliance."[76]

However, at no time in the forty years that Canadian military forces were
deployed in Germany, could the military mission of those forces be detached
from their political role. Indeed, the credibility of Canada's political role in
NATO was in large measure dependent on the perceived viability of its
military commitment. This was certainly true in the early 1950s when its
forces were first deployed, and this continued to be the case in the years that
followed. In this respect, NATO, and subsequently the German government
most especially, always regarded issues surrounding the deployment and the
equipment of Canada's forces in Europe as an essential aspect of a viable
deterrence and defence strategy in central Europe. If this basic fact was not
apparent to Canadian leaders in 1969, it should have become fully evident
in the years thereafter.

7 The German Defence Dilemma, the Enhanced Importance of Conventional Forces, and the Canadian Commitment, 1970–1989

Since 1955 the Germans had been faced with a dilemma concerning allied strategy for the defence of central Europe. This centred on the relative weight that the alliance should accord to its nuclear and conventional forces. Simply summarized, the problem was how to keep the nuclear threshold low but still sufficient to deter Soviet aggression while retaining adequate conventional forces for repelling more limited attacks. By fielding stronger conventional forces, the danger arose that the nuclear threshold required for the purpose of deterrence would be raised, thereby undermining the credibility of the threat of nuclear retaliation in the face of a conventional attack from the East. In the late 1950s and early 1960s the response had been to place the emphasis on a strategy of "stark deterrence." Believing that with the outbreak of war "the game would already be lost" (in that Germany and Europe would be either devastated in the ensuing general war or else conquered), the priority was on maximizing deterrence through reliance on nuclear weapons.[1]

However, in the course of the 1960s this view began to lose support. This resulted in a German policy decision to raise the total strength of the Bundeswehr to 500,000 men (from 350,000) and also, in response to American desires, to accept (in 1967) the concept of flexible response as the basis of NATO strategy. "Stark deterrence" was gradually supplanted by a growing emphasis on enhancing the viability of conventional defence. The dilemma of how far to go still existed, however. Helmut Schmidt, who became defence minister in 1969, had long been a "champion" of a form of flexible response or "graduated deterrence." He had argued that "Europe can only hope to avoid nuclear destruction in the event of war if strong, highly mobile conventional forces are built up … only a defence capability of this kind will put an end to the situation which has existed up till now, whereby the defence of Europe leads inevitably to the destruction of Europe."[2]

The German defence white paper of 1970 had described the use of nuclear weapons as a "last resort" and stated that the defence of western Europe "critically" depended "on maintaining conventional forces at a level which will give NATO an alternative to a nuclear response against anything but a major deliberate attack: and which, if an attack on this scale should occur, would allow time for negotiations to end this conflict and for consultations among the allies about the initial use of nuclear weapons if negotiations should fail." At present it added, "the level of conventional forces is just sufficient for this purpose."[3] It was in this context of a renewed German emphasis on the importance of conventional defence that the Defence Ministry contemplated with dismay the Canadian decision of 1969. Beyond the possible political impact that the Canadian action might have in the United States, the withdrawal of the Canadian brigade from the front-line role in the Northern Army Group was not an insignificant development from a military perspective, especially since conventional forces in the Federal Republic had been described by the Germans as "just sufficient" for mounting a reasonable conventional defence effort for a short period. These concerns were therefore emphasized by Schmidt in his meeting with the Canadian minister of national defence, Donald Macdonald, in December 1970.

In particular, Schmidt stressed how important it was, from a German perspective, that the Canadians continue in a mechanized land role within the CENTAG sector. The intention to convert the 4th Canadian Mechanized Battle Group (4 CMBG) into an air-portable formation was seen in Bonn as tantamount to an additional reduction in the capability of Canadian forces based in Europe. An air-portable force, while potentially of use to the alliance on the European flanks, had less relevance in Germany itself. While Schmidt noted his "understanding" of the Canadian desire to equip its forces in Europe in a way compatible with its forces in Canada, he made clear his preference for the deployment of a mechanized Canadian land force formation in Europe. Heavy armoured and mechanized forces were still of primary importance, both for holding a forward defence line and for counterattack.

Macdonald sought to portray the Canadian desire to reconfigure its ground force in Europe as an air-portable force as no different from earlier German moves to reconfigure some of their heavy brigades as light brigades. Schmidt, however, noted that this change had merely involved a "reorganization" of German resources. Tanks from previous heavy brigades had been retained in service and used to form independent tank battalions.[4]

Despite Schmidt's arguments, the Canadian government was at that time still officially determined to move ahead with re-equipping its forces in Europe on a compatible basis with forces in Canada. Even so, while Ottawa was opposed to acquiring a new main battle tank for its European-based forces alone, it was now also unwilling to invest the necessary additional resources to re-equip 4 CMBG as a fully capable air-mobile force available to SACEUR for deployment on the NATO flanks. As a result, it decided instead to leave 4 CMBG committed within the CENTAG sector alone. The September 1971 Canadian defence white paper, *Defence in the 70s*, stated that Canadian land forces would be "reconfigured ... for tactical reconnaissance missions in a Central Region reserve role." The Centurion tank would be retired and replaced with a light, tracked, direct-fire-support vehicle.[5] By the end of 1971, it had been decided that the British-produced Scorpion light tank was clearly "the vehicle required."[6]

A memorandum prepared for the Defence Council by Brigadier-General J.C. Gardner, director general land forces, in January 1972, outlined the proposed capabilities and missions of 4 CMBG as a tactical reconnaissance force in the CENTAG area.[7] The full strength of 4 CMBG would be 3,365 officers and men (including 265 personnel based in Canada in peacetime), consisting of two infantry battalions with M-113 armoured personnel carriers; an artillery regiment with 18 M-109 155-mm guns; an air defence battery with light surface-to-air missiles; a reconnaissance regiment with 48 Scorpion light tanks; a squadron of observation helicopters; and engineers and support elements. To reconfigure the combat group for the reconnaissance mission, it was proposed that in addition to the Scorpions, both light surface-to-air missiles and anti-tank guided weapons be purchased. (These were acquired in limited numbers in 1973 and 1974 in the form of the Blowpipe missile and the TOW anti-tank system). Although a more extensive aviation capability was also desired, the memorandum noted that the manpower ceilings imposed by the government meant that a truly meaningful air capability could not be integrated into the force which was envisaged for the post-1974 period.

With its new configuration, 4 CMBG could undertake two principal tasks. The first was a reconnaissance mission either on an independent basis or attached to allied units. In this role, but only when augmented by allied formations (especially armoured ones), it could also engage in "block and hold" operations. Second, the Canadian combat group could undertake limited security operations in which it could participate in countering minor penetrations or providing security in the CENTAG sector to counter enemy airborne or air-landed operations in the army group's rear area. The memorandum made it clear, however, that participation in the normal corps covering battle as a mobile task force would not be possible without augmentation by allied tanks, additional mechanized infantry, and additional artillery.

Within the constraints imposed by the government (especially manpower ceilings, budgetary limitations, and the retirement of the Centurion), this was the best force which could be established as well as the most meaningful set of mission options which could be considered. For the allies and SHAPE, however, it was not good enough.

General Goodpaster (SACEUR), after being briefed on the new plan in the spring of 1972, expressed his "serious reservations" about the equipment of 4 CMBG, especially its lack of armour and the reduction in the strength of the field engineers. Lack of mobility ensured that 4 CMBG would be restricted to a role in the CENTAG sector, and in that sector there were far more urgent military missions than the ones the Canadians now proposed for themselves. On the basis of the comments of General Goodpaster, the chief of defence staff, General Jacques Dextraze, recommended to the government that the proposed reorganization be reconsidered.[8]

General Dextraze, as an Army officer and World War II veteran, felt strongly that a main battle tank was essential for Canadian ground forces in Europe. Indeed, he would remark to the German defence attaché in Ottawa, Colonel Rolf Klages, in February 1973 that the Scorpion was a totally inadequate substitute for the Centurion, describing it as a "tin can which he would not even cross a corridor in." Dextraze noted that he would do "all in his power" to convince the government not to buy the Scorpion.[9] In this lengthy struggle, he had the support of both SHAPE and the Germans.

Both the SACEUR and the commander of the Central Army Group had apparently personally told Dextraze of their desire for a properly equipped and configured Canadian land force in Europe. The SACEUR had reportedly informed Dextraze that, since Canada had "volunteered" for the CENTAG reserve role, it had to follow through with the necessary procurement decision.[10] Aside from their objections on military grounds, the Germans certainly did not assess the reconnaissance role as the type of high-profile task which demonstrated a serious Canadian commitment to NATO's defence strategy in central Europe. As a result, they were willing to facilitate the rapid and relatively cheap acquisition by Canada of the Leopard I main battle tank. After the Scorpion purchase was scuttled, secret negotiations with Germany were initiated by the cabinet in the fall of 1972 for the purchase of 160 Leopard Is. These talks, however, were apparently abandoned after cabinet rejected the cost of the tanks as too high.[11]

With the reconnaissance role undesired by the central front allies and the government still unwilling to acquire a new tank, the Department of National Defence was forced to struggle along with the Centurion and to look at other long-term options. One possibility was to withdraw Canadian land forces from Europe entirely and replace them with an enhanced air commitment. In 1973 the defence minister, James Richardson, began to look at the option of taking some of the air force's CF-5 aircraft (the majority of which were in storage) and basing them in Europe to complement the CF-104s and replace the land force commitment. However, aside from the limited military utility of the CF-5 (which would likely be restricted to a close air-support role), the Europeans were all opposed to the substitution of an enhanced air commitment for the ground force commitment. As one high-ranking German official noted years later, the "symbolic quality of ground forces" could not be compensated for with air power.[12] Allied opposition was matched by the hostility of the Department of External Affairs to the plan. As a DEA memorandum noted in June 1973, "need[ed to say we too would] oppose such measures as contrary to the declared [policies and damaging our] national interests especially in terms of our efforts [to improve relations with] western Europe."[13]

The "symbolic quality" of the ground force commitment was especially important because it committed Canadian soldiers to a potential ground battle in Europe. As had been evident since 1951, it was a commitment from which the Canadian government found it difficult to walk away. The air commitment, while valuable, did not possess this quality; air power was more flexible and could generally be somewhat more easily increased and altered. The allies thus viewed the notion of Canada withdrawing its land forces in favour of an enhanced air commitment as a further indication of a continuing desire to reduce its commitment in central Europe.

Although attempts to implement the ideas of *Defence in the 70s* seemed to demonstrate that the alliance had made few gains in stabilizing the Canadian military commitment in Europe, the allies had already helped ensure that Canada's plans for re-equipping and reconfiguring its ground forces in a manner deemed undesirable (that is, in a light force configuration) were put on hold. With respect to the role and missions of the air commitment, the allies had not been as successful.

From 1 January 1972, the Canadian Air Group, with 3 squadrons of CF-104s, was oriented solely to a conventional attack/reconnaissance role. In contrast to the financial costs inherent in the proposed conversion of 4 CMBG, the dropping of the air group's nuclear mission was relatively inexpensive. Likewise, by the early 1970s, with only 24 CF-104s still dedicated to the nuclear role in peacetime and the new longer-range nuclear-tipped surface-to-surface missile (Pershing I) operational with American and German forces on the central front, the military loss to SACEUR was less than it would have been several years earlier.[14]

The political costs were greater, however. Canada was now the only NATO state (other than Luxembourg) with forces in the integrated military structure on the central front to have shed a nuclear role for its forces.[15] Given the key role of nuclear weapons in allied strategy, the Europeans in particular reacted negatively to the Canadian action. Indeed, even though Canada continued to carry out its nuclear tasks for more than two years following the 1969 decision, when the nuclear roles were discontinued in 1971–2, the country was harshly criticized in NATO military and political circles. According to John Anderson, assistant deputy minister for policy in DND at the time, Canada was "hard hit" during the examination of its defence plans in NATO's annual review in 1972. The alliance's defence committee expressed strong criticism of the Canadian decision to drop the nuclear role, and there seemed to be a perception that Canada "did not know what it was doing in defence."[16]

RESTORATION OF THE BRIGADE COMMITMENT

As discussed in chapters 3 and 5, it was the government's search for a contractual trade link with the European Community which ultimately made Canadian political leaders more sympathetic to the idea of improving the capability of the Canadian forces stationed in Europe. Having successfully forestalled both the re-equipment of 4 CMBG as a light force and the mooted withdrawal of Canada's ground forces from Europe as proposed by James Richardson, the chief of defence staff now began to look towards the improvement of the combat capability of 4 CMBG so that it could play a more effective role in the CENTAG sector.

The Central Army Group sector stretched along about 450 kilometres of the boundary between the Federal Republic and Czechoslovakia and East Germany. This front was covered by four allied army corps – two German and two American corps. CENTAG's frontage was more than double the frontage covered by NORTHAG which was also composed of four allied corps on the front line. The deployment area for 4 CMBG within CENTAG was therefore potentially a wide one. In practice, however, it was limited to the southern part of the CENTAG area because of the limited logistic capabilities of the Canadian ground force. This southern region was defended by the German II Corps (covering some 150 km) and the United States VII Corps (also covering about 150 km) (see map, p. 144).

The deployment options of 4 CMBG within these two corps areas were almost as numerous as the possible threats confronting CENTAG. Warsaw pact forces in both East Germany and Czechoslovakia were capable of mounting a large-scale offensive against NATO on very short notice. Their fifteen divisions (5 Soviet) in Czechoslovakia could have been supplemented by some of the 26 pact divisions (20 Soviet) in East Germany in any attack on the VII Corps and II Corps sectors. The main axis of advance would likely have been towards Nürnberg from Czechoslovakia and towards either, or both, Nürnberg and Würzburg from the GDR. An advance by some 15 to 20 pact divisions (including about 10 Soviet) into this sector would have constituted just the first-echelon attack because reinforcing Soviet forces from the western USSR would have added to the weight of an offensive in subsequent days and weeks.

In the aftermath of the collapse of the GDR in 1989–90, the West Germans had access to Warsaw pact documents (those not removed or destroyed) and they confirmed the offensive nature of the pact's military plans. The principal objectives with respect to one of the options for operations against the German II Corps involved securing the area from Regensburg to Munich in eastern Bavaria prior to beginning operations to destroy the capabilities of the German II Corps completely.[17]

To counter such an offensive, the German II Corps would have been able to field three divisions (one panzer, one panzergrenadier, and one mountain infantry) and likely one light 3000-man brigade of airborne infantry (drawn from the 1st German Airborne Division based in southwestern Germany). The United States VII Corps also deployed three divisions (one armoured and two mechanized infantry) and an armoured cavalry regiment (essentially a brigade-sized unit of 5000 men equipped with both main battle tanks and combat helicopters). One of the two American mechanized divisions had only one brigade based in Germany in peacetime with the remainder of the division in the United States but able to link up with pre-positioned equipment in the Federal Republic within about 10 days.[18]

In the mid-1970s, potential reinforcements in this sector were scarce aside from 4 CMBG. The French army deployed one corps with two mechanized divisions in the Federal Republic and another corps of three mechanized divisions was available as back-up in France itself. However, these forces were not under NATO command and could, especially in the case of the corps in France, also be deployed in support of allied forces farther north. It was also possible that they might not be committed at all but saved to defend France itself. Moreover, in addition to not being committed to first-echelon defence, the French army had suffered for years from the concentration of priority resources on the French nuclear deterrent. As a result, the French army of the 1970s lacked both firepower and mobility.[19]

Thus, it was because 4 CMBG was the *only* first-echelon and in-theatre reserve formation available in southern Germany that there were, in addition to the political factors, strong military reasons for proceeding with an improvement in its capabilities. The three key aspects of such an upgrading were a new main battle tank, the size of the force in a crisis, and viable deployment options.

Schmidt, Trudeau, and the Tank Purchase

The first and most widely known need of 4 CMBG was, of course, the purchase of a new tank. By the mid-1970s the Centurion had been in service well beyond the time-frame originally envisaged. For the reserve role with 4 CMBG, it was totally inadequate and its capability was significantly below that of both the German Leopard and the American m-60a3. The military requirement for a new tank was so important that it became the political symbol of a more credible Canadian commitment to the alliance.

The tank re-equipment decision, as Canada's ambassador to NATO, Arthur Menzies, noted in August 1975, had in fact become more urgent because of the perception of a growing Soviet tank threat (figures of which he provided to Ottawa) and because American tank stocks had become depleted during the 1973 Middle East War when they had been used to reinforce Israel. Menzies argued that CENTAG had far too few tank assets to phase out 4 CMBG's tanks as well. He reported that this assessment had been communicated to him by the commander-in-chief of the allied forces in central Europe, German General E. Ferber, as well as by his successor who had urged Menzies to ask Ottawa to acquire a new main battle tank at least as capable as the m-60 or Leopard.[20]

Pressure came from higher up as well. In meetings in the course of 1975 between German and Canadian ministers, the Germans made clear the importance they attached to the purchase of a new tank by the Canadian Forces. Chancellor Schmidt also raised the issue directly with the prime minister at the first opportunity. In a breakfast meeting on 31 July 1975 in Helsinki, Schmidt tried to convey to Trudeau his own perception of the military threat confronting the Federal Republic and explain why Germany believed a Canadian armoured capability to be important.

Schmidt stated his belief that any decision to use nuclear weapons in a conflict would be an exceedingly difficult one to take and the effect on the Germans, he believed, would be catastrophic. Consequently, the NATO allies had to maintain adequate conventional forces in central Europe to meet the Soviet threat. The chancellor stated that the readiness of the forces of some allied countries (France in particular) was in his opinion too low. When Trudeau suggested that the United States would perhaps opt to use its nuclear weapons if conventional defence was failing, Schmidt replied with some emotion that his government would not permit the use of such weapons in Germany. In this sense Schmidt's comments matched the views which he had already argued publicly in the period before he became Germany's minister of defence.

The chancellor did state, however, that the presence of nuclear weapons constituted a deterrent and that Canada had gone too far when it opted out of its nuclear roles in 1972. When the prime minister asked what use nuclear weapons were if the Soviet Union knew the West would not use them, Schmidt responded simply: "they think we will use them." In a nutshell, he argued that the West needed nuclear weapons to deter aggression but that it needed conventional forces for actually stopping the enemy if they tried to advance. In terms of the Canadian commitment, he stressed the importance of the "psycho-political element" and subsequently added that it was essential to show the Russians and all others that the NATO forces in Germany were not all German or American. If Canada ever concluded that it had to reduce its tanks in Germany, Schmidt stated his preference that it should be done in the context of negotiated mutual and balanced force reductions. Unilateral reductions would undercut alliance unity and a total withdrawal, the chancellor warned, would leave Canada unable to participate in the Conference on Security and Co-operation in Europe in a meaningful way.[21]

The basic thrust of Schmidt's defence thinking in the period after 1969 was generally publicly known. However, Schmidt's views and those of the Social Democratic leadership in this period were not shared in every respect by all in the German Ministry of Defence. It was therefore the ambiguity of the Federal Republic's nuclear position which would keep the Soviet Union guessing. Moreover, it was certainly a point of dispute whether the United States would ever accept the notion of a German veto over the use of nuclear weapons in the Federal Republic if American forces were facing possible destruction. Certainly on a public declaratory level, official German pronouncements continued to emphasize the importance of nuclear weapons in NATO's defence strategy. Indeed, two years later, Schmidt's call for NATO to counter what he perceived to be a growing Soviet theatre nuclear capability reinforced the public emphasis on the continued importance of a strong nuclear position.

By pointing out in no uncertain terms his personal perspective on the respective roles of nuclear and conventional forces in NATO strategy, Schmidt undoubtedly sought to convince Trudeau of the continuing relevance of a strong conventional effort on the part of the allies in central Europe. His reference to the political importance of ensuring that the allied effort in central Europe was not overly dominated by either the Germans or the Americans re-emphasized the importance of the contributions made by even strategically small forces like those of Canada. Interestingly, one month later in September 1975, the German defence minister, Georg Leber, used similar signals when he publicly rejected suggestions that the Bundeswehr be expanded to a strength of 600,000 men. This, he stated, would give the German army an "excessive weight" in the circle of West European military powers.[22]

Schmidt's line of argument was also one advanced by Menzies who stated that "it is in Canada's interest to ensure that NATO Conventional Forces are perceived by NATO and Warsaw Pact leaders and public(s) to be capable of holding [the] line so that recourse to tactical nuclear weapons will be delayed as long as possible."[23] Canada's subsequent purchase of 128 Leopard Is (114 main battle tanks and 14 bridge-layer and recovery variants) was greatly facilitated by the Germans who made them available from the German production schedule and who also agreed to loan the Canadians 35 Leopard tanks from their II Corps stocks to replace the Centurions until Canada's own Leopards were ready.[24] This tank purchase was just sufficient to re-equip 4 CMBG's armoured regiment, pre-position a small number of reserve tanks in Germany, and equip a training squadron in Canada.

The "Combat Group" again Becomes a "Brigade"

The second element in making 4 CMBG's military role more credible was to ensure that its capabilities were expanded in wartime to those of a brigade-sized fighting force rather than those of a smaller "combat group" which was largely reliant on allied support. For a long time it had been widely believed that the smallest viable independent military formation in central Europe was a brigade-sized all-arms force of at least 5000 men with tanks, self-propelled artillery, and mechanized infantry.[25] As early as 1973, General Dextraze and the current commander of 4 CMBG, Brigadier-General P.V.B. Grieve, had succeeded in getting the term "combat group" dropped and the Canadian ground forces in Europe redesignated as a "brigade group."[26] While this change was more symbolic than real, the ultimate goal was clear, and with the Defence Structure Review of 1974–5, the Canadian Forces were able to move more concretely in the direction of making 4 CMBG a credible combat formation.

In January 1976, General Dextraze was able to announce that the wartime strength of 4 CMBG would be raised by adding 1 company of mechanized infantry to both infantry battalions (for a total strength of 4 companies per battalion), 1 squadron of tanks to the armoured regiment (for a total of 3 tank squadrons), one battery of 6 guns (for a total of 4 batteries with 6 guns each) to the artillery regiment, and additional combat engineers. While not stationed in Europe, they would be provided as a flyover commitment and their equipment would be pre-positioned in Germany. This commitment helped raise the authorized wartime strength of 4 CMBG from some 3300 personnel (including some 200 on flyover) in 1971 to about 5500 (including 2250 on flyover), once the new plans were implemented.[27]

After developing these plans and discussion at the highest levels in 1976 and 1977, Canada reported in the country chapter of NATO Defence Planning, 1978–82 that it would seek to implement its goals for a brigade commitment by 1979. These "plans" became a firm commitment when the minister of national defence, Barney Danson, declared to NATO's Defence Planning Committee in December 1977 that "Canada agrees to the report of the 1977 NATO Review and in doing so accepts, as a firm commitment for 1978, the Force contributions recorded in Canada's Country chapter and its statistical Annexes."[28]

The Canadian pledge gradually returned the wartime commitment of 4 CMBG closer to what it had been before 1969. However, the build-up of 4 CMBG back to brigade strength would only occur in a time of crisis or tension, and it also required the investment of additional resources to ensure that adequate equipment and munitions were pre-positioned in Germany. The ability to move towards providing CENTAG with a full-strength brigade in wartime was a product of the decision of the Canadian government in the late 1970s to accord defence a higher priority and to devote more resources to defence so as to address, at least partially, the growing commitment-capability gap.[29] However, the need to provide a flyover commitment of more than 2000 extra personnel for Europe added to the logistics dilemmas confronting the Canadian Forces.

Deployment and Tasking Dilemmas

The third requirement for making the Canadian brigade's reserve role more credible was to ensure well-rehearsed, realistic, and workable deployment options. The location of 4 CMBG at Lahr and Baden-Söllingen very near the French border was not the most ideal for achieving this objective. To reinforce American and German units on the front line a location farther forward would certainly have been more credible militarily. In spite of this weakness, with adequate warning and reinforcement from Canada, the Canadian brigade would likely have had sufficient time to deploy.[30]

The possible deployment options for 4 CMBG were almost as numerous as the possibly military threats confronting the II and VII Corps. These options were outlined in the continuously updated General Deployment Plan which was formulated on the basis of changing intelligence assessments of Warsaw pact capabilities and plans. At one point there were eight or more potential taskings assigned to 4 CMBG, ranging from deployment options south of Munich with the German 10th Panzer Division in the direction of Passau on the Austrian border to deployment options on the northern edge of the United States VII Corps area. As the French moved in the late 1970s and 1980s to integrate their forces more closely with allied strategy, the Canadian brigade also developed deployment options with the French II Corps.

While a cabinet decision had been required to make 4 CMBG a reserve formation for CENTAG, thereafter its specific tasking was made by the CENTAG commander, acting on his own authority, without reference to Ottawa. The Department of National Defence was informed about tasking assignments, but only out of courtesy. The result was, as one senior officer noted, that the Canadian commanders in the Federal Republic (both of Canada's overall forces and of 4 CMBG) had a key role in advising CENTAG on the missions that the Canadian brigade was assigned.[31] While the capabilities of 4 CMBG put certain limitations on the missions that it could be assigned, it was also true that the assignment of Canadian ground forces to certain tasks in which their capabilities needed to be augmented by allied units put pressure on the government to ensure that 4 CMBG acquired the

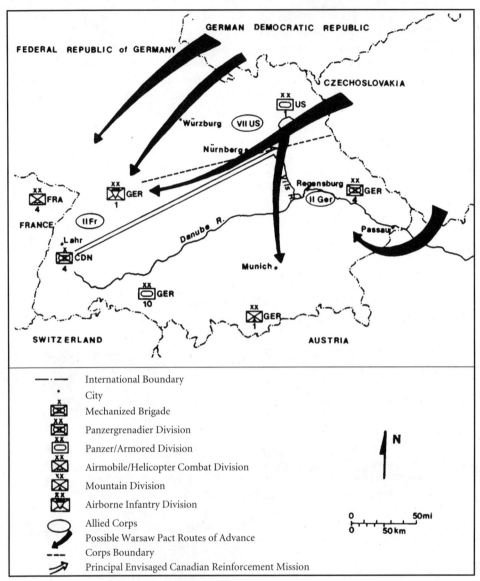

Canadian Land Forces and the Defence of Southern Germany in the mid-1980s

capabilities to carry out its assigned tasks effectively and autonomously. Thus, over the longer term, the pressure to "fulfil NATO commitments," the specifics of which may never have been discussed in Ottawa, was instrumental in influencing not only certain equipment acquisitions but also, in its own small way, the making of defence policy itself.

Despite the diverse deployment options which existed for 4 CMBG, it was the reinforcement mission in the boundary area between the II and VII Corps which evolved into the priority task. This decision was made pursuant to discussions between Brigadier-General Jack Dangerfield, the commander of 4 CMBG, and General Glen Otis, the commander of the Central Army Group in 1984. Following a visit to Canadian land headquarters in Lahr, when General Otis was fully briefed on the large number of deployment options that the Canadian brigade was expected to maintain, he ordered his staff in Heidelberg to narrow the number of tasking options assigned to Canadian ground forces.[32]

For Canadian commanders this was in many ways a most desirable and advantageous development. The small size of the brigade staff made it difficult to keep plans for the different deployment options fully up to date. Narrowing the focus of possible operations to the boundary area between the German and American corps simplified the planning process. Moreover, from both a military and political perspective, it was desirable to retain close contacts with both the Germans and the Americans. Both corps commanders, as one former brigade commander noted, wanted exclusive possession of 4 CMBG, because this would have allowed the Canadians to be fully integrated into their corps' planning and training programme.[33] The CENTAG commander himself, however, wanted to retain the option of deploying the Canadians wherever the threat seemed to be the greatest. Co-assignment allowed the Canadian military to retain professional and training links to both the Germans and the Americans.

The division deployed on the northern side of the II Corps boundary was the 4th Jäger (later Panzergrenadier) Division, while the American 1st Armored Division was responsible for defending the southern sector of the VII Corps area. In the mid-1970s Canadian liaison officers were assigned to both of these allied units. As the brigade's reinforcement options were narrowed to focus on these particular units, contingency planning became more specific in terms of the communications, logistics, and other support to be provided to 4 CMBG by the German and American divisions.

One main role envisaged for the Canadian brigade was to set up and hold a defensive position east of Nürnberg in the vicinity of the Vils River, some 30 to 60 kilometres from the Czechoslovak frontier. This defensive role suited the capabilities of the brigade, for while it possessed an offensive capability, its armoured assets were few and its logistics support strained. This limited 4 CMBG's *shock action* counterattack capability. Likewise, the brigade had to deploy to its assembly area by a mixture of road and rail transport and although an all-road move was possible if rail transport was not available, it caused heavy wear on 4 CMBG's tracked vehicles.

With only 57 Leopard I tanks when operating at full strength and lacking the armoured fighting vehicles with which both the German and American brigades were equipped by the early 1980s, 4 CMBG would be at its best when it was dug in and holding a defensive position. In this role the brigade was described as in some ways a stronger asset than its American and German counterparts because it was able to field a greater overall number of dismounted infantry than either American or German brigades. Canada's mechanized, but nevertheless lighter, infantry brigade was thus ideally suited for operations in the wooded terrain around Nürnberg.[34]

Whether 4 CMBG would be "priority tasked" to either the 1st Armored Division or the 4th Panzergrenadier Division after 1984 depended largely on the CENTAG commander and his assessment of the nature of the threat at any particular moment. In exercise scenarios towards the end of the 1980s, the envisaged threat resulted in the assignment of 4 CMBG to the 1st Armored Division on most occasions. This may have been partly a product of the greater efforts of the French after 1980 to increase co-operation between their own II Corps (based in southwestern Germany) and the German II Corps. Moreover, the formation of the French Rapid Action Force (FAR) (which included basing the 4th Helicopter Combat Division in northeastern France) increased the likelihood and the credibility of a strong French military effort from the beginning of the hostilities. The FAR consisted of five light divisions tasked with rapid intervention in the event of conflict. Its purpose was thus as much political as military. Likewise, the French army's three main corps were also extensively modernized in the late 1970s and 1980s, increasing their combat credibility. Later, the moves to form a joint Franco-German brigade pursuant to a 1987 agreement, and the large-scale joint German-French military exercise of that same year further cemented Franco-German military co-operation.[35]

Despite these positive developments, German II Corps still confronted a monumental problem in trying to defend a 150-kilometre front with only three divisions. In fact the front defended by II Corps was even broader because it was widely anticipated that the Warsaw pact would violate Austrian neutrality and try to outflank II Corps in the south.[36] If this occurred, it was envisaged that elements of the 4th German Division might have had to be shifted south to support the 1st German Mountain Division on the Austrian border.[37] Under these circumstances the Canadian brigade's role in the slot between VII and II Corps would have become more important.[38] Thus, a larger Canadian presence was clearly desirable, given the mission and role expected of the brigade. That the Warsaw pact had active plans for violation of Austrian territory to support an offensive against southern Germany was confirmed in documents available in East Germany after 1990. These plans included options for an offensive through Austria against southern Germany and possibly northern Italy. In just this type of scenario, the role of 4 CMBG, operating either in the northern part of the German corps sector or in the southern part of the American corps sector, would have been even more critical.[39]

Canada had fallen into the reserve mission in CENTAG by default after it had dropped out of its front-line role in NORTHAG. Despite the rather significant tactical military value of Canada's brigade-sized contribution now made to CENTAG, the role had always really demanded a division or even a corps. The latter option was clearly out of the question, and even a division-sized effort was a possibility few Canadian officers considered seriously given the reluctance with which Canada had committed itself to even the wartime brigade-sized obligation. Yet from a military standpoint, a division commitment would have given Canadian ground forces the capability of making a more effective contribution to the defensive effort of either the German or the American corps. Moreover, in the event of some of the potential scenarios actually developing, a division commitment could even have given the Canadian land forces a more independent and pivotal role in the protection of the flanks of the two allied corps.[40]

It was ultimately a combination of factors, however, which quite suddenly made the option of a division commitment seem to be a more realistic one toward the end of the 1980s. For one, the allies had been undertaking more strenuous efforts to improve the quality of their forces. As well as the more credible French effort in the 1980s, the Federal Republic and the United States jointly moved to improve significantly the credibility of the American reinforcement commitment. Under the Wartime Host Nation Support agreement of 1982, the United States moved to pre-position equipment for more of its home-based divisions in Germany so as to ensure a rapid (about 10 days) deployment by air while the Germans agreed to provide 90,000 additional reservists to give these divisions the necessary logistics support and rear-area security once deployed.[41] However, an equally important factor in moving Canada towards a division-level effort was the evolution of political events in Canada. Ironically, the precursor to this development was yet another review of the country's military commitments in central Europe which actually had as its goal the complete withdrawal of Canada's land and air forces from Germany.

THE NIELSEN DEFENCE REVIEW

In opposition, the Progressive Conservative party had long been critical of the Liberal government's defence policies. In particular, it had deplored the government's inadequate funding of defence and the resulting inability properly to fulfil NATO commitments. Aside from Luxembourg and Iceland, Canada devoted a lower percentage of its gross domestic product to defence than any other country in the alliance (see Appendix Five). The Mulroney Conservatives, on their election in September 1984, were thus pledged to provide significantly greater resources for defence.[42] It soon became apparent, however, that other matters (most particularly, the attempt to institute budget deficit reductions) were to have a greater priority and defence appropriations were actually cut to a level below that which had been envisaged by the Liberal government for 1984/5.[43] It thus become impossible to improve the capabilities of the Canadian Forces to meet their commitments solely through an increase in resources.

In terms of Canada's alliance commitments, the commitment-capability gap was evident most particularly in the pledge to provide NATO in a crisis with both a mechanized brigade in central Europe and a second brigade to reinforce northern Norway. Similarly, the air forces were tasked with the responsibility of providing one air group of three attack squadrons in Germany and another two CF-5 squadrons to northern Norway. These pledges created an enormous logistics burden for a country such as Canada and its limited defence budget, especially in terms of its ability to sustain these forces (in two widely separate theatres) once they were committed to combat. Many defence analysts as well as military officers favoured resolving this dilemma by consolidating the country's NATO commitments to serve one area or the other: either central Europe or the northern flank. The question was which commitment to drop and which to retain.[44]

For several years the idea of a northern defence orientation had been gaining support among defence analysts and some defence decision-makers. This idea included a proposal that Canada make a more credible commitment to reinforce northern Norway. This task had always been a militarily difficult one. Because foreign forces could not be based in Norway in peacetime, reinforcements would have to move there by sea and by air once a crisis was imminent. Canada's Air-Sea Transportable (CAST) brigade would take 21 to 30 days to deploy to northern Norway, and most military analysts questioned the realism of moving the brigade's heavy equipment to Norway by sea after hostilities might have already erupted. Pre-positioning equipment in Norway and maintaining an all-air reinforcement commitment had long been proposed, but Canada lacked the resources to purchase the two sets of equipment which would be necessary to pursue this course. In any case, the logistical problems of supporting both the CAST brigade in Norway and 4 CMBG in Germany would remain.

Those who argued for a northern defence orientation held that in the past Canada had paid insufficient attention to the defence of its own territory, including its air and sea approaches. The maintenance of forces in Europe, many of these analysts argued, afforded the country little strategic advantage while constituting an unacceptable drain on the defence budget. Instead, resources should be concentrated on defence tasks in North America, which in itself was a crucial region of the alliance, and on the North Atlantic region, including northern Norway. The northern flank was vitally important strategically because it faced a significant military threat from Soviet ground, naval, and air forces based on the Kola Peninsula. Even a single Canadian brigade and supporting air squadrons would have a strategic relevance on this flank that they could never possess in central Europe. Therefore, since the entire NATO defence strategy in the Atlantic was itself dependent on a successful defence of northern Norway, Canada had an immediate and major interest in helping to defend this region.[45]

Critics of the northern defence orientation stressed the vital *political* importance of the central region, and especially of Germany, in the East-West balance of power. They argued that if Canada was to have a credible voice in the alliance and in Europe, there could be no substitute for the physical presence of Canadian soldiers on the ground in Germany. These political rationales, which had strong support within the Department of External Affairs, were buttressed by military arguments (chiefly from the army) that held that while the central European role could be made militarily credible (because of the large Canadian base in southern Germany), the commitment in northern Europe would never be viable in the absence of either pre-positioning or peacetime basing in Norway.

Discussions in NDHQ

Erik Nielsen, who became minister of national defence in March 1985, was determined to address the commitment-capability gap.[46] Generally, he was in favour of a strategy which would have adjusted government spending priorities and accorded defence a higher priority. Nielsen was a rarity as a Canadian defence minister in that he was a senior member of the government serving simultaneously as deputy prime minister and a member of the cabinet's most powerful committee, priorities and planning. While the readjustment of government spending priorities remained an ultimate goal, it soon became apparent that Prime Minister Mulroney and the rest of the government were not prepared to take the political risks associated with seriously curbing Canada's runaway spending on domestic programmes and redirecting those resources to other areas (such as defence – see table 2 at p. 164).[47] Nielsen was therefore prepared to consider different ideas for consolidating the country's defence effort.

In the summer of 1985, on the initiative of the chief of defence staff, General Gerard Thériault, several meetings were held within the Department of National Defence between Nielsen, the deputy minister, D.B. Dewar, the assistant deputy minister for policy, John Anderson, General Thériault, and his vice-chief, Lieutenant-General Jack Vance, to discuss policy options. It was generally agreed, as noted in a discussion paper submitted by Anderson, that there were four strategic imperatives to which Canadian defence policy should seek to contribute: the avoidance of nuclear war, friendly control of the ocean approaches to North America and Canada, denial of hegemonic control of Europe and Asia to any single power which might then directly threaten North America, and friendly relations with the United States.

Then, on the basis of another paper and presentation made by General Thériault in the first of these meetings, it was agreed, as long argued by many defence analysts, that Canada had devoted insufficient attention to the defence of its own territory and its air and sea approaches. Moreover, Thériault reiterated that Canada was far overextended in terms of its European commitments. He proposed an alternative force posture based on a northern defence orientation and an Atlantic strategy which would see Canada withdraw its land and air forces from Germany, pre-position much of 4 CMBG's equipment in Norway, and contribute a more credible ground and air force reinforcement effort in northern Norway.

At this time disputes between Canada and the United States over Canadian sovereignty claims in Arctic waters meant that the nationalist flavour of a northern defence orientation found favour with Nielsen who apparently became convinced of its appeal domestically. He evidently also became convinced of its strategic logic. He asked that a plan be drafted which could be taken to the prime minister. This plan included the following elements:

1 A phased withdrawal, over three years, of all Canadian ground and air forces from Germany. The air force's new CF-18 fighters would be used to augment the aircraft available for air defence in North America and committed to the northern flank. Much of the army's equipment from Germany would be pre-positioned in northern Norway and the troops withdrawn to Canada. The plan included the option of setting up a logistics base or facility in the United Kingdom.
2 The Canadian commitment to the North American Aerospace Defence Command would be strengthened through the construction of new radars and the possible acquisition of airborne warning and control system (AWACS) aircraft.
3 The construction programme for the navy would continue, and it was proposed that additional long-range patrol aircraft also be acquired.
4 Some additional equipment would be purchased to ensure that ground forces now based in Canada, but with pre-positioned equipment in northern Norway, could continue to train effectively.
5 The air force would be given the capability to transport troops to Europe more rapidly.

These were, of course, only proposals and certainly those dealing with equipment were only a wish list. Nevertheless, Mulroney apparently granted permission for Nielsen to sound out key NATO allies on their views. The defence minister was reportedly determined not to proceed unless the allies were generally in agreement with the Canadian plan.

Talks with the Allies

In late August 1985, Nielsen travelled to Washington to meet with the American secretary of defense, Caspar Weinberger. It was expected that the most sympathetic response to Canada's proposals would be in Washington, but even so it was decided that Nielsen should speak to his American counterpart in a relatively informal setting without advisers present. In the meeting (with only their chiefs of staff present) Nielsen explained the Canadian plan to the secretary of defense and stressed it was a rational refocusing of Canadian resources for the greatest benefit to the alliance. Weinberger was said to have been generally supportive though he stressed that he would have to consult with his own advisers before offering his formal support. Whatever the truth regarding the degree of Weinberger's interest in the Canadian ideas, Nielsen certainly came away with the impression that the Americans were not hostile to the Canadian proposals.

Encouraged by the positive response from the Americans, Nielsen decided to visit Europe immediately to sound out the British and German defence ministers on his proposals. General Thériault cautioned Nielsen that the reaction of the Europeans to the plan was unlikely to be as positive as Washington's and suggested that he should go to Europe first to prepare the ground and sound out European views. In this way the strategic merits of the plan could be more carefully presented and the impression avoided that yet another hasty Canadian review was under way to "welsh out" of commitments previously agreed to. Nielsen, however, decided to proceed to Europe without any preliminary groundwork.

General Thériault's own general views on Canada's defence dilemmas had already been discussed in varying degrees of detail with the SACEUR, General Bernard Rogers, and with several NATO service chiefs, including General Wolfgang Altenburg, the inspector-general of the Bundeswehr, and Field Marshal Bramall, the British chief of defence staff. On an informal basis, Thériault had made known his personal preference for a northern defence orientation for the Canadian Forces. None of these individuals had actively opposed his ideas, although Rogers noted the importance of 4 CMBG to CENTAG[48] and Altenburg stressed the particular political sensitivity of the issue for the Federal Republic.

With their knowledge of the views of Canada's chief of defence staff, the European military chiefs must certainly have had their suspicions about the direction that a Canadian defence review was likely to take. Yet, while allied military officials were likely aware of the ideas evolving in DND, it seems that Canada's diplomats were not. Certainly, neither the Canadian ambassador in Washington, Allan Gotlieb, nor his counterpart in Bonn, Don McPhail, was informed of the reason for Nielsen's visits. Gotlieb reportedly was "furious" on learning of its purpose after the fact.[49]

It is likely that Joe Clark, the secretary of state for external affairs, knew of Nielsen's démarche, because the cabinet's priorities and planning committee had met just prior to Nielsen's visit to Washington. Given Nielsen's belief in cabinet solidarity, it is unlikely that he would have failed to inform his colleagues of his plans. Certainly if Clark did know of the proposals, they ran counter to assurances he had given to the German foreign minister, Hans-Dietrich Genscher, back in September 1984 that the Conservative government did not intend to make any "dramatic changes" in Canada's defence policy.[50]

For Manfred Wörner, the German defence minister, the Canadian proposals must have come as a surprise. In March 1985, when Nielsen became defence minister, it had been announced that Canada would actually be increasing its forces in Germany by some 1200 personnel, or about 20 per cent. This move, to be implemented in 1986, would bring the combat arms elements in 4 CMBG to full strength and reduce the size of the flyover commitment. Similarly, Canada had invested resources in the infrastructure to support the new CF-18 multi-role fighter in Germany and conversion of the three CF-104 squadrons to the CF-18 had begun during 1985. The Germans had been very satisfied with these developments and saw them, quite rightly, as indications that Canada was confirming its presence in Germany. Less than six months later, the proposals for a complete withdrawal of these forces made Canadian defence policy appear "jumpy" and unreliable. From the German perspective the timing of the proposal was particularly bad, coming in the immediate aftermath of the searing debate over the deployment of intermediate-range nuclear weapons in the Federal Republic. Moreover, since the proposals of American Senator Sam Nunn to reduce American troops in Germany were at that time under active consideration in the United States, Bonn was anxious that no questions be raised regarding the credibility of any other allied commitment in central Europe.

On 9/10 September, Nielsen began his unpublicized visit to Europe, stopping first in London to meet the British defence minister, Michael Heseltine. Nielsen's approach was to try to convince the allies that by withdrawing forces from Germany, Canada was simply seeking to shift those resources within Europe to the northern flank where they would be more useful. It was hoped that this argument might secure British support since the British themselves had military commitments to the northern flank. Moreover, Nielsen's discussion would include the option of possibly setting up a logistics facility in the United Kingdom. However, Heseltine, who was facing pressure of his own to reduce forces in Germany, was not at all receptive. The atmosphere of the meeting was in fact reported to be tense from the outset, and Canadian hopes of securing British support were rather abruptly crushed.[51]

The next day Nielsen flew to Bonn for a meeting with Manfred Wörner. The embassy there had been informed about three days earlier of Nielsen's intended visit, but, as noted, they had no idea of the proposed subject matter – though it was assumed that Canada's troops in the Federal Republic would be discussed. That evening the ambassador was told that there was a review of Canada's troop presence in Germany but not any of the details, and his request to attend the meeting with Wörner was turned down.

Nielsen's presentation of the Canadian plan was apparently a skilful one. Again it was emphasized that the moves should be seen as ones which would strengthen the alliance as a whole by focusing the Canadian effort in Europe and making it more realistic militarily. Some years earlier (1977–8), when Canada had been considering cutting the CAST commitment to the northern flank in favour of an enhanced central front commitment, the Germans, perhaps somewhat surprisingly, had urged Canada to continue to task a reinforcing brigade to the northern flank. A memorandum from the defence relations division of DEA in the autumn of 1978 had explained that the unique political and strategic circumstances prevailing on the northern flank had forced the Germans to curtail their own military activities in northern Europe because of a negative Soviet and Finnish reaction to the prospect of an enhanced German role in the defence of northern Norway. As a result, since the Germans were said to believe that support for Norway was of tremendous political importance to the alliance as a whole, they were apparently strongly in favour of a continuing Canadian commitment.[52] Indeed, the issue had been viewed as important enough that it had been raised both during Chancellor Schmidt's 1977 state visit to Canada and by the German defence minister, Georg Leber, with the Canadian defence minister, Barney Danson in the same year.[53]

Although Nielsen and Wörner, who were both pilots, reportedly got along reasonably well, Wörner, like Heseltine, expressed his opposition to the Canadian ideas. In fact, after being told of Weinberger's general, if only informal, support for the Canadian plan, he later telephoned the American ambassador in Germany, Richard Burt, to express his strong objections. Burt raised the issue directly with the State Department, and his telegram, which was shown to one Canadian official, was apparently extremely negative towards the Canadian proposals. Following the intervention of the State Department, Weinberger reversed his earlier position in support of the Canadian plan. Nielsen thus left Europe having been unable to convince the two major European allies of the desirability of the proposed changes to Canada's force posture. And once it was clear the Americans were now opposed as well, he was no longer prepared to proceed with the plan.

With the Nielsen plan no longer viable, other options for the consolidation of the country's defence effort were considered. One was to move Canadian forces from southern Germany north to Schleswig-Holstein. Canadian forces would continue to be based in the Federal Republic, but since this area of Germany was part of NATO's Northern European Command (AFNORTH), these troops could be said to be assisting directly in the defence of northern Europe, thus fulfilling the thrust towards a more "northern-oriented" Canadian defence effort. While NATO forces there, as everywhere else, could use reinforcement, such a move would take time and cost money. New bases would have to be found and doubtless new facilities for Canadian personnel and their families would have to be constructed. After hundreds of millions of dollars had already been invested in Lahr and Baden-Söllingen, this was not a welcome prospect. Asked for his thoughts on the idea, the commander of 4 CMBG, Brigadier-General Jack Dangerfield, noted that his studies indicated that the base facilities in Schleswig-Holstein were full. Moreover, on a political level he advised that while in CENTAG the one-star commander of 4 CMBG participated in planning conferences with three-star German and American corps commanders, in Schleswig-Holstein the Canadian brigade would form only one small element within an integrated Danish-German corps. A Canadian move from southern Germany to the far north of Germany could thus involve some potential loss of the influence which was currently enjoyed.[54]

The Germans likewise pointed out some of these difficulties in the annual staff talks between German and Canadian officers in 1986. They preferred the Canadians to stay right where they were, because a move north by 4 CMBG would deprive CENTAG of its only in-theatre reserve and because of problems involved in facilitating such a major redeployment. However, General Wolfgang Altenburg, inspector-general of the German armed forces, had already told the Canadian defence attaché in Bonn, Colonel Gerry Hirter, shortly after Nielsen's visit in 1985, that if the Canadians were intent on moving, the Germans would certainly prefer a move to Schleswig-Holstein, where he acknowledged that German forces were weak, rather than out of Germany entirely. Indeed, a German staff paper had reportedly already been produced in the autumn of 1985, looking at the implications and the costs involved in such a move.

The origins of the Schleswig-Holstein option are uncertain. It almost certainly did not emanate from the senior policy-making circles of DND (that is, from the minister's office or the chief of defence staff). It is possible that the Germans may have produced the proposal as an alternative to the Nielsen plan, but this too is uncertain. Whatever its origin, the plan was never adopted, nor it seems ever seriously considered in the department.

THE SHORT-LIVED DIVISION COMMITMENT

With Nielsen's retirement in June 1986 and the subsequent retirements of both John Anderson and General Thériault by the end of the summer, the thrust of the defence review changed course. The consolidation of the commitments in Europe was still the goal but the focus shifted to reversing the logic of the Nielsen review and concentrating Canada's commitment in Germany instead of on the northern flank. It was no secret that the army had never been very enthusiastic about the commitment in Norway, and it now had an opportunity to advance its case for a division-level commitment to CENTAG. The tactical military importance of the reserve role in the

CENTAG sector has been noted. In addition, Canada already had the bases in southern Germany to provide a division-sized force with the logistics support necessary to sustain operations for a longer period. These military arguments were of course bolstered by political factors which had for a long time pointed to the desirability of making a more credible defence effort in Germany.

From August to October 1986, Canada exercised the deployment of the CAST brigade to Norway for the first time and the results confirmed what everyone already suspected: the reinforcement commitment to the northern flank was beset by problems, especially without the pre-positioning of military equipment in Norway. In September the Land Doctrine and Operations Section of DND thus began planning for a division-level effort in Germany. The political fallout associated with consolidation in Germany and abandonment of the Norwegian role was not as serious as that from the reverse scheme. Although the Norwegian defence minister visited Canada in February 1987 and made a reportedly strong political pitch for Canada to remain committed to the northern flank,[55] the Norwegians did not have the political clout in the alliance that the Germans did. Thus, despite its strategic value, the CAST commitment was abandoned.

The initial concept for a consolidated commitment in central Europe was based on an armoured division which would be composed of four regiments – two of tanks and two of mechanized infantry. The costs associated with this option, particularly the acquisition of a main battle tank and an armoured fighting vehicle rapidly caused it to be discarded. Instead, as announced in the 1987 defence white paper, it was decided to settle on a two-brigade mechanized division based mostly on existing units.[56]

However, even the creation of a division based on this more modest structure would also be tremendously expensive, especially since new equipment would be required virtually across the board in the 1990s. Despite some improvements, Canada's brigade was already really operating with obsolescent equipment in the 1980s. Canada had bought few major items of new equipment in the 1970s and 1980s (see Appendix Two), and the acquisitions it had made had been limited in numbers and really only barely supported the maintenance of a modest front-line capability. There was little or no thought given to reinforcement capability, or to the need to have some war reserve capability so as to provide front-line forces with depth.

In marked contrast, the Germans and the Americans had made major acquisitions during the same period. Both had deployed second-generation main battle tanks more capable than the Leopard I (the M-1/A1 Abrams by the Americans and the Leopard II by the Germans). Both countries also deployed new armoured fighting vehicles (the Bradley with the United States Army and the Marder by the Germans), and the Americans acquired new combat helicopters (the Apache). None of these types of weapon system was held by 4 CMBG. The Canadian failure to keep up was a shortcoming which undermined the military effectiveness of the brigade and, by extension, the political credibility of the country's commitment. If Canada was to move to a tenable divisional-level effort in the 1990s, new equipment would have to be purchased and on a much larger scale than before.

One new system that had already been ordered in 1986 was the self-propelled dual air-defence/anti-tank missile system (ADATS). Originally designed to protect both the CAST brigade and 4 CMBG, all ADATS systems were now to be consolidated in Germany where they would form a division-level regiment to provide a strengthened anti-tank capability and greatly improved low-level air defence. Until this point, the only air-defence capability possessed by 4 CMBG was the hand-held Blowpipe surface-to-air missile acquired in the early 1970s.

Other necessary equipment would include some 250 new main battle tanks, eventually "several thousand" new armoured personnel carriers of various types, new artillery (both heavy artillery and multiple rocket launchers), and new helicopters. Moreover, to sustain the division up to thirty days, extensive amounts of munitions and supplies would have to be purchased. Likewise, to provide credible reinforcement and logistics support as well as casualty and equipment replacements once engaged in combat, the reserves had to be expanded. Initially, it was planned to provide 25 per cent of the division's wartime strength from the reserves.[57]

Indeed, much of the $17-billion army re-equipment programme envisaged in the 1987 white paper would go to re-equip the Canadian division in Germany. In light of the difficulty that previous Liberal and Conservative governments had had in sustaining a consistent level of defence expenditures, many of the allies were justifiably sceptical. One officer on the staff of the German defence minister, whose task it was to prepare a summary for Wörner of the Canadian defence white paper, had already reportedly commented that it was the proposals for funding in the white paper which made him the most doubtful of the Canadian government's plans.[58]

Canada phased out its northern flank reinforcement role in the two years following the release of its white paper in June 1987.[59] The air division of 5 CF-18 squadrons (3 in Germany and 2 in Canada) was established in 1988, while the army division took up its commitment to the central front in November 1989 (the same month that the Berlin Wall fell). The white paper had outlined a plan which would have seen Canada's 5500-man wartime brigade commitment tripled to a 16,500-man wartime division commitment. With this plan the Canadian army in Germany was to assume a much larger and comprehensive role in NATO's defence strategy, with a ground force commitment much more suited to the task at hand. Even so, in initial discussions between the Canadian embassy in Bonn and German authorities on the provision of wartime host nation support for the enhanced Canadian effort, the Germans reportedly expressed some scepticism about the long-term seriousness of the Canadian commitment. Some Germans inquired whether Canada was really intent on moving ahead with its plans, given the changes then already under way in Soviet foreign policy.[60]

By this time, the revolutions in Eastern Europe were beginning, and it would soon become apparent that the reinforcement role for the 1st Canadian Division within CENTAG was already obsolete. While this certainly could not have been foreseen by political and military planners in 1987, the division commitment had in fact become a hollow one even before that when the government very abruptly, and with no consultation with DND or DEA, all but abandoned the white paper's goals in April 1989 by cutting defence appropriations to the point where most of the white paper's objectives became unrealizable. As a result of the April 1989 budget, the division's envisaged capabilities were significantly scaled back and the overall wartime size reduced from 16,500 to 12,500 personnel. In many eyes, the scope of the cutbacks and the cancellation of almost all the equipment replacement programmes envisaged in the white paper made the proposal to provide a division to CENTAG little more than a paper commitment in the waning months of the Cold War.[61]

CANADA'S MILITARY COMMITMENT, 1970–89: AN ASSESSMENT

The role that Canada's forces took on in the defence of the central front after 1969 was determined by domestic political factors and by economics. The withdrawal of 4 CMBG from a front-line role within NORTHAG had been forced by the compromise solution reached within the Trudeau cabinet in 1969 which had significantly reduced the size of Canada's forces in Europe and made the maintenance of a full-strength brigade in the NATO front line no longer tenable. In turn, the basing of Canadian ground forces in CENTAG sector at the two Canadian air bases in southern Germany and the retention of their recently acquired mechanized equipment was a product of the inability to afford a reconfiguration of Canadian ground forces as an air-mobile force. The reserve role in the CENTAG sector was thus one which Canada took on by accident rather than by intent. Over the longer term a combination of service and professional interests (in this case in the army) as well as allied pressure gradually restored the Canadian commitment to provide NATO with a mechanized full-strength brigade in Germany in wartime.

The government's movement towards this revision of Canada's NATO roles in the 1970s was almost entirely ad hoc and reactive. Cabinet itself had no part in determining the specific missions of 4 CMBG in the CENTAG area but subsequently did feel the pressure to configure and equip Canadian ground forces to carry out these missions. What was always lacking was a realistic and workable security policy strategy which would have integrated defence and foreign policy objectives in a common framework. Even after the Defence Structure Review of 1974–5, when the government reluctantly agreed to accord NATO a higher priority and to invest some additional resources in defence, there was no willingness on the part of the Trudeau government to follow what had been its own objective back in 1968–9: to ensure that defence policy was properly supportive of foreign policy objectives. The Defence Structure Review seemed designed more to ensure that defence did not continue to act as a hindrance to the government's other objectives than to look seriously at how it might serve to provide those goals with a significant boost.

Indeed, after the Leopard tank purchase and the signing of the contractual link with the European Community in 1976, there was no initiative to utilize politically the obvious allied and German interest in the construction of a more viable military commitment. In fact, many of the measures which were undertaken to improve the military viability of the Canadian Forces (such as the restoration of a wartime brigade commitment and the search for more credible missions within CENTAG) were initiated from within the military itself. As one officer put it: "The military had to go out and sell itself within CENTAG," in the best way that it could given the assets which it had been assigned.[62]

While Canada's reserve role within CENTAG had developed in an entirely ad hoc fashion and while there were legitimate questions about whether this was the right role for Canada to be performing within NATO, the mission nevertheless ended up inadvertently providing Canada with some degree of real influence. In terms of the air contribution, the Canadian Air Group commander, as a one-star officer within the 4th Allied Tactical Air Force (ATAF), was a participant in commanders' conferences with four German and American commanders of two-star rank and the German commander of 4 ATAF who was of three-star rank. Moreover, within 4 ATAF headquarters, a Canadian officer always held the position of deputy chief of staff for operations, giving him a day-to-day influence over operational planning. This position was described by General Brian L. Smith (who served as deputy chief of operations and later as commander of Canadian Forces Europe) as more influential in matters of force employment than even that of the commander of Canadian Forces Europe.[63]

After the conversion from the CF-104 to the CF-18 and the subsequent build-up to a wartime commitment of one air division of five squadrons, the credibility of Canada's air commitment in central Europe increased. Moreover, the multi-role CF-18, unlike the CF-104, could perform the air-to-ground mission as well as an air-defence mission and as such it was a highly prized asset both by 4 ATAF's Allied Tactical Operating Centre 4 (responsible for offensive operations) and Sector Operating Centre 4 (responsible for defensive operations). Thus, as was the case for 4 CMBG, the subordinate allied headquarters in 4 ATAF to a certain extent competed for the Canadian air assets.[64]

Canada's not inconsequential role within the alliance's integrated military structure was complemented from the late 1970s by a closer bilateral military relationship with the Federal Republic as well. The Leopard tank purchase and Canada's search for a closer economic and political relationship with Germany had also sparked a new series of high-level military contacts. In 1977 Canada and Germany held the first in a series of annual staff talks between the two military establishments. Discussions at the two-star level (between the associate assistant deputy minister for policy at DND and the director of the military policy staff in the German Ministry of Defence) focused on policy questions of common interest, the role of the Canadian Forces in Europe, German training in Canada, and collaborative armaments projects. In these talks the Germans from time to time noted their interest in seeing Canada increase its efforts in central Europe, particularly by stationing more personnel in Germany to bring 4 CMBG closer to its wartime strength.[65]

The Canadian government also received similar advice from other sources, including the Senate's Sub-Committee on National Defence in 1982,[66] but it was not until 1985 that substantive measures were announced to begin to move in this direction. Given Canada's larger political and economic objectives in Europe in the late 1970s and early 1980s, and notwithstanding the fact that Canada's reserve role in CENTAG had arisen for many of the wrong reasons, the move to a division-level effort after 1976 could have greatly facilitated some of the country's wider objectives within Europe. This could have been done through focusing the procurement for the re-equipment programmes which would have been required on Europe and possibly through collaborative arms development projects.

However, instead of a strategically directed and planned approach, Canada backed inadvertently into its division-level commitment some ten years later as the result of a failed attempt earlier in the defence review process to withdraw Canada's forces from Germany entirely. Devoid of the larger political and economic rationales necessary to support the investment of billions of dollars in the move to a division-level effort in central Europe, the project failed to survive as a viable government policy for even two years.

In the process, the CAST commitment, which was both strategically and politically important, was discarded as well. It should have been possible to find the resources to maintain both commitments in a viable fashion. However, when compared with other areas of federal spending (see table 2, at 164) not only were the resources allocated to defence in the 1970s and 1980s inadequate, but the requisite attention to policy from Canada's leaders was also always lacking. In consequence, it was all but impossible to establish the most important requirement for sound policy: a stable policy environment.

The military role of Canadian forces in the defence of central Europe and the Federal Republic up to 1989 was certainly a modest one from a strategic perspective. However from a tactical military perspective, Canada's forces would have made an important contribution to the defence of their sector wherever they had been deployed. Such was the reality of NATO's weakness in conventional forces on the central front. This aspect of Canada's military role in Germany was never properly appreciated in political decision-making circles. In consequence, the existence of Canadian forces in Europe was never exploited to its fullest potential.

PART FOUR

Canadian-German Relations
in the Post–Cold War Period:
Whither Transatlanticism?

8 The Politics of the Demise of Canada's Military Commitment in Germany

In 1989–90 the West won the Cold War when the communist order collapsed from within. Ensuring the security of Europe and the North Atlantic area for some forty years was a major accomplishment of the alliance and, as a member of NATO, Canada shared in this success. Yet, having won the Cold War it was also important to win the "peace" that followed. All member-states were faced with the task of re-evaluating their contributions and determining, in concert with their allies, the most effective contribution that could be made in the future.

In Canada, however, even as revolution was sweeping Europe and the old international political order was giving way to a new one, the political agenda was increasingly dominated by domestic concerns centred on the country's constitutional and budgetary problems. As a result, Canada's political leaders paid even less attention than before to international affairs. The time that Canadian leaders did give to external affairs and defence matters was by and large dominated by the mistaken belief that the country had earned a "peace dividend." This meant that Canada's foreign engagements and defence commitments were easy targets for cost-cutting.

In fact government retrenchment in these areas had been signalled even before the collapse of the Berlin Wall in November 1989. Bolstered by its election victory in the autumn of 1988, the government of Brian Mulroney turned its political attention to trying to bring Canada's deficit and debt under some measure of control. However, an unwillingness to consider any fundamental reforms or cuts to the country's increasingly expensive domestic social programmes led the government to apply many of its cost-cutting measures disproportionately to the weakest federal government departments. There were few departments as weak as National Defence.

Table 2
Canadian Government Spending, 1984/5 to 1995/6, in $Billions and as Percentage of Total
Expenditures

	1984/5	1989/90	1995/6
Social Programmes*	$37 (33.9%)	$47.22 (33%)	$53.6 (32.8%)
Other Fiscal Transfers†	$16.9 (15.5%)	$20.3 (14.2%)	$23.1 (14.1%)
Defence	$8.8 (8.1%)	$11.3 (7.9%)	$10.3 (6.3%)
Foreign Aid	$2.1 (1.9%)	$2.4 (1.7%)	$2.2 (1.3%)
All Other Programme Spending‡	$22 (20.1%)	$22.2 (15.5%)	$24.6 (15%)
Public Debt Charges	$22.5 (20.6%)	$39.4 (27.6%)	$49.5 (30.3%)
TOTAL	$109.2	$142.9	$163.5

Figures have been rounded.
* Refers to federal transfers to the provinces for health, post-secondary education, and social welfare as well as
   direct payments to individuals for unemployment insurance, pensions, and family allowances.
† Includes equalization payments to provinces, business subsidies, and payments to Indians and Inuit.
‡ Includes funding for all other government departments and agencies and funding for crown corporations.

Beginning with the April 1989 budget, DND was hit with a series of major spending cuts. In the first round of cuts, the department was forced to bear 37.2 per cent of the government's overall budgetary reductions, even though defence spending represented only some 7.9 per cent of all federal spending. Then in 1990/1 the department bore 29.4 per cent of government cutbacks. In total, projected defence spending increases were cut by some $5.6 billion over the five years following the 1989 budget. Signifying the generally low political priority the government attached in practice to its overseas commitments, international development assistance was also seriously pared back.[1]

Spending restrictions fell disproportionately on the Department of National Defence (see table 2). By 1995/6, defence spending had been reduced to just 6.3 per cent of the federal budget. (By way of contrast, defence spending by the German federal government declined from 18.3 per cent of the budget to 10.9 per cent between 1981 and 1993.[2]) The relatively small size of Canada's defence budget meant that the cuts to defence spending in Canada were not sufficient in and of themselves to provide a significant reduction in the federal government's deficit and debt. The failure to address the problem of rising social and other programme spending in any serious way resulted in increasing deficit and debt levels throughout the period in question (see table 3). Serious restrictions on social programme spending were not in fact announced until the 1995 federal budget.

Even though these cuts necessitated the complete abandonment, in all but name, of the defence white paper issued only two years earlier, this did not create any serious domestic political consequences for the government. Its actions, and the lack of reaction to them, yet again showed that the question

Table 3
Canada's Federal Debt and Deficit Levels ($billions)

Year	Deficit	Debt
1985/6	34.6	242.6
1989/90	28.9	358.8
1993/4	42.0	508.2
1994/5	37.9	546.1
1995/6	32.7	578.9

Source: Canada, Department of Finance, annual budget estimates.

of relevance related to Canadian defence policy was in many ways even stronger than it had been in the past. Although many of the programmes in the defence white paper, especially those related to the control of the air and sea approaches to Canadian territory, addressed strategic weaknesses which were in many ways independent of the existence of the Cold War, the defence budget was nevertheless cut across the board, without any attempt to address these problems.

In spite of the comprehensive nature of the defence cuts, the most vulnerable target for even deeper reductions was the Canadian military presence in Europe. Since the late 1950s the withdrawal of these forces had been considered on different occasions by nearly every national government. Each time political considerations had intervened to keep Canadian forces in Europe. With the end of the Soviet military threat, however, the traditional military basis for the political arguments supporting this commitment had very suddenly been removed.

THE FOREIGN AFFAIRS AND DEFENCE POLICY REVIEW

Early in 1990 the Mulroney government began a review of Canada's foreign policy. On 5 February, the secretary of state for external affairs, Joe Clark, announced a reassessment of the country's European policy intended to "define Canadian interests in Europe and to develop a strategy to secure those interests." As he admitted several months later, however, "Canada's wishes will not necessarily determine Canada's role": "Powerful new economic and political forces are at work, forces over which Canada has limited influence. A European role will not be bestowed upon us because we decide it is in our interest. It must be earned. That requires imagination and realism and hard work."[3]

Canadian officials and diplomats responsible for Canada's relations with Europe for the most part continued to believe in the importance and relevance of Canada's military role in Europe. "Security in Canada has no meaning without security in Europe," Clark stated. This Pearsonian commitment to Canada's active engagement abroad continued to be the dominant rationale within the Department of External Affairs for the country's international diplomacy no less during the Mulroney years than in earlier times. In this sense, the importance of Canada's military presence in supporting Canada's wider diplomatic objectives was emphasized. Again, as Clark noted: "The primary Canadian bridge to Europe has been our contribution to the North Atlantic Alliance. That contribution has involved thousands of Canadian troops on the ground in Germany, troops whose lives have been put on the line daily in defence of freedom. In a real sense, that contribution of Canadian lives can have no substitute and no parallel."[4]

Thus DEA officials emphasized above all the need for prudence concerning changes to the Canadian military commitment. Quite rightly, they viewed this commitment both as a symbol of Canada's continued interest in a transatlantic approach to common European and North American political and security problems and as a vehicle for promoting and supporting the country's diplomatic, economic, and trading interests in Europe.

Nevertheless, despite the strong preferences of DEA, the pressures on the government for a total Canadian withdrawal mounted. Continuing budgetary outbacks loomed over the Department of National Defence for the foreseeable future. This unstable budgetary situation dictated a need for some hard choices and for several reasons Canada's military presence in Europe was regarded as a "luxury" the country could not afford.

First, there was a widespread perception in many quarters that the country's political and economic interests were shifting away from Europe. By 1990, 75 per cent of the country's exports were destined for the United States, while 64.5 per cent of imports came from that single source. Each country was the other's largest trading partner. While trade with all of Europe (including the USSR) remained large in absolute terms (some $36 billion in 1990), it only amounted to 12.6 per cent of Canada's total world trade – about equal to that with the Asia-Pacific region.[5] Moreover, under terms of the Free Trade Agreement with the United States which came into force in 1989, Canada was committed to an economic and trading strategy which sought to deepen and strengthen the North American trading relationship. (This trend would be enhanced with the entry into force of the North American Free Trade Agreement (NAFTA) in 1994 which extended the free trade zone to include Mexico.) The "strategy" of the 1970s which had sought to reduce Canada's dependence on the United States market and to strengthen trade links with Europe as a counterweight had long been abandoned.

In other issue-areas as well, such as culture and the environment – and indeed in virtually every realm – the relationship with the United States totally overshadowed Canadian life and therefore Canada's external relations. Thus, although Canada's other international links (especially with

Europe in a cultural, political, economic, and military sense) remained important, their profile on Canada's domestic political agenda remained weak by comparison.

A second pressure for the withdrawal of forces in Europe arose from those who had long believed that Canada devoted insufficient resources to the defence of its own territory and continent. Certainly, the 1985 defence review had revealed the strong desire which existed in the Canadian defence establishment to improve capabilities in North America. The white paper of 1987 had really been the first of Canada's post–World War II defence policy statements to take a serious look at the country's unique strategic and military interests and requirements and to prescribe policies based on those needs. This orientation was especially evident in the white paper's evaluation of Canada as a "three-ocean country" and in its analysis of the strategic importance of the Arctic to Canada.[6] After the 1989 budget, however, the desire of the Canadian military to improve its capabilities in North America was no longer realistic, and the focus was simply on endeavouring to maintain a reasonable level of military capability in the face of continuous budgetary cutbacks.

In this respect, the cancellation of many of the "continentalist" defence programmes originally forecast in the 1987 white paper (including nuclear-powered submarines envisaged principally to give the Canadian navy a three-ocean capability) reinforced concerns in DND over the erosion of the country's ability to protect its own territory. Thus, although the Canadian military has had strong professional interests in staying in Europe, the budgetary and equipment dilemmas confronting DND moved the department in the direction of prioritizing its defence commitments. With an estimated $1.3 billion spent annually on Canada's NATO forces and ever declining defence resources, the commitment in Europe soon began to look like an increasingly attractive place to make reductions since cuts had to be made. Moreover, because the maintenance of a viable force in Europe would require a major re-equipment effort in order to discharge the new tasks and requirements of the alliance related to rapid deployment, military opinion became increasingly convinced of the need to consolidate the country's defence effort in North America.[7]

The debate which took place in Canada between 1990 and 1992 pitted an increasingly financially strapped Department of National Defence, which believed that in the existing budgetary situation the country could no longer afford to maintain a viable military force in Europe, against a Department of External Affairs which continued to view it as politically essential to retain Canadian military forces in Europe or risk the country's complete marginalization within the Atlantic alliance and the "continentalization" of Canada's foreign and defence policies. Both DND and DEA were correct. But in the absence of any firm direction from the country's political leaders, no firm decisions could be made. Instead, the government tried once again to "muddle through." In the end this only compounded the political damage that the country would suffer before financial realities made the government's decision for it.

In Canadian diplomatic circles Germany had long been perceived as Canada's most important partner in Europe – even though the country's political leaders were often unaware of this fact. Beginning in 1990, the realization that Canada's very position in Europe would now come under increasing domestic challenge caused DEA officials to redouble their efforts to strengthen Canada's political relationship with Europe and with Germany most particularly. The recognition that the military dimension of Canada's relationship with Europe would decline in the coming years led its diplomats to promote a strengthened CSCE structure with a strong North American involvement and to try to ensure that its economic and trade interests in Europe were fully protected after the establishment of a unified internal European market at the end of 1992. Canada also endeavoured to stress its willingness to assist in the reconstruction of eastern Europe, noting in particular that Canada's multicultural make-up put it in a strong position to engage itself there by drawing on and building on contacts which already existed between ethnic communities in Canada and their former homelands. Here and in other areas, such as the provision of expertise related to arms control verification or peacekeeping operations, Canada sought to present itself as able to fill a niche in the construction of a new European security order.

On the German side, Canada's diplomatic initiatives were viewed in a positive light because they mirrored perceptions in governing circles in Bonn as to the type of active engagement necessary to help ensure political, economic, and social stability in eastern Europe. Indeed, in an April 1990 visit to Ottawa in which he met with Clark and other officials, the German foreign minister, Hans-Dietrich Genscher, supported and "underscored Ottawa's growing commitment to participation in the CSCE and European institutions."[8] The Federal Republic and Canada had also both been long-standing proponents of introducing stronger military confidence-building measures into East-West relations and of providing military manœuvres in both NATO and the Warsaw pact with greater "transparency." In support of this effort, Canada offered to host an "open skies" conference in Ottawa in the middle of February, a conference to be attended by foreign ministers from the West as well as from the now collapsing Soviet bloc.

Early in February 1990, the Canadian ambassador in Bonn, Thomas Delworth, was informed by Genscher that the open skies forum should also be used as an opportunity to reaffirm the importance of the transatlantic relationship.[9] For the Germans, then entering the most difficult stage in their unification discussions with the Soviet Union, such a declaration would emphasize the importance Bonn attached to maintaining its Western links. It would also confirm North American support for those objectives. The European Community was suggested as the best partner-institution for a joint transatlantic declaration between Europe and North America which would reaffirm the mutual commitment of both European and North American states to consultation and to strengthening the mechanisms for discussions on issues of common concern.

Canada was immediately interested in two declarations – one between the United States and the EC and the other between Canada and the EC. In keeping with traditional Canadian policy, such a format would re-emphasize Canada's symbolic equality with the United States. The Canadian embassy reportedly vigorously lobbied the Foreign Office in Bonn to support the idea of two accords. German support actually proved to be crucial in convincing a reluctant Italy (which held the presidency of the EC in the second half of 1990) to agree to transatlantic declarations with both Canada and the United States. Italy was apparently unconvinced of the necessity of these declarations, but with German support accords were signed between the EC and the two North American states in Rome in November 1990. They symbolized the continuing diplomatic interest on both sides of the Atlantic for the maintenance of the transatlantic political relationship.[10]

Despite this diplomatic success and the evident interest of Germany in a continued strong relationship, Canada's own diplomatic and military policies seemed once again to be unco-ordinated. In October 1990 the defence minister, William McKnight, announced that yet another review of Canada's defence policy was under way and that Canada's military commitment in central Europe would be under discussion. It was also announced that the government was moving to withdraw some 1400 of Canada's 7900 troops in Europe. Although both the review and the decision to withdraw forces from Germany were not unusual developments, the objectives of DND in conducting its review were at odds with the policy being pursued by External Affairs.

For instance, during the negotiations on the Conventional Forces Treaty, finally signed in Paris in November 1990, Canada had fought hard to exempt its forces in Europe from being assigned any reductions as part of the NATO cuts on the central front. It had argued that Canada's military deployments in Germany were so small that any treaty restrictions would risk making those forces militarily unviable. This diplomatic objective was in fact achieved and the ceilings set for the Canadian Forces allowed the country to maintain the force in Europe at its existing strength (the only NATO power thus exempted from major equipment reductions in central Europe). Canada then decided nevertheless to go ahead with a proportional cut to the strength of its forces in Germany. The army brigade would reduce its armoured, infantry, and artillery elements through the withdrawal of one company from each of the four battalion-sized units it had deployed to Germany. The nature of these reductions made it evident that once again in the making of Canadian defence policy, the left hand had no idea what the right hand was up to, for the cuts made were exactly the type which Canada might have been assigned in the Conventional Forces Treaty and which Canadian negotiators had sought so hard to avoid.

This "salami-slice" approach to force reductions was typical of the force reductions that Canada had made over the previous thirty years. While the overall readiness and effectiveness of the forces in Germany were reduced by cuts of this type, it was believed that this kind of reduction would be less likely to cause Canada unwanted diplomatic problems which might be associated with a more comprehensive reconfiguration of the forces and their mission.

The specific nature of the equipment ceilings assigned the Canadian forces under the Conventional Forces Treaty hindered any ideas that might have been put forward to reconfigure the brigade in Europe to meet the new strategic and political challenges confronting the alliance. The ceilings made little allowance for the most likely future changes that Canada might want to make to the configuration of its forces to suit the post–Cold War environment. Most specifically, the restrictions agreed to for Canadian land forces under the treaty greatly limited the option of converting the brigade into a helicopter-equipped air-mobile formation.

During the Cold War such a "light" role for the brigade had been largely incompatible with the military requirements of defending the central front, but in the post–Cold War era such a role for the Canadian brigade appeared more compatible with NATO's new emphasis on strategic mobility. Mobile forces were now needed to respond to unexpected crises which might arise anywhere in the NATO area or even outside it (as in Yugoslavia). In 1991, the alliance had created a Rapid Reaction Corps (RRC) to meet the requirement for a rapidly deployable force. This corps has come include air-mobile formations from Britain, Belgium, the Netherlands, and Germany. Together these formations make up a multinational division within the corps.[11]

In 1995 the British element of this division (24th Airmobile Brigade) was deployed to Bosnia as part of the allied rapid response force created to protect United Nations peacekeepers there. A few months later, the headquarters of the RRC was given responsibility for commanding the 60,000-strong NATO force sent to police the Bosnian peace agreement signed in Dayton, Ohio, in November 1995. Instead of being able to provide a full combat-effective brigade to this allied effort, Canada's contribution was limited to just 1000 troops serving in an integrated multinational brigade.

In 1989, a report of the Senate's Special Committee on National Defence, had recommended that the government give serious consideration to converting Canadian forces in Europe to fill the air-mobile role. One might therefore have expected Canadian negotiators at the talks leading to the Conventional Forces Treaty to ensure that the ceiling on combat helicopters set for Canadian forces in Europe be sufficiently high to allow for this possibility. However, while the eventual ceiling of 13 combat helicopters did not totally preclude such a reconfiguration, it nevertheless allowed for little flexibility.[12] Since the option of converting the brigade in Germany into a more viable formation was never given serious consideration, the raison d'être of the Canadian contingent in Germany declined even more rapidly.

DND's objectives in the 1990 defence review were in fact almost exclusively budgetary. Having been saddled with large reductions in both the 1989/90 and 1990/1 budgets, the department was forced to make cutbacks in areas of lower priority so as to continue to fulfil all of its agreed commitments. Europe was now re-graded as an area of lower military priority.

For officials in Bonn, particularly in the Ministry of Defence, the stationing of Canadian forces in Germany was still the most important symbol of Canada's Atlanticist commitment. From their perspective, the multinational dimension in Western security and defence policy remained a crucial guarantee of the stability of central Europe in the post–Cold War years. A complete withdrawal by any of the nations engaged in central Europe was not seen to be in the German interest, especially not the withdrawal of the second North American member of the alliance. As a result, the Germans took all available opportunities to inform the Canadians that a continued military presence remained important. During a visit to Bonn in late September 1990 De Montigny Marchand, the under-secretary of state for external affairs, had been so informed by the Defence Ministry's state secretary, Ludwig-Holger Pfahls.[13]

NATO and German planning late in 1990 was focusing closely on the creation of the several multinational corps called for in the new alliance strategy. These corps would form the basis for a continued multinational military policy in central Europe. With regard to the Canadian role, the Germans were looking at options which included the creation of a multinational American-German-Canadian corps in southern Germany or possibly a joint German-Canadian division. The highly regarded and professional Canadian brigade was considered a great asset, especially in the context of the generally lower level of conventional forces which would now be fielded by the alliance.[14]

Yet this initiative was undermined in the autumn of 1990 by the Germans themselves who were also occasionally prone to sending out mixed signals. Although publicly, the importance of the allied troop presence in Germany was always emphasized, new unilaterally imposed training restrictions were beginning to send a different message. These restrictions, which coincided with the start of new negotiations on the future status of allied forces in Germany, raised the prospect that the training opportunities for both allied ground and air forces would be seriously limited in the future.

A unilateral ban on low-level flying (below 300 metres), imposed for internal political reasons in Germany, was bitterly received by the Canadians, and the ambassador in Bonn was instructed to deliver a letter of protest from the defence minister to the German Defence Ministry. Later, in a September meeting in Washington, Louis Delvoie, DND's assistant deputy minister for policy, reiterated to Major-General Klaus Naumann, the director of the Bundeswehr's military policy staff, Canada's great distress at the German decision which risked undermining the air force's effectiveness.[15] While Naumann apparently assured Delvoie that the Canadian deployment remained both essential and desired by Germany, German words and actions seemed contradictory.

These developments raised questions in many minds as to whether Canadian forces would really be welcome in the FRG in the future. The Canadian military in particular tended to view the restrictions as a signal that while the Germans wanted the allies to remain, they would in future remain largely confined to their bases. To most Canadian officers, such an arrangement would make the forces' presence untenable, and, in fact, indicated a decided lack of German interest in the Canadian and allied presence.[16] This action, when coupled with the much more serious political mis-signals sent out by the Germans in the following year (related to the formation of the so-called Euro-Corps with France outside the NATO command structure), may have been instrumental in contributing to a perception in North America and in the United Kingdom that German interest in the Atlantic alliance was declining.

Given these developments, especially in the light of budgetary realities, it appeared that the Canadian military had virtually won its case for a complete withdrawal from Germany. Early in 1991 one of the leading advocates within the government of the value of a continued Canadian military presence, Joe Clark, was replaced as secretary of state for external affairs by Barbara McDougall. Reversing Clark's earlier emphasis on the importance of the military presence, McDougall stated at the spring 1991 NATO ministerial meeting that "given the other roles we play [in NATO], I don't think that it's critical to Canada's participation to maintain troops in Europe." At the same time, the new defence minister, Marcel Masse, indicated his desire to move quickly towards a defence review decision and promised to make such an announcement by the end of June.[17]

For the Germans, the prospects of a Canadian withdrawal caused serious concerns. Despite the policy mis-steps that had been and were continuing to be made, Germany's political leadership remained committed to the transatlantic link. A military presence in the Federal Republic was still regarded as the most important element in this link. Bonn had made great diplomatic efforts to stabilize both the French and Belgian military commitments in Germany following announcements from Paris and Brussels which suggested that all French and Belgian forces would soon be withdrawn. These announcements had raised the prospect of a sudden unravelling of the defence structure in central Europe before NATO's new multinational corps structure could be put into place.

The Germans had an equal concern that the American, British, and Canadian forces remain on the continent. As one very senior German officer noted, while the continental allies of Germany were committed to Germany's defence by the "reality of geography," the United States, Canada, and Britain were not. As a result, the Anglo-Canadian-American commitment was more important in a symbolic and political sense because strategic detachment from Europe by these states was always feasible.[18]

The Germans therefore turned up the diplomatic pressure in 1991 in an endeavour to ensure some Canadian presence in Europe after 1995 (the date when all Soviet forces were to be withdrawn from East Germany under the 1990 unification treaty). In May Genscher paid a short visit to Ottawa in which he apparently made a pitch to Canadian leaders for a continued Canadian commitment in central Europe.[19] Then in June, during a state visit by Prime Minister Mulroney to the Federal Republic, Chancellor Helmut Kohl publicly underscored the importance that Germany continued to attach to the presence of Canadian forces. In private discussions between the prime minister and both Kohl and Genscher, the German views in this respect were outlined in greater detail.

Whether or not their arguments were decisive in convincing Mulroney (temporarily at least) of the continued importance of basing Canadian forces in Germany, he nevertheless pronounced himself "swayed and impressed" by the chancellor's arguments. And in a public address in Berlin on 14 June, the prime minister declared that a Canadian troop presence would be maintained in the Federal Republic: "Canada will not be withdrawing completely from Europe. Canadian forces will remain as long as there is a residual threat to European and Canadian security and as long as we are needed and welcome." Although Mulroney declined to be more specific (and if his decision was made on an ad hoc basis, he probably could not be), the pledge to maintain a presence after 1995 was explicit and was certainly seen as unequivocal by the German side.[20]

The problem was how to fulfil the prime minister's political pledge to maintain a viable force in Europe and still deploy credible forces in North America, within a shrinking defence budget which would in all likelihood continue to be under pressure for the rest of the decade. The option of retaining a brigade-sized force (previously regarded as the minimum militarily and therefore also politically credible force) was likely soon ruled out as unaffordable because of re-equipment costs. Furthermore, the costs of continuing to operate one of Canada's two bases in Europe had probably caused that option also to be rejected early on. The only option which remained was to base a battalion or regimental-sized force at an allied base. This unit would then be available for rapid deployment as part of an allied composite force in the NATO area. A land force commitment was preferred over an all-air one because of the political necessity of making any commitment as credible a symbol as possible of Canada's support for European security. Over the past forty years the ground force element in Canada's military presence had taken on such a symbolic quality. While such a limited presence was sub-optimal in both a political sense (with regard to maintaining a distinctive and recognizably Canadian presence in Europe) and a military one (since the force would be a sub-brigade size), it nevertheless would fulfil the *minimum* objective of continuing publicly to commit Canada to the importance of a North American presence in Europe.

On this basis, the minister of national defence finally announced the results of the long-awaited defence review in September. In it, Canada pledged to maintain a "task force" of 1100 personnel in Europe to be stationed at an allied base. Canada's own bases at Baden-Söllingen and Lahr would close in 1994 and 1995, respectively. In terms of reinforcement elements for NATO in a crisis, Canada pledged to continue to commit a battalion group to Allied Command Europe's mobile force and an additional Canada-based brigade and two fighter squadrons.[21]

In public, the reaction of NATO officials such as Secretary General Wörner to the Canadian decision was one of relief that the withdrawal would not be a total one. Privately, however, the reaction was less polite. Previously, an all-arms brigade-sized force had been regarded as the minimum acceptable commitment. This "task force" would be considerably below that strength and thus made little sense to most NATO and German military officials. What especially raised the ire of the alliance was that once again Canada had set a new troop level without formally consulting its allies. This violated a principle formulated as early as 1954 when Canada had agreed not to change the status of forces assigned to SACEUR without consultations.

Officials at the highest level in the German Foreign Office informed the Canadian ambassador that Bonn was not happy that Canada had chosen not to consult its allies, either on a multilateral or on a bilateral basis. A close transatlantic partnership was of great significance at this time, they argued, and the principle of intra-alliance consultations thus assumed greater importance. The Germans noted that even the Soviet Union, at the Vienna conventional force talks, had come to recognize the importance of consultations prior to taking decisions. For his part, the ambassador argued that both the domestic political situation and time pressures within Canada had contributed to the quick fashion in which this decision had been taken.[22]

At NATO, Canada's permanent representative, James Bartleman, briefed his colleagues at a private luncheon of NATO ambassadors. He apparently argued that the Canadian decision should be assessed from the perspective of the serious budgetary difficulties facing the government and in light of the earlier possibility of a complete pullout. The allied reaction was, on this occasion, restrained. Even so, the American representative reportedly stated that the political impact in the United States would now have to be awaited. This impact could, he said, either be positive, given that Canada had decided at least to maintain a reduced force in Europe, or negative, given the sharp nature of the reductions announced. The German ambassador apparently agreed with these remarks, acknowledging that all the allies knew that the Canadian decision could have a great impact on the United States debate on its troop presence in Europe. This was why the alliance had underscored the great importance of the continued American presence in its earlier ministerial meeting in Copenhagen. Nevertheless, recognizing Canada's serious internal difficulties, the German representative expressed his relief that Canada would be retaining a symbolic presence on the continent.[23]

Although Canada had now made a public declaration of its future plans for troop deployment in Europe (a declaration which was repeated by the prime minister to the NATO heads of government and state meeting in Rome in November[24]), it seems unlikely that this commitment was ever a very deep one. If only 1100 troops were to be retained on the continent, many began to wonder whether the "decoupling threshold" had not finally been reached.[25] From the perspective of the armed forces, even the maintenance of a 1100-personnel "task force" together with several thousand civilian dependents was looking like a proposition which would be too expensive. Certainly the military utility of the force was now seen to be limited and the political benefit to Canada marginal. "Our flag pole is going to have to be an awfully long one to be noticed," one senior officer remarked.[26] Nevertheless, it was the government's basic indifference to the whole question which ultimately ensured that the policy to retain some forces in Europe was reversed.

As in 1989, it was a Canadian budget which led the government to reverse its latest declaration on defence policy. In late February 1992, the finance minister, Don Mazankowski, announced that the government had decided to cut another $2.2 billion from the defence budget, spread over a five-year period. Canada's previous plan to retain troops in Europe would now be abandoned and the two bases in Germany would close even earlier than planned. The reaction of NATO and of individual allies, both publicly and in private, was astonishment. The secretary general stated: "I have noted ... [the Canadian decision] with considerable regret, given the political and military importance of the presence of Canadian forces in Europe ... There will now be formal consultations within the alliance on the Canadian decision."[27] In Bonn, planning and consultations between the Ministry of Defence and the military attaché's staff at the Canadian embassy had been under way for some time on how to accommodate the reduced Canadian military presence. Through their contacts, Canadian officials were informed that the Germans were very upset that these discussions, on which considerable time and staff work had been spent, had proved to be a waste. Indeed, although the Germans always conducted themselves in a professional manner, Canadian officials were asked whether the embassy had known in advance of the government's decision. It proved embarrassing to explain that the decision had caught the embassy as much by surprise as everyone else.[28]

Canada explained its decision to the NATO Council on 26 February. Mr Bartleman apparently argued that the sole reason for the decision was financial, and that it did not signify any change in Canadian security policy or imply a lessening of the country's commitment to the alliance. Indeed, he stated that Canada would continue to make available forces for emergency reinforcement of the NATO area and to stand by its commitments to support the NATO infrastructure.

The response of NATO representatives was to express total dissatisfaction with the Canadian decision and the explanation of it. They let it be known that they foresaw the gravest potential political repercussions from the Canadian decision. The secretary general spoke of "far-reaching political consequences," particularly in the form of an undesirable impact on the debate in the United States and with regard to the maintenance of a North American presence in Europe. The German ambassador echoed these views, apparently arguing that this decision could well have a negative effect in the United States, coming as it did from one of only two North American states within the alliance. These German fears were confirmed by the American representative, William Taft. Indeed, even the French ambassador allegedly spoke of the serious negative consequences which could ensue from the Canadian decision.

Not surprisingly, given existing British concern over the weakening of the transatlantic link, the British reaction was probably the most negative. The British representative to NATO, Sir John Weston, apparently voiced his utter "dismay" at the decision.[29] The British government subsequently made a formal request, through its high commissioner in Ottawa, for the Canadian government to reconsider its decision. The Canadian high commissioner in London was also called to the Foreign Office "to hear British objections." The British initiative was supported by a declaration from the meeting of NATO's Defence Planning Committee early in April at which Canada was again heavily criticized. Then in May the British made a last-ditch effort to keep a Canadian presence in Europe, suggesting that a force of just 300 troops be left which would integrated into a larger allied force.[30]

However, Canada was not to be moved, and the decision was confirmed by the defence minister soon thereafter. Even if it had been reversed, there was no guarantee that it would not have been re-reversed by the Mulroney government or by the Liberal government of Jean Chrétien which would certainly not have felt bound by the decision of its predecessor. The simple fact was that, despite the Canadian ambassador's protestations before the NATO Council to the contrary, far more than financial factors lay behind Canada's decision. The very fact that a public pledge made by the prime minister in Germany in June and reiterated to all the NATO allies at the Rome summit in November could be so easily reversed clearly indicated that the relevance Canadian leaders attached to the country's Atlantic connections had waned considerably.[31]

Interestingly, although the official German response to the most recent Canadian defence review had been one of concern and even anxiety, the reaction of the German élite to the 1992 announcement seemed to suggest only limited interest. In comparison, for instance, with the wide coverage which the Trudeau government's 1969 decision had received, the events of 1991–2 got only scattered coverage in the German national press. In fact, for many it seemed that the Canadian decision merely confirmed that both NATO and Atlanticism were in trouble. In April 1992 the *Frankfurter Allgemeine Zeitung* stated that Canada's decision reflected the failure of the alliance to define a new and convincing function for itself in which "loyal allies like Canada" would find a new and meaningful role.[32]

Nevertheless, this seeming indifference was not universal in Germany, and in Atlanticist circles the decision was viewed in a particularly negative light. One analyst, for instance, spoke of the dangers of a possible "Canadianization" of American policy, meaning that budgetary realities might fuel a future American decision to withdraw. Likewise, the noted political analyst and historian, Michael Stürmer, warned that the Canadian decision might herald the beginning of an erosion of the whole Atlantic system.[33]

The implications for Canadian-German relations were, of course, potentially far reaching. Certainly to the extent that Canadian troops were seen to be an important symbol of Canada's commitment to Atlanticism, their withdrawal had an enormous impact on the Canadian-German political relationship. For forty years, Canada's forces in Europe had given a wider meaning and significance to Canadian-German relations. Canada had acquired a direct stake in developments in central Europe while the Federal Republic developed an interest in continued Canadian military engagement and in the form and substance of that engagement.

To be sure, for the time being Canada will continue to be engaged politically as well as militarily in NATO – through its reinforcement commitment, by contributing to the manning of NATO's AWACS force, and through its maritime forces. However, these activities will not likely be an effective substitute for the physical presence of a credible Canadian land force in Europe. Limited co-operation and interaction between forces which rarely, if ever, exercise and train together in any meaningful way and are based on opposite sides of the Atlantic is no substitute for the daily interaction engaged in by the multinational forces based in Germany.

Nor is the effect only on a military level. It will also have a significant political impact. One of the key lessons of the forty-year Canadian military presence in Europe is that this commitment gave a meaning and significance to the country's diplomatic initiatives that they would not otherwise have had. Even the specific military configuration of the Canadian contingent has had an influence on Canada's political standing with its allies. Thus, there may well be a significant impact on the influence that Canada will have in both NATO and the CSCE and its successor, the Organization for Security and Co-operation in Europe. Canada's political leverage in such organizations has always been seen by others as closely tied to its military commitment. Indeed, as Helmut Schmidt warned Pierre Trudeau in 1975, Canada's influence in an organization like the CSCE was directly linked to the continuation and nature of its military presence on the continent.

Once the decision for withdrawal was made, the question of whether it might provoke the unravelling of other bilateral and multilateral transatlantic links had to be faced. For example, while Germany did renew the agreement under which it trained military forces in Canada in 1993, this is likely to have been mostly because the Germans have already invested considerable resources in establishing the necessary land and air training facilities in Canada. Certainly, the past political meaning and importance of these German activities is now in question. German training in Canada was, after all, originally a product of a political desire on the Federal Republic's part to demonstrate its interest in a more balanced transatlantic relationship with Canada. In this sense, the withdrawal of Canada's forces from Europe after forty years will change, potentially on a fundamental level, the political framework and context of Canada's relationship with both Germany and Europe.

Between 1992 and 1995 the government tried to argue that its commitment to peacekeeping in the former Yugoslavia represented the country's strong and continued interest in European security. However, this commitment was always a temporary one and in a region of Europe outside NATO's area of responsibility. Even Canada's commitment of some 1000 troops to the NATO force deployed to Bosnia at the end of 1995 is a temporary and limited operation.

After the withdrawal of these forces, Canada will still be the only one of the NATO states previously engaged in central Europe to have abandoned the allied stationing regime in Germany. In the longer term, this political fact will always outweigh any temporary military commitments assumed by

Canada in Europe, however valuable and worthwhile they may be. Indeed, Canada's influence in the making of allied policy on the former Yugoslavia after 1992 was probably hindered more by the decision to withdraw from Germany than it was advanced by the move to join the United Nations force in Yugoslavia. Interestingly, the German defence white paper of 1994 states that it is the willingness shown by allied states to contribute to the integrated multinational forces of the alliance which ensures that "each ally has political influence and a voice."[34] Thus, reduced Canadian influence in NATO – the inevitable consequence of the withdrawal decision – undermines the country's role in the making of allied policy even in cases like Yugoslavia where Canadian lives were at risk.

With the withdrawal decision, Canadian-German relations are now on a different footing. On the one hand, Germany occupies a new position in Europe. It has a new relationship with the East and its role in the West is in transition. Its new responsibilities in eastern Europe and its changing relationship with western Europe have reinforced the importance of international and European affairs for its political decision-makers. Canada, on the other hand, is focused more than ever before on internal problems and its relationship with the United States. It seems likely that many aspects of the co-operative Canadian-German political relationship, forged in the post–World War II era and strengthened in the 1970s, will not carry over into the post–Cold War era. Had a deeper and more comprehensive economic and industrial relationship been developed between the two countries in the 1960s and 1970s, that relationship might have helped to mitigate some of the current trends towards "continentalism" on both sides of the Atlantic, but in North America most especially. However, in the absence of such comprehensive links, there has been little interest in Canada in resisting the pull of "continentalism."

On the most fundamental level of all – the future of the Atlantic alliance – to the extent that the Canadian decision has undermined the allied stationing regime in Germany and contributed to the perception that North American and European interests are drifting apart, it has been particularly harmful. Especially important is the longer term influence of the Canadian decision on the debate in other countries, particularly the United States. As indicated in table 4, almost all of the allies with troops in Germany, including the United States, have sharply reduced their forces since 1990 and further cuts seem likely. As force levels continue to decline, pressures for a complete withdrawal are certain to mount. In this regard, it is the policies of the non-continental states (the United States and the United Kingdom) that will be most important.

While the final impact of the Canadian decision on the debate will not be evident for some time, the fact that NATO decision-makers already interpret the decision as an erosion of interest in the transatlantic link in Canada and

Table 4
Standing Allied Ground and Air Forces in Germany: 1990 and 1995

	1990		1995*	
	Ground Forces	Air Forces	Ground Forces	Air Forces
Belgium	1 corps HQ 2 brigades plus corps units (25,000 troops)	Nil	1 brigade (4300 troops)	Nil
Canada	1 brigade (4400 troops)	3 fighter squadrons (54 combat aircraft)	Nil	Nil
France[†]	1 corps HQ 3 divisions Berlin garrison (53,000 troops)	Nil	1 division (15,000 troops – future under review)	Nil
Germany[†]	3 corps HQ 12 divisions (308,000 troops)	15 fighter wings (450 combat aircraft)	2 corps HQ 9 divisions with 23 brigades[‡] (234,000 troops)	10 fighter wings (400 combat aircraft)
Netherlands	1 brigade (5700 troops)	Nil	1 light brigade (3000 troops)	Nil
United Kingdom	1 corps HQ 3 divisions Berlin brigade (56,000 troops)	12 fighter squadrons (150 combat aircraft)	1 division (24,000 troops)	6 fighter squadrons (78 combat aircraft – all to be withdrawn by 2002)
United States	1 army HQ 2 corps HQ 4 divisions 5 independent brigades and regiments (203,000 troops)	4 fighter wings (300 combat aircraft)	1 corps HQ 2 divisions (71,000 troops)	1 fighter wing (96 combat aircraft)

* By 1995 allied forces in Germany were integrated in multinational corps formations. The British-commanded Rapid Reaction Corps was headquartered in Germany. Likewise American V Corps and German II Corps comprised German and American divisions while a multinational corps (at Münster) under rotating German/Dutch command consisted of both German and Dutch forces. German IV Corps commanded German forces in eastern Germany. German forces were also integrated with Danish forces in a joint corps and, outside NATO command, in the Euro-Corps (with French, Belgian, and Spanish forces).

† Both Germany and France also contributed to the Franco-German Brigade, which was forming in 1990 and operational by 1992.

‡ In 1995 only 7 of 23 German brigades were at full strength in peacetime. The rest relied on reserve mobilization.

Sources: The Military Balance, 1990–91 and 1995–96 (London: International Institute for Strategic Studies 1990 and 1995); Federal Ministry of Defence (Germany), White Paper 1994.

in North America is already of considerable importance. Indeed, Canada's budgetary explanation for its 1992 decision raises the fear in Europe that economic factors may eventually also influence an American decision. Certainly most decision-makers in France and many in Germany already believe in the likelihood of an ultimate American withdrawal from Europe.[35] If the Canadian decision has further encouraged a European belief in the eventual withdrawal of the United States, then regardless of events in the United States, European (and particularly Franco-German) actions in anticipation of a possible American pullout may help make predictions of an ever-widening Atlantic become a self-fulfilling prophecy.

9 Canada, Germany, the Widening Atlantic, and the Future of Canada's Foreign Policy

History will record the revolution of 1989 as one of those events which ushered out an old order and heralded a new era. The internal disintegration of the world's second superpower was in most ways without precedent. Never before had a great power collapsed so rapidly and (at least up until 1995–6) in such a relatively peaceful fashion.

The dissolution of the Soviet empire forced the Atlantic alliance to face in reality a series of questions which had been asked on only a theoretical basis since 1949. Could the alliance survive the disappearance of the Soviet threat? More specifically, could the transatlantic relationship survive the collapse of the Soviet threat? Was the alliance more than simply a military alliance? Was the political dimension of NATO sufficiently strong, or, alternately, could it be sufficiently strengthened, to provide the alliance with a continuing raison d'être? What importance, for individual and particular member-states, would the Atlantic alliance have in a post–Cold War order? On a more general level, were the interests of North American and West European members of the alliance different or similar in this respect? And to what extent? Could a West European or pan-European security alternative now supplant NATO?

These questions were all centred on the most important dimension of the alliance – the relationship between Europe and North America. This "core relationship" had already been under pressure in the decade prior to 1989. In fact, this tension had been in many ways a permanent feature of transatlantic relations since the alliance was founded. "They tell me the alliance is in disarray; when has it ever been in array?" Harold Brown, a former American defense secretary, is reported to have remarked.

However, the changed international environment of the 1990s forced the alliance to consider its utility in the absence of any immediate external threat. The ability to maintain alliance unity in the new strategic environment was thus crucially dependent on prevailing perceptions and attitudes, in both Western Europe and North America, about the future value and importance of the Atlantic alliance. Germany's key position in Europe meant that its policy with regard to the Atlantic link would in all likelihood continue to be especially decisive in determining Europe's general policy orientation on this whole question. The evolution of German policy will of course be closely determined by the extent to which German interests are perceived in Berlin/ Bonn to be advanced by the alliance's continued existence.[1]

THE BALANCE IN GERMAN FOREIGN POLICY SINCE 1989

As discussed in chapter 2, in the years after 1949 German security policy came to be structured around four principal themes: first, the importance of the Atlantic link and the country's relationship with the United States – this dimension being in fact the crucial and ultimate guarantee of the Federal Republic's security throughout the Cold War; second, the idea of European unity and reconciliation with France; third, the restoration of Germany to a position of complete equality in the international community; and, finally, the ultimate goal of national reunification but only in the context of a peaceful and stable relationship with the Soviet Union. The maintenance of an effective balance among these themes became central to Bonn's efforts to manage the various dimensions of the "German Question" as they manifested themselves in the Cold War period. The nature of the balance may have changed depending on the international and domestic political climate, but all these dimensions of German security policy remained key components of Bonn's external policy framework throughout the Cold War.

Despite the end of the Cold War, this principle of balance is still basic to Germany's security policy. In the aftermath of the country's reunification, there have been three areas of focus for German security policy:

1 The continued promotion of the goal of a more united Europe, which depends as before on the closest co-operation with France;
2 The great importance of constructing a new and stable framework for relations with Russia and the states of eastern Europe; and
3 The preservation of a close partnership with the United States and other allies in the Atlantic context.

These themes in post-1989 German security policy have increasingly been identified with particular multilateral institutions. The goal of European unity has been most directly associated with the evolution of German policy with respect to the European Union (eu) and the Western European Union (weu). Likewise, the development of Germany's bilateral relationship with France has been tied to the creation of a joint military corps and to the further growth of institutional links between the two countries under the rubric of the Elysée Treaty of 1963.[2] In pursuing the need to build broader and more encompassing security structures which will extend co-operative links to Russia and eastern Europe, the key institutions are the Organization for Security and Co-operation in Europe (osce) (which changed its name to "organization" from "conference" in 1994–5) and, to a lesser degree, the North Atlantic Cooperation Council (nacc), created at the end of 1991. Finally, the preservation of the Atlantic link and of the close relationship with the United States remains directly identified with nato. The Germans continue to view the organization as especially important to ensure the alliance's aims and activities are relevant to Europe's political and security problems.[3]

As in the past, the construction of an effective balance among these different dimensions and institutions within the German security policy framework has been a complex and difficult undertaking. It has been complicated because of Germany's pivotal position in European affairs since its reunification in 1990. Germany is now the single most influential power in western Europe and its position in the east has grown rapidly to fill the vacuum created by the demise of the Soviet Union. As a result, the evolution of German policy is central to the construction of Europe's future security architecture.

The European Pillar

In the security sphere, a distinctly European security and defence identity (esdi) has generally been perceived in Bonn in three ways. First, it has been regarded as an important element in the long-term goal of building a united Europe. Second, throughout most of the Cold War period, it has been closely associated with the maintenance and advancement of a close co-operative military and security relationship with France. Indirectly, this has also been seen as fostering the objective of tying France more closely to the North Atlantic alliance. Thus, the bilateral security and defence relationship with France has always been an integral aspect of the Europeanist dimension of German security policy. Finally, the Europeanist option has also been regarded as an important hedge against unanticipated and undesirable developments in United States policy. It has been perceived to provide both a measure of reassurance against the possibility of a downgrading of the United States security commitment as well as a lever with which to influence the development of United States and alliance strategy in a manner compatible with German interests. All these dimensions of a European security option continued to be important in influencing the development of German policy in the aftermath of 1989.

These views have also been the basis of the policy orientation of Germany's principal partner in Europe, France, but French security policy has been premised first and foremost on the vital need to tie the Federal Republic as closely as possible to the West. Thus, Paris initially reacted with suspicion and caution to Chancellor Kohl's initiatives on German unification in the autumn of 1989. Once the French saw that unification was inevitable, however, Paris became anxious to ensure that this dramatic event was accompanied by a simultaneous deepening of European integration so as to bind the enlarged German federation even more tightly to the West.[4] Bonn was sensitive to these French concerns, and almost immediately after the fall of the Berlin Wall, Kohl was stressing that his government would endeavour to promote a deeper European unity "with all of its power."[5] This led to the joint French-German initiative, presented at the special European Community conference in Dublin in April 1990, for the negotiation of, and movement towards, European monetary and political union.[6]

In the first years after the fall of the Wall, the relative importance Bonn attached to the ESDI definitely increased. German initiatives for a strengthened European defence identity focused on three areas: on deepening and expanding the political union (specifically, widening the competence and authority of the EC in the making of a common foreign and defence policy); on the promotion of the WEU as the security arm of the Community; and on strengthening the bilateral military relationship with France (principally through the formation of a joint army corps).[7]

In the latter two areas most especially, German policy came into ever greater conflict with both American and British policies in 1991 and 1992. From the French and German perspective, the need to revitalize the WEU as the "defence component" of the EC and to create the "Euro-Corps" arose when the goal of giving the EC direct competence over defence questions became unreachable in the Maastricht negotiations of 1991 because of the opposition of Britain and some other Community members.

To the United States and the United Kingdom, however, these developments, when coupled with statements by German and, especially, French leaders suggesting a need to create some insurance against the possibility of an eventual American withdrawal, raised concerns over the ultimate direction of Bonn's policy and about that country's commitment to the Atlantic link. The American view was effectively outlined in 1992 by the permanent representative to NATO, William Taft. He noted that while the concepts of Europeanism and Atlanticism were seen in the United States as mutually reinforcing, the strength of the Atlantic alliance should not be undermined by the development of a European defence identity. Thus, he argued: "In designing the relationship of the European Security Identity and the Western European Union (WEU) to NATO, in particular, it is vital that this corresponds to the relationship followed by those nations participating in the Defence Planning Committee and the integrated military structure rather than the anomalous French pattern."[8] The British were even more suspicious of German intentions. The view in London was that German policy was increasingly being pulled into the French orbit and that, contrary to the German claim that its policy was designed to tie the French closer to NATO, it was more likely that Germany would be increasingly pulled away from the alliance.[9]

The reaction in London and Washington to the formation of the Euro-Corps was hostile. Certainly, the German position itself has often appeared ambiguous, with Bonn arguing that the Euro-Corps would "strengthen the alliance" while simultaneously stating that the corps constituted an integral element in the construction of a viable European defence identity.

Whatever the ultimate intentions of German leaders with respect to the European option in the immediate aftermath of unification, events since 1992 have shown that many obstacles remain in the path of developing Europe's political and security institutions. The resurgence of nationalism in Europe in the early 1990s is one problem. Because of national policy differences, European countries and their institutions were completely incapable of ending the war in the former Yugoslavia. Likewise, the construction of a deeper European union has continued to be problematical as all states have demonstrated a reluctance to surrender sovereignty. This was illustrated in the 1992 referendum results in Denmark and France which nearly killed the Maastricht Treaty, in the continued underdevelopment of the WEU as a defence organization, and by the hesitance of many states, including Germany, about the wisdom and practicality of proceeding with a common European currency as called for in the Maastricht Treaty. Thus, while the European alternative remains on the agenda and will likely continue to be a policy objective of both the French and German governments, for the present the European option remains a weak one, especially in the defence and security sphere.[10]

Relations with the East

After 1989 Germany's relationship with eastern Europe was revolutionized. The artificial barriers constructed after 1945 as an impediment to normal relations between the Federal Republic and its eastern neighbours were broken down. Germany emerged as the leading regional power in central Europe. As a result, the reunified Federal Republic is looked to by all of the former communist states for assistance in making the transition to a democratic and free-market system. Indeed, Timothy Garton Ash has put forward the idea of

"Model Germany" – the concept that in a number of different areas Germany is perceived as both the model on which to pattern the shift to a post-totalitarian order as well as the most important facilitator of that process.[11]

On the economic side, Germany has emerged as the leading trading partner for all the central European states, in large measure replacing the former trading relationships between these states and the former Soviet Union. Between 1989 and 1992, trade between Germany and Poland doubled, while Germany emerged as the leading trading partner of Czechoslovakia (accounting for some 50 per cent of that country's total world trade in 1992). Similarly, 30 per cent of Hungary's foreign trade was oriented to Germany by 1992.[12] Germany's strong presence was also felt in the investment sector, even if it was temporarily constrained by the priority of reconstructing the GDR's economy (an effort which had absorbed tens of billions of dollars every year since 1990–1).

In a broader political sense, Germany has, in large measure, become the leading spokesman in the West for the interests of the states of central and eastern Europe. For those countries, the road to Brussels (and membership in NATO and the EU) is clearly seen to lie through Berlin. In friendship treaties signed with each of the eastern states in 1991 and 1992, the Federal Republic pledged to work towards the eventual admission of these states to the European Union. Likewise, in 1993 and 1994, the Germans emerged as the leading advocates for the entry of the "Visegrad states" (Poland, the Czech Republic, Slovakia, and Hungary) into NATO.

Germany's revitalized relationships and responsibilities in the East create a dilemma: how to balance Germany's Western relationships with the enhanced role that it is playing in the eastern half of the continent. On one side, Western unity remains a cornerstone of German foreign policy. On the other side, the perception that more urgent measures are needed to stabilize eastern Europe have increasingly influenced some of the specific aspects of German policy, thereby inevitably raising questions about the ultimate orientation of Germany.

These questions and concerns were very evident in the unification diplomacy of 1989 and 1990. Early in the process, for instance, the German foreign minister, Hans-Dietrich Genscher, appears to have been willing to consider trading concessions with respect to the terms of Germany's alliance membership for Soviet agreement on unification. Indeed, in March 1990, when Genscher publicly called for the "transformation of NATO and the Warsaw Pact" into a new system of collective security, Kohl reportedly angrily rebuked him in a letter which stated that Genscher's statements contradicted the government's emphasis on the "necessity of the Alantic alliance and Germany's integration therein."[13]

Since 1989 the development of German policy towards the East has raised Western concerns in a number of respects. The mutual non-aggression clause included at Moscow's insistence in the German-Soviet friendship treaty of November 1990 reportedly aroused alarm, especially in France. Bonn's unilateral decision to recognize the independence of the breakaway Yugoslav republics of Slovenia and Croatia in 1991 also created serious strains on its relations with its Western allies.

However, the most important dimension of Germany's future relationship with eastern Europe centres on the nature of its relationship with Russia. Since 1989, an opportunity has emerged to overcome the legacy of Russo-German war and conflict which has characterized virtually the whole of the twentieth century. The construction of a co-operative German-Russian relationship therefore formed a cornerstone of Bonn's policy in the unification diplomacy of 1989–90 and in the subsequent period. Early on, Bonn concluded that there was no hope for long-term stability in Europe without the facilitation of successful democratic and free-market reforms in Russia.

However, while there are solid policy reasons for pursuing a closer and more co-operative relationship with Russia, the ultimate desirability of constructing a new European security architecture has also influenced the evolution of Germany's eastern policy. The appeal of the construction of a new European security architecture was grounded in ideas which originally gained popularity with the German left in the 1980s. These ideas were most especially manifest within the Social Democratic party and in its commitment to the concept of "common security" as well as in the rising popularity of the ecological Green party. Ending the East-West military confrontation and constructing a new co-operative relationship with the Soviet Union was always central to the common security approach. In this sense, for most common security adherents, the policy of the Western alliance based on collective defence and nuclear deterrence had to be overturned.[14]

In the post–Cold War period, this belief in the ideal of common security continued but was matched by a new enthusiasm for the Conference/Organization for Security and Co-operation in Europe as the ideal institutional framework within which to construct a pan-European security architecture. The development of the c/osce received cross-party and élite support in the Federal Republic in the aftermath of unification. Although events in Yugoslavia in 1991 and the rise of nationalism in Russia dampened much of the earlier optimism, the foreign minister was still able to comment in 1992 that the "strengthening of the elements of cooperative or common security via the csce" was the only solution which offered any hope for permanently resolving the continent's security problems.[15]

Russia's own European policy was also strongly based on the importance of the c/osce. The government of President Boris Yeltsin envisaged the c/osce as the primary forum for managing the continent's political and security problems. It also apparently believed it would be able to use the c/OSCE to limit the influence of the West in Russia's "near abroad" – the countries of eastern Europe and the former Soviet Union.[16]

Despite many disappointments related to the development of the c/OSCE after the fall of the Berlin Wall, many in Germany continued to argue for a common security policy approach which relied on the further development of the c/OSCE. This was certainly the policy of the Social Democrats in the 1994 election campaign. In the platform adopted in November 1993, it declared that the party supported "the step-by-step development of the CSCE in the direction of a collective security system."[17] To facilitate this goal, the Social Democrats pledged to work towards the withdrawal of all nuclear weapons from Europe and to support the convening of a conference focused on the goal of general and complete nuclear disarmament. As a first step, the party committed itself to securing the removal of all NATO's nuclear weapons from German territory.[18] Such a development would make NATO superfluous and gradually establish a new balance in Germany's political relationships with the West and with Russia. Indeed, in such a context a "special" political and security relationship between Berlin and Moscow (with all of the broader implications that would entail) would be sure to follow.

In essence there are two visions of the OSCE in the current German policy debate. The present official view held by the governing coalition is that the OSCE (together with the NACC and the Partnership for Peace created in 1994) is a necessary complement to NATO and the EU, but one which nevertheless has certain limitations. Both the OSCE and the other institutions facilitate the deepening of eastern and western political and military interaction and co-operation, but are not by themselves ever likely to be replacements for NATO. The other vision of the OSCE (popular in sections of the Social Democratic party and in alternative German political parties like the Green party and the Party for Democratic Socialism) looks on the organization as the nucleus of an eventual new European security architecture, one which will progressively transcend and replace the Atlantic alliance. As part of this vision, it is believed that Germany must begin to give greater weight to the eastern dimension of its foreign policy and to the bilateral relationship with Russia.

Germany's new Ostpolitik is thus faced with a multitude of challenges in the medium to long term. On a practical and everyday level, there are the difficulties associated with facilitating the resolution of the numerous economic, social, political, and security problems which plague the countries of eastern Europe. On a more fundamental level, however, there is the broader question of the balance of priorities in Germany's overall foreign policy and the future position of Russia in Bonn/Berlin's foreign policy framework. The way in which Germany deals with these challenges will therefore be of great interest to its allies and neighbours.

The Atlantic Link

In the intense period of diplomatic activity leading to the reunification of Germany in 1990, the importance of Germany's transatlantic partnership with the United States was once again underscored. From the moment of the fall of the Berlin Wall in November 1989, American diplomacy was the most supportive of German objectives as they evolved in the course of the following year. In contrast to the initial positions adopted by the British and French, the United States, both through its ambassador in Bonn and through meetings and contacts with German officials, stressed its commitment to the goal of unification under conditions in which the Federal Republic's links with the West would remain unaffected.[19] As events unfolded, bilateral consultations between the Germans and Americans, including both face-to-face meetings and telephone conversations between Chancellor Kohl and President Bush, cemented American political support for Germany's diplomatic initiatives.[20]

As discussed in chapter 2, historically the United States has often proved to be the ally most understanding and supportive of the political interests of the Federal Republic. Moreover, the continuing value of the American military presence and of the NATO alliance in addressing the variety of common military and political challenges which confront the alliance collectively in Europe is especially stressed by German Atlanticists. NATO remains the only viable means of counterbalancing the nuclear and conventional military capability of Russia, a country which still controls more than 75 per cent of the Eurasian land mass and one whose future external policy orientation is still very much an unknown quantity. As Kohl argued in May 1992: "The experiences of this century have taught us: Europe needs America, but America also needs Europe." "NATO alone," he continued, "can guarantee the necessary presence of the United States – and the necessary, lasting and substantial presence of American troops – in Europe ... [In a time of change] the Atlantic alliance remains the irreplaceable fundamental of freedom and peace in Europe."[21]

This statement, made in the immediate aftermath of the announcement of the Franco-German Euro-Corps, was designed to repair some of the damage which resulted from that decision and to re-emphasize Germany's interest in a close transatlantic relationship. While perhaps initially slow to recognize British and American worries with respect to the seeming increased emphasis that Germany was placing on the ESDI, from 1992 on Bonn did finally make concerted efforts to respond to Anglo-American concerns. First, the Germans sought to ensure that any defence arrangements concluded with France were compatible with those of NATO. This effort culminated in an agreement, signed by the French and the Germans with NATO's supreme commander in Europe in January 1993, which emphasized that the Euro-Corps could be placed under the command of the alliance in a crisis.

Second, the Germans increasingly took pains to stress their continued interest in a revitalized North Atlantic alliance. On the one hand, the new foreign minister, Klaus Kinkel, sought to place immediate emphasis on the importance of the North Atlantic dimension in German foreign policy by stating in one of his first interviews that "NATO remains, without reservation, for the foreseeable future, the guarantee of our security."[22] Furthermore, in both the Foreign and Defence Ministries there was a renewed emphasis on shoring up the non-military dimensions of the alliance. For example, Frank Elbe, the head of the planning staff in the Foreign Office, advocated in an article for the *Frankfurter Allgemeine Zeitung* in June 1992 that the transatlantic relationship be reconstructed on the basis of a new treaty which would give enhanced emphasis to economic and political co-operation.[23] This approach, which seemed to be oriented towards the goal of a revised transatlantic partnership framework agreement, was attracting considerable political support from the other allies by 1994–5.

Likewise, from 1993 on the Germans began to place more emphasis on the expansion of both the EU and NATO to include Poland, the Czech Republic, Slovakia, and Hungary.[24] The primary goal of this initiative, announced by the defence minister, Volker Rühe, was the transformation of the alliance into a more effective instrument for creating stability in eastern Europe. With this proposal, the Germans were responding primarily to a perceived desire in the United States that the alliance remain an effective collective policy instrument in the new European order. Believing that the United States would remain interested in NATO only as long as it remained an effective policy tool, the Defence Ministry in particular was most anxious to demonstrate the German desire to adapt the alliance to new realities.[25]

However, while there did appear to be a congruence of opinion between Rühe and certain groups in the United States Congress, the Clinton administration initially refused to commit itself on the matter of NATO membership for the Visegrad states. Instead, at the alliance summit in Brussels in January 1994, the United States floated its compromise Partnership for Peace proposal which, while moving towards deeper military co-operation with the eastern European states, stopped short of any public commitment on the question of full membership.[26] Only one year later, however, the Clinton administration had warmed to the idea and full NATO membership for eastern European states is again high on the agenda for active consideration by the allies.

A third area of convergence between German and American policy occurred over the war in the former Yugoslavia. In 1993, the policy shift accompanying the transition from the Bush to the Clinton administration led to closer American and German co-operation on the question of the war in Bosnia. Both governments proved to be strong advocates of a firmer policy, a fact which was revealed at the time of the June 1993 EU summit in Copenhagen when Germany alone among EU states supported the United States proposals to lift the arms embargo against Bosnia's Muslims and commence air strikes to enforce United Nations Security Council resolutions. Indeed, United States and German co-operation on this question remained very close after 1993, much to the consternation of both the French and the British whose policy positions were decidedly opposed to moving beyond peacekeeping to active military intervention in the conflict.[27]

Finally, the Kohl government also moved at a measured pace to extend German involvement in Western military activities outside the NATO area. This action was necessary both to reinforce the credibility of German diplomacy and to ensure that in some future crisis, Germany's lack of involvement did not become a source of political tension and animosity between the allies. In the Gulf War most especially, the limitation of German involvement to the provision of financial assistance and logistics support had caused some acrimony and tension in the German-American relationship. Thus, the ruling by the German Constitutional Court in July 1994 that the country's Basic Law did not restrict the ability of the government to deploy forces on defensive missions outside the NATO area was a welcome development, even if domestic political realities – including the requirement for German parliamentary approval of each new mission – and historical factors would continue to make combat deployments by German forces difficult undertakings.

While in the short term the importance of NATO and the relationship with the United States in German policy has been strengthened by these factors, the medium to longer term situation is difficult to assess. The overarching reality of the disappearance of the Soviet threat will continue to raise questions about the relevance of NATO's collective defence role. Whether the less dramatic role of the alliance as the principal co-ordinating mechanism for maintaining the unity of the West's political and military policies in Europe will continue to have value depends both on the evolving policy priorities of the German government and on the interest attached to NATO by other allied governments, including those on the western side of the Atlantic.

German Policy Options and the Canadian Connection

Since 1989 Germany has endeavoured to construct its post–Cold War security policy on three complementary pillars, each of which has served as a vehicle for the promotion of Germany's policy interests in different forums. As in the pre-1989 era, the belief that it is not in the country's interest to place too great a reliance on any single pillar of that policy framework has continued to command a consensus of support among the country's political leaders. However, the distinct political interests linked to each of the three main institutional forums in which it operates raise the very real prospect that Germany may in the future have to make some basic policy choices. For the present, however, the government is seeking to ride several horses simultaneously.

While in the past a complementary approach was also characteristic of German security policy, the transatlantic link nevertheless always served as the larger framework within which Germany's efforts to build Europe's unity and to improve relations with the Eastern bloc were situated. The role of the United States was akin to that of a regional hegemon; it guaranteed European stability and the balance of political relations among the major European states. During the Cold War era the principal function of the United States was to deter and defend against any aggression from the Soviet bloc. While in the post–Cold War period the American role is not as overtly dramatic, it is no less important. The United States continues to guarantee Europe's political equilibrium and is therefore a principal force for ensuring that a re-nationalization of defence policy does not occur. Likewise, its political role (based on its continued military presence) is one which reassures Europe's smaller powers, particularly the fledgling democracies of eastern Europe.

However, this view of the role of the United States and of the Atlantic link is under serious scrutiny and question. In Germany, the popular view since the end of the Cold War has been that NATO's military role – at least in terms of its mission to defend western Europe against attack – is now largely unnecessary, if not irrelevant. While this view was stronger in the immediate aftermath of unification than it is now in the middle of the decade, it illustrates the difficulties NATO has had in finding new roles.[28] Should this problem persist, NATO will continue to be weakened. If this occurs, it is not likely at present that either the European Security and Identity alternative or the pan-European collective security option would be able to replace the role played by the alliance.

The continuation of a viable transatlantic relationship requires political support from both sides of the Atlantic. No country has been entirely without blame for contributing to a widening Atlantic and conflictual intra-alliance relations in recent years. The British government's deeply suspicious reaction to the prospect of German unification in 1990, the unilateral German decisions with respect to the recognition of Croatia and Slovenia in 1991, the lack of consultation with other allies by Bonn and Paris with respect to forming the Euro-Corps in 1992, and the various unilateral actions by the Clinton administration with regard to the war in the former Yugoslavia (culminating in the decision late in 1994 to break ranks and suspend American enforcement of the United Nations arms embargo on the government of Bosnia-Herzegovina) – all of these actions heightened tensions within NATO and thereby undermined allied unity. This very view was expressed in

November 1994 by the German ambassador to NATO. In a telegram leaked to the German press, Baron Herman von Richthoven warned of emerging "cracks" within the alliance over a variety of political issues, most especially the war in Bosnia.[29]

Canadian policy was also not very helpful for those seeking to maintain a strong North Atlantic alliance. Once one of the strongest champions of Atlanticism, Ottawa effectively marginalized its position within both the alliance and its bilateral relationship with Germany by its decision in 1991–2 to withdraw its forces from Europe. Indeed, even two years after this decision was taken, the German ambassador to NATO noted that the move had contributed to divisions and to a weakening of alliance cohesion. Despite Canada's decision to contribute to the United Nations force in the former Yugoslavia, the ambassador argued that by withdrawing its forces from Germany Canada had in fact "left Europe militarily."[30] The integrated command structure uniting NATO forces in Germany remained one of the most important elements in NATO's continued viability. Without a military organization centred on integrated forces in Germany, the most fundamental element in the collective approach to defence problems would disappear. Re-nationalized defence policies would become more likely.

In Canada, the future relevance of Atlanticism in Canadian foreign policy has for a long time been directly tied to both the stationing issue and the bilateral relationship with Germany. Since Germany is the most important power in Europe, the nature of Canada's relationship with it is – as it has been for nearly forty years – a crucial indicator of the strength of Ottawa's commitment to the very idea of the Atlantic link.

On a broader policy level, Canada's dispute with the EU over Spanish overfishing just outside Canadian waters in 1995 symbolized a new willingness on its part to pursue a policy of confrontation with its allies across the Atlantic on specific issues, regardless of the consequences for the country's broader relationship with Europe. This conflict, which escalated to the point where both Canada and Spain deployed patrol vessels and (in Canada's case) major surface warships and possibly submarines, was only resolved because of pressure on Spain from its EU partners to back down. Although resolved peacefully, the dispute offered a taste of the potential consequences of a breakdown in the Atlantic security system and a re-nationalization of foreign and defence policies.

The orientation of Canadian policy continues to be perceived in many circles as an indicator of the possible strength of similar perspectives in the United States. Therefore recent developments in Canadian policy have been of some importance in this negative sense. European countries will only remain committed to the alliance as long as it is perceived to be supported in North America. Once NATO is regarded as largely irrelevant in North

American policy circles, its importance in Europe will also fade. The reverse is of course true. Europeans must be seen to be committed to the continued value of the alliance. The persistence of Atlanticism is in fact dependent on the mutual support afforded to that concept by decision-makers on both sides of the Atlantic. The credibility and value of the alliance in addressing the common political and military problems which confront the North Atlantic community will only remain strong if both Europeans and North Americans demonstrate their belief in the organization's continuing worth. (The peace enforcement mission taken on by the alliance in Bosnia in 1995 largely at American insistence will be a crucial, if unintended, test of NATO's continued relevance and viability.) The developments in Canadian-German relations in the years immediately following the end of the Cold War were certainly not auspicious for the future of Atlanticism.

CANADA'S POST–COLD WAR
FOREIGN AND DEFENCE POLICY AND
THE DRIFT TOWARDS CONTINENTALISM

As discussed in chapter 2, the theme of counterweights has been a central one in Canadian foreign policy since the end of the Second World War. In particular, wider international engagement has been viewed as a way of counterbalancing the influence of the United States. The relationship which developed between Canada and the Federal Republic of Germany in the 1960s and the 1970s emerged from Canada's search for a more diversified series of multilateral and bilateral policy relationships. Even if the country's decision-makers were not always fully conscious of the fact, Germany, Europe, and the Atlantic alliance were at the core of Canada's search for balance in its external relationships.

For the last decade however, and especially since the end of the Cold War in 1989, there has been a decided shift away from Europe and from the Atlantic alliance in the direction of a firmly continentalist policy orientation. The rather ignominious end of Canada's European military commitment in 1992, which was as much a product of government indifference as anything else, was the final confirmation of this change. However, fearful of the obvious implications of political and economic dependence that an overt shift to continentalism implies, Canadian officials have, since 1992, again sought to stress the country's continued commitment to an active, independent, and multilateral world role as a counterbalance to the country's relationship with the United States. Much like Finland in the Cold War period, Canada, for different reasons, has come to see the various dimensions of its international engagement as an expression of the country's distinct identity and as a means for rhetorically asserting its independence.

"Common Security" and Liberal Idealism

In an address to parliament in March 1994, the new minister of foreign affairs,[31] André Ouellet, stated that Canada's foreign policy would now be more "independent" because the new government would have the courage to "say what we think" in foreign affairs, "sometimes in spite of others ... often before others, but also to always say it better than others."[32]

This strongly liberal approach to international affairs stressed the theme of an economically interdependent world in which power was not to be measured primarily in military terms. In fact, traditional yardsticks for measuring power were regarded as decidedly unimportant in the post–Cold War international arena. As one adherent of this liberal-idealist approach argued: "Diplomacy – not military force – will be the most important instrument for preserving security as Canada conceives it in the new international environment."[33]

The approach is essentially based on the concept of "common" or "co-operative" security, and it combines the liberal/neo-realist emphasis on economic factors and trade with the idealist stress on building a new and better world order. It is a perspective which draws on both the tradition of Pearsonian internationalism as well as more recent neo-realist ideas. While the perspective does not command complete support among élite opinion in Canada, it is nevertheless in large measure the dominant and prevailing world-view within the Canadian foreign policy establishment, in many academic circles, and among Canada's political leaders. In Germany, as in many other countries, the common security ideal is a challenging view of some influence in that country's foreign policy. However, despite this challenge, it is a "realist" perspective which has always been dominant in the area of security policy. As the German defence white paper of 1994 states:

Action in the field of security policy must be based on interests. Interests determine priorities for action. They are the expression of the policies of a sovereign state, a point of departure for assessing risks and deciding what action is required in a particular situation and a prerequisite for the reconciliation of interests, cooperation and international stability ...

Germany's defence policy is based on a capability to conduct national defence, and to defend its allies as a form of extended national defence. It is supplemented by the ability to participate in cooperative multinational conflict prevention and crisis management. German security policy is determined by the holistic combination of two basic functions: protection against risks and threats and the active shaping of stability and peace.

Germany is not impacted by all risks to the same extent. Its security is directly affected by how the situation in Central, Eastern and Southeastern Europe develops. It is indirectly affected by unstable conditions in the Mediterranean, the Middle East

and Southwestern Asia. German security is also affected by destabilizing developments in other parts of the world.

Germany's security policy endeavours to establish priorities based on the
national interest. It seeks to use both diplomacy and economic power,
supported by an effective military capability, to achieve political objectives.
German policy is concentrated and focused on Europe first and then on
regions bordering Europe in which events and conditions might have an
impact on the Federal Republic. "The core of German security policy," it is
noted in the white paper, "is a firm and deep friendship and close cooperation with our allies."[34]

By way of contrast, in Canada the notion of common security is the
dominant perspective of the governing élite. As the Chrétien government's
foreign policy statement, *Canada in the World*, asserted in 1995: "While
military capacities might will [*sic*] remain important factors in the international system of the future, international affairs will be rooted increasingly
in economic and trade relations between countries and regions."[35] This helps
ensure the continuation of a Canadian foreign and defence policy which
lacks military and political co-ordination and often ignores the national
interest.

The popularity of the common security idea is evident in government
policy and is also found in many influential studies done outside of government, such as that of the Canada 21 group of academics and former government ministers who submitted a report in 1994 calling for the entrenchment
of the common security idea in Canadian foreign policy.[36] The report of the
Special Joint Parliamentary Committee Reviewing Canadian Foreign Policy,
issued in November 1994, noted that the "central theme" of its study was
that "the most important global requirements of the 90s and beyond are for
shared security, shared prosperity and shared custody of the environment."[37]
Likewise, in a speech delivered at the United Nations in September 1994,
Ouellet asserted his belief that Canada shared common concerns with virtually every country in the global community. These "interests" included the
need to promote economic development, justice, democracy, human rights,
and protection of the environment.[38]

This liberal-idealist approach constitutes the basis of the external policy
adopted by both the Mulroney Conservatives and the Chrétien Liberals.
Under this rubric, Canadian foreign policy is in fact being formulated on
two distinct planes. The first stresses the goal of protecting the country's
position in the global trading order while the second emphasizes the need
to build a better and more just international order and environment.

On the economic plane, the growing importance of developing international trading relationships is a persistent theme. As argued in the report
issued by the joint committee, an "international orientation" for Canadian

business is essential to protect the country's wealth and prosperity. While the term "counterweights" no longer appears to be fashionable, the new "international business approach" is nevertheless driven, in part, by a similar impetus. The committee's report asserted: "Without a concerted national effort Canada is fated to play a diminishing economic role in the world. Such a decline would threaten not only our international standing and prestige, but also our standard of living and prosperity."[39]

The primary focus of this new trade policy orientation is on East Asia, but other regions such as Latin America and the Middle East will be more and more important. On the surface at least, this policy orientation appears to have a high level of support. This was most dramatically signalled late in 1994 and again early in 1996 when huge Canadian trade delegations headed by the prime minister and most of the provincial premiers visited Asia. In many ways this is a welcome development and one which seems to stand in some contrast to the evolution of much of Canadian policy with respect to Europe, Germany, and NATO in the decades before.[40]

On a second plane, Canada's diplomatic policy is oriented towards multilateral engagement in almost any forum that is available both to assert Canada's distinct identity and to try to work constructively towards the building of a better world order. Indeed, in keeping with this stress on multilateralism, the prime minister was himself directly involved in several international gatherings in 1993–4 alone, including two meetings of the Asia-Pacific Economic Cooperation (APEC) group, one NATO summit meeting, the annual G-7 summit, and a CSCE meeting.[41] The perception that Canada is a major player in these forums (or even a "principal power") constitutes an important aspect of the liberal-idealist analysis and approach.

Pitfalls in the Liberal-Idealist Approach

There are fundamental problems with both dimensions of the liberal-idealist approach. First, as is evident in this book, military/strategic factors and security/defence issues usually constitute one dimension of the most important international relationships maintained by any state. They can certainly not be divorced from Canadian foreign policy. Contrary to the idealist view, as expressed in the common security approach, traditional measurements of power do still matter in the international system. They matter because nearly all other countries in the international system act in a manner which is in keeping with such a belief.[42]

The continued importance of military power in the traditional sense became very evident for Canada itself early in 1995 when, in a very rare occurrence for the country, it deployed elements of its maritime forces to protect its offshore interests against intrusion by Spain. The decision to escalate Canada's confrontation with Spain and employ armed force in this dispute was certainly not in keeping with the concept of common security. However, in the main, the impetus for this policy action seems to have come from outside the foreign policy establishment – from within the Department of Fisheries and Oceans and as a result of domestic agitation and pressure, especially from the Atlantic provinces which had long suffered from predatory foreign overfishing off the east coast. The "turbot dispute" once again brought into question one specific assertion often made by liberal-idealist analysts, namely, that allied and liberal democratic states do not employ force against one another. As was demonstrated in this instance (and as has been evident in certain other cases as well), this view cannot be considered an uncontested premise of international politics. This has been the case for the last fifty years only because an alliance has been created among sixteen European and North American countries to protect their security and to promote a collective approach to the political, security and defence problem which they confront. The more that a collective approach to political, security, and defence questions among Western states erodes, the less of an axiom it will be.

A second flaw in the liberal-idealist approach concerns the view held by its adherents about Canada's relative ranking and status internationally. Despite the assertion of liberal/neo-realists that Canada's economic capability and diplomatic standing make it a major player internationally, the fact is that most of the major powers do not consider Canada to be a particularly important state when issues of high politics are discussed. The country simply does not carry sufficient weight in either a military or a political sense to be a major player. That it is not is partly a product of geography. The country's position as the second power in North America ensures that it is totally overshadowed by the United States on the international stage. This is true in economic and trade terms, in a cultural sense, and also politically and militarily. Canada has sometimes been called a regional power without a region, and in many ways this description indeed hits the mark.

However, Canada's limited profile and influence internationally has been very much reinforced by the general and pronounced decline in resources available to support the conduct of the country's external relations. By 1998/9 the defence budget is to be reduced to less than $9.3 billion from $10.3 billion in 1995/6.[43] This downward trend is going to continue, resulting in manpower cuts, training restrictions, and severe limits on badly needed equipment purchases. Funding for the Department of Foreign Affairs and International Trade including the foreign aid budget is also to be reduced. These cuts come on top of reductions already implemented in previous budgets since 1989. A country which seeks to retain some influence internationally cannot do so on rhetoric and diplomacy alone.

The extent to which these cuts have undermined Canadian influence internationally is most evident on the military side, and in terms of the deficiencies which exist in the country's specific commitments to international organizations like the United Nations and NATO. On an official level, the United Nations is the centrepiece of Canada's post–Cold War multilateral diplomacy. In particular, peacekeeping is seen as a "fundamental" strand of Canadian policy. As the minister of foreign affairs stated in 1994, the government does not view this commitment simply as "a question of continuing a tradition for which Canadians have a deserved international reputation." Rather, "it is a question of making a concrete and key contribution to international security at a time of instability in many parts of the world."[44] Picking up on this theme, the 1994 defence white paper contains this assertion:

As a reflection of the global nature of Canada's values and interests, the Canadian Forces must contribute to international security. We should continue to play an active military role in the United Nations, the North Atlantic Treaty Organization and the Conference on Security and Cooperation in Europe. We should develop our defence relationships with the nations of the Asia-Pacific region and Latin America, and contribute, where possible, to the security of the Middle East and Africa.[45]

However characteristic of the common security perspective, there has been little effort to rank Canada's external interests on the basis of strategic or political factors. Instead, it has simply been asserted that "the global nature of Canada's values" demands that the country be prepared to contribute anywhere and potentially in any capacity, to fight "alongside the best, against the best," as the white paper puts it.[46] This policy reveals a basic failure to focus on regions of the world of real strategic and political importance to Canada. Indeed, the one regional multilateral organization in which Canada had played a modestly significant role over the past forty-five years has been virtually forgotten. The white paper announced the end of the country's remaining substantive NATO commitment in favour of an elusive and unrealistic internationalist role. While there is new rhetoric about enhancing military co-operation with Latin America, the Middle East, and even Africa, the remaining defence commitment to Norway has been eliminated (again apparently without consultation) while funding for the NATO infrastructure programme has been scaled back.[47]

This policy approach is unrealistic and inadvisable from both a political/ economic and a military perspective. The lesson of the twentieth century, it can be convincingly argued, is that the security of Canada (and North America) is directly tied to the stability of Europe. To some degree the same might be said of the link between security and stability in East Asia and North America (owing, in part, to the volume of economic and trading links between these two regions). However, most other regions of the world are peripheral to Canada, or are ones with which the country has few historical ties. Military operations in regions of the world which are of minor importance to the country are always dubious undertakings. In this regard, there were no Canadian political, economic, or strategic interests to warrant the deployment of the Canadian Forces to Somalia in 1993 or Haiti in 1994–5. Both deployments were more about maintaining the country's "image" in the United Nations and about supporting the domestic political agenda of the governing party.

Most particularly, any operation which has a high potential for significant casualties must be undertaken only if it is seen to be in the country's vital national interest. These interests are determined, first and foremost, by political, economic, and strategic factors. In the long term, the Canadian public will be less likely to support major peacekeeping missions in areas of the world where Canada's interests are in fact limited. Certainly, when peacekeeping missions give way to "peace-restoring" or "peace enforcement" operations, no Canadian military commitment can be justified in the absence of vital national interests at stake. This is especially true of commitments which may become sustained and open-ended. In the post–Cold War era, Bosnia is the most notable example of such a questionable commitment of Canadian forces.

While the mission in the former Yugoslavia (including both Bosnia and Croatia) could be justified on the basis of the interests that Canada has in contributing to the security of Europe and the North Atlantic area, it was nevertheless questionable whether the specific nature of the missions assumed in Bosnia were ones for which the Canadian Forces were really adequately equipped or prepared. The first mission, taken on from 1992 to 1995 and involving the delivery of humanitarian assistance in the circumstances of full-scale war, was agreed to in a typically reactive fashion in the summer of 1992 without any proper consideration of strategic factors or of the ultimate objectives and parameters of the mission. By 1995, when war returned to Croatia, Canadian soldiers on the ground increasingly found themselves pawns in a larger game being played by regional countries and the great powers.

The second mission in Bosnia, assumed at the end of 1995 to enforce the terms of the Dayton accord, was taken on principally in response to the perceived importance of showing political solidarity with Canada's NATO allies. However, while this was indeed important, the extent to which the Canadian Forces were prepared and equipped for such a peace enforcement mission, should enforcement (that is, combat operations) actually be required, is certainly open to debate.

During the Cold War period the argument was often made that any regional conflict was potentially of political and strategic importance to Canada because of the need to avoid possible superpower involvement and confrontation, but this danger no longer exists. Therefore involvement in peacekeeping or peace enforcement operations (especially where a significant commitment of resources is required) must be limited to those regions where there is a significant risk that a conflict will have a direct and negative impact on Canada's own political and security interests.

On another level, it also seems unlikely that the budgetary dilemmas confronting the Canadian military will improve in the next several years. It is therefore improbable that Canada will have the necessary economic and military resources to sustain the same level of commitment to United Nations peacekeeping that it has been endeavouring to maintain since 1989. Thus, beyond extremely limited military assistance and training agreements, largely symbolic port visits by ships or occasional military consultations, a tangible expansion of the country's military links with Asian-Pacific, Latin American, Middle Eastern, or African countries will simply not be possible.

By 1999 the Canadian Forces are to be reduced to a strength of just 60,000 regular and 23,000 reserve personnel (from a strength in 1994–5 of 73,000 regular and 29,500 reserve troops). While it is planned to increase the strength of the regular land forces within this reduced total (to about 24,000 soldiers from 21,000), the ability to provide major military units (of battalion group size, or about 800–1500 troops) for rotational peacekeeping assignments will nevertheless remain limited.[48] In comparison with the Bundeswehr, for example, the Canadian Forces remain far too top-heavy and inefficient (see Appendix Four). As is evident from the data in Appendix Five, Germany has never devoted a particularly high percentage of its gross national product to defence, but its larger absolute resources have, for the most part, been used in a more cost-effective fashion. Likewise, the environment for German defence policy-making, unlike the environment in Canada, has been much more stable, which has allowed for more credible and consistent long-term planning.

Recognizing how rapidly the international strategic and political environment can change, the white paper has stressed the primary need to maintain "combat-capable forces."[49] However, the maintenance of a basic "core capability" to defend the air and sea approaches to Canadian territory as well as to ensure that the army maintains an effective expeditionary ability and potential is not an inexpensive proposition. For instance, a continued ability to participate in so-called "second-generation peacekeeping" (sometimes referred to as "peace-restoring" or "peace enforcement" operations) will require an all-arms capability and a major re-equipment of the land forces, not just with new armoured personnel carriers as called for in the white paper and ordered by the Department of National Defence in August 1995, but also with new or modernized artillery and tactical command, control, and communications systems. However, instead of considering options to fill these needs, DND is being forced to move in the opposite direction, shedding its ADATS air-defence/anti-tank system vehicles and having no prospect of replacing its main battle tank or of acquiring improved air and sea transport capabilities.[50]

Declining defence resources when combined with the failure of the 1994 white paper to clearly define Canada's political and strategic interests undermine the effectiveness of Canada's post–Cold War role. Given the historical experience with past white papers, it also remains doubtful whether the policy relevance of the 1994 white paper will last any longer than that of any of its predecessors. Indeed, by the middle of 1995, cabinet already appeared to be balking at some of the defence projects to which it had supposedly committed itself only six months before.[51] In this respect, the "question of relevance" with respect to Canadian defence policy remains alive and well, and it is doubtful that the floor of defence cutbacks has yet been reached.

Canada's weaknesses on the military side are matched by political and economic disadvantages which also suggest a reduced international role in the years to come. On the economic side, although Canada has a large GNP in absolute terms, trade is concentrated on the United States. This fact, coupled with the recent creation of a single North American trading bloc, means that internationally the Canadian economy is perceived, by and large, to be an extension of that of the United States. Canada's rather isolated geographic position in the northern hemisphere makes its economic position in the external trading framework of most other countries largely peripheral. The only country that has a very large trading relationship with Canada is the United States. Canada's overall economic significance to even the most important of its other trading partners is limited (table 5). This is true of both the G-7 countries and other rising trading partners. Certainly, the percentage of German trade with Canada is lower than at any time in the 1970s or 1980s (see table 1, p. 101). The continentalist orientation in Canadian trade policy has never been stronger.

By 1994, exports to the United States had actually increased to about 81.5 per cent while total two-way trade had climbed from 70 per cent in 1992 to 75 per cent. Trade with other partners fell correspondingly. Trade with Germany, for instance, fell from 1.8 per cent in 1992 to only 1.6 per cent of the country's total trade in 1994.[52] Matching the decline in Canadian-German trade, German investment in Canada has also dropped dramatically in the last several years. German investment in Canada had averaged some $350 million per year in the 1980s, but it totalled only $11 million in 1993.[53] The declining economic relationship with Germany and Europe cannot fail to affect political relations.

On the diplomatic side, most of the major powers have not accorded Canada a very high priority. For instance, in Germany Canada continues to have a low profile in the ranking of foreign policy concerns. In the last ten years, the Canadian desk in the Foreign Office has been part of a larger

Table 5
Total Trade (Imports and Exports) between Canada and Major Trading Partners,
1992

Country	Canada's Trade with State Concerned (%)	That State's Trade with Canada (%)
G-7 COUNTRIES		
United States	70.0	19.0
Japan	5.6	2.6
United Kingdom	2.3	1.5
FRG	1.8	0.68
France	1.4	0.80
Italy	0.93	0.75
RISING TRADING PARTNERS		
China	1.5	1.5–2.3*
South Korea	1.1	2.1
Mexico	1.1	2.8
Brazil	0.42	1.6
Chile	0.10	1.2

*   IMF figures suggest that 1.5 per cent of China's total trade was with Canada. However, a
figure of 2.3 per cent might be more accurate because Canada's overall volume of international trade is higher than that of China.
Source: International Monetary Fund, *Direction of Trade Statistics Yearbook, 1993.*

section, be it the British and Scandinavian or the North American section.
Thus the head of this section spent only a small amount of his time on
Canadian affairs. Moreover, out of six ranking levels for German missions
abroad, the post in Ottawa reportedly stood at the third level from the
bottom. The decision to pull the forces from Germany lowered Canada's
profile even farther. By way of contrast, and typically inconsistent with the
1992 withdrawal decision, the Canadian embassy in Bonn is still seen in
Ottawa as one of the top five Canadian posts abroad.[54]

Canada's low international ranking restricts the country's overall influence in the multilateral institutions and organizations of which it is a member. In the past, Canada has often played a more significant role
internationally by concentrating its diplomatic efforts on building coalitions
with other like-minded countries. Ottawa used this strategy successfully over
the years in the United Nations, in NATO, and at the CSCE. Canada was most
successful with such a strategy in the late 1940s and 1950s when it was able
and willing to concentrate significant economic, diplomatic, and military
resources in support of its larger political goals. In the past, even if many of
the country's leaders were largely unaware of the fact, an integrated Canadian policy approach and a focus on Europe and the North Atlantic alliance
allowed the country to achieve a level of influence beyond what it might
otherwise have been.

Table 6
The Regional Focus of Canada's Bilateral External Development
Assistance, 1994

Region	Total Bilateral Aid (US$ millions)	Per cent of Total
Africa	332.47	23.2
Americas	144.31	10.1
Far East	124.16	8.7
South Asia	144.17	10.1
Middle East	16.34	1.1
Oceania	4.16	0.3
Europe*	11.8	0.8
Unspecified Less Developed Countries	654.02	45.7
TOTAL	1431.44	

* An additional $89.5 million was allocated to eastern European countries
  in 1994. The revised figure of $101.3 million in Canadian aid for eastern
  Europe is 6.7 per cent of a slightly higher figure for total Canadian external assistance.

Source: Canadian response to Questionnaire from the Development
Assistance Committee of the OECD on the nature of foreign development
assistance provided by member-countries of the United Nations in 1994.

However, the ability to pursue an integrated policy approach has been
progressively discarded. Because of this, current Canadian political and
economic initiatives lack meaningful depth. Potentially positive Canadian
contributions, such as, for instance, the efforts being made to support countries in eastern Europe in their efforts to democratize and establish free-
market economies, will probably fail to yield the longer term closer bilateral
relationships between Canada and the nations concerned that should normally accompany such assistance. The level of assistance being provided by
Canada is simply too small. Greater resources are available, but Canada's
bilateral development assistance is, like the other aspects of the country's
foreign policy, insufficiently concentrated on facilitating larger political or
economic objectives in regions of vital importance to Canada. As table 6
shows, most of Canada's aid is destined for countries in the Third World
with which Canada has no substantial trading links and little prospect of
developing them. In 1994, the formerly communist countries of eastern
Europe were provided with only some US$11.8 million in assistance from
Canada's US$1.4 billion aid budget. While this trifling amount was topped
up by an additional US$89.5 million in special assistance, the long-term
strategic and trading importance of the region to Canada warranted a re-
evaluation of Canadian policy and a greater concentration of the country's
reduced resources in that region.[55]

This example illustrates a crucial aspect of the Canadian foreign policy dilemma in the post–Cold War period. There are today no areas, aside from the country's relationship with the United States, in which political, economic, and military interests and resources come together in a significant fashion. There are no Canadian political and military ties of any real significance to East Asia, Latin America, or the Middle East, as there once were with Europe. As a result there is little opportunity for an integrated and multidimensional policy approach to take shape.

Canada's internal financial difficulties and problems of national unity further restrict the government's freedom of action in the foreign and defence policy sphere. The combined federal and provincial debt totalled about 94 per cent of the country's total gross domestic product in 1994, the second highest (after Italy) of any country in the Organization for Economic Co-operation and Development.[56] The federal government's priority is therefore likely remain the reduction of the deficit and although the debt and deficit problem was certainly not caused by high defence and external affairs spending, it is nevertheless in those areas that spending cuts cause the least domestic fallout.

Whether Quebec remains in the Canadian federation is still to be settled. The ultimate outcome of this constitutional and political struggle, which also encompasses the dissatisfaction felt by other regions and provinces and by Canada's native peoples, will have a significant impact on Canada's international position. The narrow victory by federalist forces (by only one percentage point) in Quebec's sovereignty referendum in October 1995 demonstrated the precarious nature of the country's continued unity. The issue of Quebec sovereignty is certain to re-emerge in only a short period of time. If Quebec eventually secedes, Canada's position on the international stage (if the country does not entirely disappear) will fade to one of complete irrelevance. Even if Canada remains intact, the incremental devolution of federal power to the provinces (including perhaps some additional authority in the realm of foreign and trade policy formulation) is very likely to change the way in which Canada interacts with the rest of the world. In any event, the attention of Canada's political leaders will remain entirely preoccupied with this domestic concern as the country struggles towards the twenty-first century.

CLOSING THE BOOK
ON THE CANADIAN-GERMAN
SECURITY RELATIONSHIP

The Canadian-German security relationship emerged in the unique circumstances of the Cold War. Ultimately, it proved to be a relationship which was peculiar to the Cold War era and it was unable to survive the transition to a new international system. Several external factors were key contributors to this failure: the disappearance of the Soviet military threat; growing tensions in the transatlantic relationship; the pull of continentalism in both Europe and North America; and the rising internal political and economic problems confronted by Canada in the 1980s and 1990s. However, the demise of the security relationship was also a product of poor management of the bilateral link by the Canadian side. Governments of all political persuasions failed to recognize its intrinsic value and the wider potential of the relationship to facilitate broader Canadian policy objectives. This failure had its roots most fundamentally in a lack of understanding in Canada of the role played by military power in the broader policy framework.

The failure to cultivate this relationship for its wider political and economic potential has had other far-reaching consequences. The bilateral links with Germany, if they had been utilized to their full potential, might have enabled Canada to develop its larger European relationship into a more viable and credible counterweight to the United States. Today however, no such credible counterweights appear to exist. Thus one could argue that in the demise of the Canadian-German security relationship one was able to witness the final failure of Canada's postwar search for counterweights. Continentalism remains the only viable alternative. To be sure, this reality is not one which simply emerged overnight. It is also not simply, or even largely, the product of the failure to fully cultivate the country's relations with Germany and Europe. Rather it is a reality towards which Canada drifted slowly and to which the failure to develop the nation's relationship with Europe certainly contributed.

What continentalism will ultimately mean for Canada's own identity and, indeed, its independence is something which will only be determined over the longer term. However, if Canada is to avoid becoming nothing more than a protectorate of the United States – if, indeed, such a fate can now be avoided – then the country will have to develop policies and strategies (which must integrate strategic and defence issues in a larger and comprehensive policy framework) that conform to and suit the overarching reality of continentalism. It will also have to learn to accept and work within an international environment in which Canada has much less freedom of manoeuvre that it once did and within which it will have even less ability to influence the international events which affect it than it has had in the past.

APPENDIX ONE

Canadian and German Political Leaders and Foreign and Defence Policy Officials, 1949–1995

HEADS OF GOVERNMENT

Canada		Germany	
Louis St. Laurent	1948–57	Konrad Adenauer	1949–63
John Diefenbaker	1957–63	Ludwig Erhard	1963–6
Lester Pearson	1963–8	Kurt Georg Kiesinger	1966–9
Pierre Trudeau	1968–79	Willy Brandt	1969–74
Joe Clark	1979–80	Helmut Schmidt	1974–82
Pierre Trudeau	1980–4	Helmut Kohl	1982–
John Turner	1984		
Brian Mulroney	1984–93		
Kim Campbell	1993		
Jean Chrétien	1993–		

SECRETARIES OF STATE FOR EXTERNAL/ FOREIGN AFFAIRS AND FOREIGN MINISTERS

Canada		Germany	
Lester Pearson	1948–57	Konrad Adenauer	1951–5
Sidney Smith	1957–9	Heinrich von Brentano	1955–61
Howard Green	1959–63	Gerhard Schröder	1961–6
Paul Martin	1963–8	Willy Brandt	1966–9
Mitchell Sharp	1968–74	Walter Scheel	1969–74
Allan MacEachen	1974–6	Hans-Dietrich Genscher	1974–92
Don Jamieson	1976–9	Klaus Kinkel	1992–

Flora MacDonald	1979–80
Mark MacGuigan	1980–2
Allan MacEachen	1982–4
Jean Chrétien	1984
Joe Clark	1984–91
Barbara McDougall	1991–3
Perrin Beatty	1993
André Ouellet	1993–6

DEFENCE MINISTERS

Canada

Brooke Claxton	1946–54
Ralph Campney	1954–7
George Pearkes	1957–9
Douglas Harkness	1960–3
Gordon Churchill	1963
Paul Hellyer	1963–7
Léo Cadieux	1967–70
C.M. Drury (acting)	1970
Donald Macdonald	1970–2
Edgar Benson	1972
J.E. Dubé (acting)	1972
C.M. Drury (acting)	1972
James Richardson	1972–6
Barnett Danson	1976–9
Allan MacKinnon	1979–80
Gilles Lamontagne	1980–3
Jean-Jacques Blais	1983–4
Robert Coates	1984–5
Joe Clark (acting)	1985
Erik Nielsen	1985–6
Perrin Beatty	1986–9
Bill McKnight	1989–91
Marcel Masse	1991–3
Kim Campbell	1993
Tom Siddon	1993
David Collenette	1993–

Germany

Theodor Blank	1955–6
Franz-Josef Strauss	1956–63
Kai-Uwe von Hassel	1963–6
Gerhard Schröder	1966–9
Helmut Schmidt	1969–72
Georg Leber	1972–8
Hans Apel	1978–82
Manfred Wörner	1982–8
Rupert Scholz	1988–9
Gerhard Stoltenberg	1989–92
Volker Rühe	1992–

CANADIAN AND GERMAN AMBASSADORS

Canadian Ambassadors in Bonn
T.C. Davis   1950–4
(Held rank of minister until 1951)

German Ambassadors in Ottawa
Werner Dankwort   1951–6
(Initially held rank of minister)

Charles Ritchie	1954–8	Hasso von Etzdorf	1956–8
Escott Reid	1958–62	Herbert Siegfried	1958–63
John Starnes	1962–6	Kurt Oppler	1963–7
Richard Bower	1966–70	J.F. Ritter von Schwerin	1968–70
Gordon Gale Crean	1970–5	D. Baron von Mirbach	1970–2
John Halstead	1975–80	Rupprecht von Keller	1972–5
Klaus Goldschlag	1980–3	Count Max Samlich	1975–9
Don McPhail	1983–7	Erich Strätling	1979–83
Thomas Delworth	1988–92	Wolfgang Behrends	1983–91
Paul Heinbecker	1992–	Richard Ellerkmann	1991–3
		Hans-Günter Sulimma	1993–

Canadian Forces in Germany, 1951–1994

1951–1969

Location	Brigade deployed in northern Germany and assigned to British Army of the Rhine (BAOR), Northern Army Group (NORTHAG) sector.
Mission	Under the operational control of the BAOR, its role was to contribute to the defence of the NORTHAG sector. From the latter 1950s, this meant contributing to the strategy of forward defence in the allied front line.
Strength	Brigade maintained a strength of between 5000 and 6600 men. Strength peaked at 6600 troops in the aftermath of the Berlin crisis of 1961 when the allies demanded that a more effective combat-capable force be deployed.
Major Equipment Acquisitions	In keeping with the shift from a purely infantry to a mechanized role, the brigade was re-equipped in the 1960s with armoured personnel carriers (M-113 type) and heavy self-propelled artillery. It also acquired an integral nuclear delivery capability in the form of the Honest John rockets deployed in 1961.
Reinforcement Commitment	Canada was obligated to provide the balance of a division (two additional brigades) 30 days after mobilization. This commitment was a relatively hollow one because the units based in Canada were widely dispersed. In 1958, the headquarters commanding this rein-

forcement division was disbanded and from the latter 1950s, Canada-based brigades were only provided with training scales of equipment. Under terms of the 1964 white paper, the Canada-based brigades were re-equipped but no longer automatically tasked to the central front. In 1968 the reinforcement commitment for Germany was ended. One of the two remaining brigades was then tasked to the northern flank instead of the central front.

1970–1974

Location	Under terms of the Trudeau defence review, Canadian ground forces were redeployed to southern Germany to operate in the Central Army Group (CENTAG) sector.
Mission	Tasked directly to the CENTAG commander, the combat group's role was to contribute to the security of the army group's rear area and, when reinforced by allied units, to engage in reconnaissance or "block and hold" operations.
Strength	In keeping with the terms of the Trudeau review, strength levels were reduced by half to some 2800 to 3000 soldiers and the brigade itself was redesignated a "combat group."
Major Equipment Acquisitions	Hand-held surface-to-air missiles (Blowpipe), anti-tank guided weapons (TOW), and observation helicopters (Kiowa).
Reinforcement Commitment	A few hundred extra personnel were to be deployed in an emergency to bring the combat group to a strength of some 3300 men.

1974–1989

Location	Southern Germany in the Central Army Group (CENTAG) sector.
Mission	The combat group was retitled "brigade" and, based on plans to increase numbers of personnel in wartime, given a front-line reinforcement role. The wartime tasking of the brigade was narrowed in the mid-1980s to the forward boundary area between the German II and United States VII Corps.
Strength	Some 3200 personnel. Peacetime strength levels were increased by some 1000 troops (to a total of just over 4000) in 1986.
Major Equipment Acquisitions	Main battle tanks (Leopard I) acquired in the 1970s; improved TOW anti-tank guided weapons acquired in the 1980s.

Reinforcement   With the move to a brigade commitment, troops were earmarked
Commitment   in Canada to reinforce 4 CMBG to a total strength of 5000 to 5500
                personnel in wartime. Some of the equipment for these troops was
                pre-positioned in the Federal Republic.

1989–1994

Location   Southern Germany in the Central Army Group (CENTAG) sector.

Mission   The forward defence role remained the primary tasking but became
                practically irrelevant with the collapse of the Berlin Wall in Novem-
                ber 1989. In the post–Cold War era, Canadian bases were used for
                a short time to support new missions outside the NATO area. Per-
                sonnel were deployed to the Middle East in 1990–1 at the time of
                the Gulf War. In 1992, Canadian ground combat units from Ger-
                many deployed to peacekeeping duties in the former Yugoslavia.

Strength   The defence review of 1990 reduced the strength of the brigade in
                the following year by some 1000 troops to just over 3000. As a result
                of the withdrawal decision announced in 1991, troop levels were
                gradually run down until the closure of CFB Lahr in 1993–4.

Major   Air-defence/anti-tank missile system (ADATS) ordered in 1986.
Equipment
Acquisitions

Reinforcement   From November of 1989, Canada was again obligated to provide a
Commitment   division in central Europe in a crisis. However, the April 1989 budget
                had made this commitment hollow even before it began. The rein-
                forcing brigade and divisional troops would have theoretically
                brought the total strength of Canadian ground forces in Germany
                to some 12,500 when deployed. The reinforcement commitment was
                terminated with the decision to close Canadian bases in Germany.

AIR FORCES

1951–1963

Location   Southern Germany and eastern France as part of 4 Allied Tactical
                Air Force.

Mission   Air defence

Principal   Air division with 12 day fighter squadrons in place by 1953 (eventu-
Units and   ally included 300 F-86 Sabres); 4 day fighter squadrons converted
Equipment   to the all-weather interceptor role in 1955–6 (re-equipped with
                72 CF-100s).

1963–1971

Location	Southern Germany with 4 Allied Tactical Air Force (Canadian air forces were asked to leave France in 1966–7).
Mission	Nuclear strike/reconnaissance (conventional attack capability added under terms of the 1964 white paper).
Principal Units and Equipment	Eight squadrons converted to the CF-104 Starfighter in 1962–3 (144 aircraft). Natural attrition and the Trudeau defence review reduced numbers to only three squadrons with some 40 aircraft in theatre by 1970. Bases in Germany reduced from three to two.

1972–1985

Location	Southern Germany assigned to 4 Allied Tactical Air Force.
Mission	Conventional attack/interdiction.
Principal Units and Equipment	Air group with 3 squadrons (some 36 operational CF-104 aircraft in theatre).

1985–1992

Location	Southern Germany assigned to 4 Allied Tactical Air Force.
Mission	Multi-role – attack or air defence. Missions terminated with the withdrawal of air combat units in 1992.
Principal Units and Equipment	Air group with 3 squadrons converted to CF-18 aircraft in 1985–6 (some 54 fighters). Three squadrons were consolidated into two in 1991 (with some 48 aircraft).
Reinforcement Commitment	In 1988, 1 Canadian Air Division was re-established with two additional CF-18 reinforcement squadrons in Canada.

Principal German-Canadian Arms Transfers and Projects, 1955–1995

TRANSFERS FROM CANADA TO GERMANY

1956	F-86 Mk 6 day fighter of American design; built on licence in Canada	225 Mk 6 aircraft supplied; 75 older model F-86 Mk 5 aircraft also supplied as mutual aid; pilots trained in Canada
1965	CL-89 reconnaissance drone	German-Canadian joint project begun in 1965 following conclusion of Research, Development, and Production Agreement of 1964
1976	CL-289 reconnaissance drone	German-Canadian joint project also joined by France in 1977; corps-level reconnaissance drone only to be acquired by Germany and France
1984	Canadair Challenger VIP transport aircraft	7 aircraft purchased by Luftwaffe

TRANSFERS FROM GERMANY TO CANADA

1976	Leopard I main battle tank	114 tanks plus 14 bridge-layer and recovery variants (delivered 1978–9)
1983	Iltis light truck	1900 vehicles built on licence in Canada
1984	Heavy trucks 10-ton-trucks	42 trucks supplied to support Canada's mechanized brigade in Germany
1990	Badger armoured engineer variant of Leopard I	9 vehicles supplied in 1990

Source: Canada, Department of National Defence, *Defence Canada,* various years.

Personnel Levels and Rank Breakdown, Canadian and German Forces, 1995

	Bundeswehr	Canadian Forces
STANDING FORCES		
Generals/Admirals	212 (0.06%)	86 (0.13%)
Other Officers	38,101 (11.3%)	14,461 (22.1%)
Warrant Officers/Senior NCOS	70,441 (20.9%)	15,082 (23%)
Junior NCOS	46,093 (13.7%)	31,976 (48.9%)
Enlisted/Conscripts	181,588 (53.9%)	3,781 (5.8%)
SUB-TOTAL	336,435	65,386
RESERVE FORCES	418,988*	24,157*
TOTAL (standing and reserve)	755,423	89,543

HEADQUARTERS PERSONNEL[†]		
	German Ministry of Defence	NDHQ, Canada
Military	1,540 (0.46% of regular force total)	3,357 (5.1% of regular force total)
Civilian	3,200[‡]	4,084[‡]

* In addition to the primary reserve force, a supplementary reserve exists in both countries numbering about 2.5 million personnel in Germany and about 45,000 in Canada.
† Some of the functions performed at NDHQ in Canada are performed at subordinate commands, offices, and agencies outside the Ministry of Defence in Germany.
‡ German civilian personnel are in the process of being reduced from some 160,000 to no more than 150,000 while Canadian civilian personnel are being reduced to 20,000 from a previous total of 32,000.

Sources: Office of the Canadian Defence Attaché, Canadian Embassy Bonn, Germany; Germany, Ministry of Defence, *White Paper 1994*; Canada, Department of National Defence, *Special Commission on the Restructuring of the Reserve, Report,* 1995. Additional information on rank breakdowns provided by Department of National Defence, Ottawa, and German Ministry of Defence, Bonn.

German and Canadian Defence Expenditure as a Percentage of GNP/GDP, 1955–1995

| Year | Germany† | | Canada‡ | |
	Percentage of GNP/GDP*	Rank in NATO	Percentage of GNP/GDP*	Rank in NATO
1955	4.8	8 of 14	7.2	4 of 14
1960	4.6	7 of 14	4.9	6 of 14
1965	5.0	6 of 14	3.5	10 of 14
1970	3.7	9 of 14	2.8	12 of 14
1975	3.5	6 of 14	2.1	13 of 14
1980	3.4	7 of 14	1.9	13 of 14
1985	3.4	6 of 15	2.1	13 of 15
1990	2.8	8 of 15	2.0	13 of 15
1995	1.7	11 of 15	1.6	13 of 15

* Figures for 1955 through to 1970 are given as percentage of GNP and from 1975 to 1995 as percentage of GDP. Figures for 1975, 1980, and 1985 are averages of the years 1970–4, 1975–9, and 1980–4 respectively. Figures for 1995 are estimates. Iceland is not included in the above list because it has no armed forces.

† In 1985, the level of German defence spending as percentage of GDP was equal to that of Portugal and in 1995 it was estimated to be equal to that of Belgium. Despite a declining percentage of GNP/GDP devoted to defence, the absolute defence budget has been relatively high due to a rapidly rising GNP/GDP. The GNP/GDP has grown from US$44.6 billion in 1955 to US$388.8 billion in 1975 to an estimated US$1.83 trillion in 1994.

‡ In 1965, the level of Canadian defence spending as percentage of GNP was equal to that of Belgium and in 1970 it was equal with that of Denmark. In 1985 the percentage of Canadian spending was equal to that of Italy. In most of the 1970s and 1980s, Luxembourg was the only state to rank below Canada in terms of the percentage of GDP devoted to defence. Since 1990 both Luxembourg and Spain have ranked below Canada. Canada's absolute defence budget has also been relatively high (but lacking cost-effectiveness) in the NATO context due to a rising GNP/GDP. The GNP/GDP has grown from about US$25 billion in 1955 to US$143.5 billion in 1975 to an estimated US$548.4 billion in 1994.

Sources: NATO *Facts and Figures* (Brussels: NATO Information Service 1976), 317; NATO *Handbook* (Brussels: NATO Office of Information and Press 1995), 358; "Documentation," NATO *Review* 44 (January 1996), 32; *The Military Balance,* 1975–76 and 1995–96 (London: International Institute for Strategic Studies 1975 and 1995), 20–2 and 41 and 48, respectively; and author's calculations based on figures in *Britannica Book of the Year,* 1956, 62 and 139.

Notes

ABBREVIATIONS

AA   Auswärtiges Amt [Foreign Office], Germany
DEA   Department of External Affairs, Canada
DHist Directorate of History, DND
DND   Department of National Defence, Canada
NA   National Archives, Canada

CHAPTER TWO

1 Belgium, Canada, Denmark, France, Iceland, Italy, Luxembourg, the Netherlands, Norway, Portugal, the United Kingdom, and the United States were the
  founding members of the North Atlantic Treaty Organization. Greece and
  Turkey joined in 1952, the Federal Republic in 1955, and Spain in 1982.
2 See, for instance, Dalma, "The Risks of a Détente Policy to Central Europe,"
  103–4.
3 Joffe, Limited Partnership, 173.
4 Hill, Political Consultation in NATO.
5 See, for instance, figures cited by Bark and Gress, From Shadow to Substance,
  279 and 285.
6 See Taylor, Struggle for the Mastery of Europe.
7 Dahrendorf, Society and Democracy in Germany.
8 Iggers, The German Conception of History; also Meinecke, The German Catastrophe, and Zuckerman, "The Germans: What is the Question?"
9 Bull, Anarchical Society, 3–52.

10 For further discussion, see Rempel, *The Meaning of the German Question in the New Europe.*

11 For a discussion of the imperatives and interests guiding German policy during the Adenauer years, see Bandulet, *Adenauer zwischen West und Ost.*

12 For discussion on this theme, see Hanrieder, *Germany, America, Europe,* 254–62; also Grosser, *Deutschlandbilanz,* 444–55.

13 Bandulet, *Adenauer zwischen West und Ost,* 31–4, 51–2.

14 Discussed by Snyder in "The Security Dilemma in Alliance Politics," 461–95.

15 One of the best accounts of allied interaction during these crises is Richardson's *Germany and the Atlantic Alliance.*

16 Buteux, *The Politics of Nuclear Consultation in NATO,* 14–49.

17 Brandt, *A Peace Policy for Europe,* 24.

18 Brandt, "German Foreign Policy," 370–2.

19 For a further discussion of German policy in this period, see, for example, Windsor, *Germany and the Management of Détente.*

20 Under the Nixon doctrine formulated in 1970, the United States proposed that its key regional allies take a greater role in carrying the burden of containment and in maintaining regional security: Kelleher, "The Federal Republic of Germany," 144; also discussion in Morgan, *West Germany's Foreign Policy Agenda,* 32–5.

21 The major issue which damaged American-German relations was the Carter administration's decisions, first, to lobby vigorously for German acceptance of the deployment of the neutron bomb in central Europe and then, once it had been reluctantly accepted, to cancel the deployment.

22 For Schmidt's impressions of the United States and of the fluctuations in American policy, see his *Men and Powers,* 123–7.

23 For the debate in the FRG on the Strategic Defense Initiative, see Bluth, "SDI: The Challenge to West Germany," 247–64.

24 See: Smouts, "External Policy of Mitterrand," 155–67; Gnesotto, "Die französischen Parteien und die sicherheitspolitische Zusammenarbeit mit der Bundesrepublik Deutschland"; and Kolboom, "Im Westen nichts Neues? Frankreichs Sicherheitspolitik, das deutsch-französische Verhältnis und die Deutsche Frage."

25 See, for instance, Vano, *Canada: The Strategic and Military Pawn*; also Roy, "The Canadian Military Tradition," and Preston, "Military Influence on the Development of Canada."

26 Nossal, *Politics of Canadian Foreign Policy,* 63–5.

27 Vano, *Canada: The Strategic and Military Pawn,* especially 71–110.

28 See Byers, *Canadian Security and Defence,* 5, 13, and for further discussion, Rempel, "The Need for a Canadian Security Policy," 38–42.

29 Sutherland, "Canada's Long-Term Strategic Situation," 199.

30 Pearson, *Democracy in World Politics,* 6.

31 Pearson, *Peace in the Family of Man,* 54.

32 See, for example, Holmes, *Shaping of Peace,* vol. 2.

33 Crane, *Introduction to Canadian Defence Policy*, 35.

34 DND, *Defence Canada 80*, 15, 17.

35 Memorandum – February 1957, DND, DHist, Raymont Papers, #767.

36 The theme of the question of relevance in Canadian defence policy was intro-
duced by Colin Gray in his *Canadian Defence Priorities*.

37 Quoted in McLin, *Canada's Changing Defense Policy 1957–1963*, 88, 80.

38 Vano, *Canada: The Strategic and Military Pawn*, 109–10, 144.

39 The best discussion of the defence policy of the Diefenbaker government is
McLin, *Canada's Changing Defense Policy 1957–1963*.

40 *Damn the Torpedoes*, the memoirs of Paul Hellyer, who was minister of
national defence under Pearson, offers a first-hand account of the defence
debates of the 1960s. Not surprisingly, the discussion in his book is dominated
by issues of budget and organization, specifically the problem of how to make
a Canadian military contribution fit the requirements of both NATO and the
United Nations in a time of declining resources. There is almost no discussion
of how any specific contribution might fit with or contribute to Canada's strategic or political interests.

41 The 1964 white paper had based its re-equipment plans for the forces on the
savings that were expected from the integration and unification of the three
services, a policy announced in the white paper. However, these savings never
materialized. See Kronenberg, *All Together Now*, 20, 110–13.

42 See, especially, Thordarson, *Trudeau and Foreign Policy*, 111–13, 123–7. See also
the article by James Eayrs ("Future Roles of the Armed Forces of Canada") in
which he argues for a Canadian policy which would in essence take a "free
ride" on the United States.

43 DND, *Defence in the 70s*, especially 12.

44 Douglas Bland argues an especially interesting thesis that, since the Trudeau
era, governments have taken a "management approach" to defence problems
in Canada, an approach which often ignores military realities and requirements. See Bland, *Administration of Defence Policy in Canada*, 56–85, 187–215.

45 DND, *White Paper on Defence – March 1964*, 21.

46 For a good account of this process, see Byers, "Defence and Foreign Policy in
the 1970s." For Peyton Lyon's original article on the concept of a Trudeau doctrine, see his "The Trudeau Doctrine."

47 The Gallup poll released on 19 June 1976 showed some 23 per cent of Canadians supportive of neutrality while the Gallup of 26 May 1986 showed 26 per
cent in support. In Gallup surveys, numbers have remained within that general area. However, much would seem to depend on the question asked and
on how it is asked. For instance, on 26 October 1989, when Canadians were
asked their views on the need for NATO, 78 per cent said it should be maintained and only 8 per cent thought it no longer necessary.

48 A sample of these arguments can be found in *The True North Strong and Free?*
and in Head and Trudeau's critique of realism in *The Canadian Way* (310–19).

See also Langille's argument (in *Changing the Guard*) for the "common security" approach to defence policy and his (rather bizarre) warning about the growing power of Canada's "military-industrial complex."

49 See Hillmer and Stevenson, eds., *Foremost Nation*; Dewitt and Kirton, *Canada as a Principal Power*; Gotlieb, *Canada and the Economic Summits*.

50 See, for instance, Sokolsky, "Parting of the Waves?"; also Ross and Langdon, "Towards a Canadian Maritime Strategy in the North Pacific Region," and Buteux, "NATO and the Evolution of Canadian Defence and Foreign Policy." More recently, Joseph Jockel and Joel Sokolsky have used this realist perspective to argue that with the end of the Cold War, Canada's strategic situation and the lack of external threats makes a policy of neo-isolationism more feasible if Canada should so choose: Jockel and Sokolsky, "Dandurand Revisited."

51 Interview, General Gerard Thériault, September 1990. For a discussion of the position of the defence minister within the executive and in defence policy-making, see Middlemiss and Sokolsky, *Canadian Defence Policy*, 59–111, especially 64–8; also Bland, *Administration of Defence Policy in Canada*, 87–146, 239.

52 Tucker, *Canadian Foreign Policy*, 227–8.

53 See, for instance, Keating and Pratt, *Canada, NATO and the Bomb*.

54 DEA, *Annual Report 1989/90*, 17. Canada's two-way trade with Europe, in contrast, amounted to only 12.2 per cent of its total world trade in 1989.

CHAPTER THREE

1 See Canada's submission on the German peace settlement, January 1947, DEA files, 50,173–40, file pocket vol. 5.

2 Cited in Eayrs, *In Defence of Canada: Growing Up Allied*, 327–8.

3 Pearson, *Mike*, vol. 2, 75.

4 German ambassador, Ottawa, to Foreign Office, Bonn, 12 November 1959, AA, 305 83.20–84.20. Siegfried's impression of Canadian policy as naive and amateurish seems to have arisen from an earlier meeting with the new secretary of state for external affairs, Howard Green. He noted in a report to Bonn that he had had to correct Green's mistaken view that the Federal Republic was a member of the United Nations! German ambassador, Ottawa, to Foreign Office, Bonn, 29 September 1959, AA, 301 81–04, vol. 123.

5 German embassy, Paris, to Foreign Office, Bonn, 13 November 1959, AA, 305 83.20–84.20.

6 Hasso von Etzdorf to German ambassador, Ottawa, 19 November 1959, AA, 305 82.20–82.21, vol. 141.

7 "Zusammenarbeit mit Kanada innerhalb der NATO," AA, 305 82.21–91.20.

8 Concern over Adenauer's leadership is reflected in the reports of the Canadian ambassador in Bonn, Escott Reid, and in a memorandum written by Norman Robertson, the under-secretary of state, in June 1959. Robertson's memorandum referred to Adenauer's actions as those of a man who was "losing his sure and confident grip in affairs," while Reid suggested that they reflected "clouded

judgement." Reid even suggested that the chancellor might have reached the early stages of senility. "Adenauer's Decision to Remain Chancellor," memorandum for the minister, 5 June 1959, DEA files, 50,173–40, vol. 10, and Canadian embassy, Bonn, to DEA, Ottawa, 26 June 1959, DEA files, 12,086–40, pt. 1.

9 Escott Reid's memoirs are instructive. He reveals that while Canadian policy remained officially supportive of the alliance position, discontent over the long-term viability of this strategy was considerable: *Radical Mandarin*, 304–19. A more detailed discussion of Canadian-German relations in this period is found in Rempel, "Canada, Germany and Alliance Relations in the Crisis Years of 1958–61," 85–100.

10 Communications between the high commission in Ottawa and the Commonwealth Office in London, 23 and 26 January 1959, Public Record Office, London, PREM 2712.

11 Quoted in Spencer, "Canada and the Origins of the CSCE," 21.

12 "Address by Prime Minister Lester B. Pearson to the Permanent Representatives to the NATO Council, Paris, January 17, 1964," in Gellner, *Canada in NATO*, 87–8.

13 "NATO and the Atlantic Community," briefing for Erhard visit to Canada, 1 June 1964, NA, RG 25, 20–GRF–9–Erhard.

14 Canada provoked some criticism – in Germany – in the summer of 1965 when it seemed to suggest that NATO's internal nuclear arrangements could become a subject for discussion at the Geneva conference. Conservative Christian Democratic politicians, including Adenauer, criticized the attitudes of both Britain and Canada in this respect. See "Bonn sucht Gespräch mit Kanada," *Frankfurter Rundschau*, 28 August 1965; also Burns, *A Seat at the Table*, 213–14.

15 See Legault and Fortmann, *Diplomacy of Hope*, 210–11.

16 Discussed in "Germany and Berlin," briefing for Erhard visit to Canada, 2 June 1964, and DEA to embassy, Bonn, 17 June 1964 (telegram S-310), both in NA, RG 25, 20–GFR–9–Erhard.

17 DEA to embassy, Bonn, 17 June 1964, NA, RG 25, 20–GFR–9–Erhard.

18 "NATO and the Atlantic Community," briefing for Erhard visit to Canada, 1 June 1964, NA, RG 25, 20–GFR–9–Erhard.

19 Communiqué issued during Erhard's visit to Canada, 10 June 1964, "Verstärkte Zusammenarbeit zwischen Kanada und Deutschland," *Bulletin*, no. 93 (12 June 1964): 853.

20 DEA document.

21 Interview, John Halstead, 25 January 1991.

22 Kovrig, "'European Security' in East-West Relations," 11–12.

23 Spencer, "Canada and the Origins of the CSCE," 25.

24 Canadian ambassador, Bonn, to secretary of state for external affairs, 8 December 1966, NA, RG 25, 20–1–2–GFR, vol. 3.

25 Paul Martin to Willy Brandt, 23 December 1966, NA, RG 25, 20–1–2–GFR.

26 Hockin, "External Affairs and Defence," *Canadian Annual Review for 1966*, 227.

27 Willy Brandt to Paul Martin, 10 January 1967, NA, RG 25, 20–1–2–GFR. With regard to the Canadian support of German policy with the Polish government, the embassy in Bonn had noted in an earlier communication that the "Secretary of State's support of German interests during his visit to Warsaw has been much appreciated in German official circles and such press comment that has appeared has singled out this aspect of Mr. Martin's trip." Canadian ambassador, Bonn, to secretary of state for external affairs, 8 December 1966, NA, RG 25, 20–1–2–GFR, vol. 3.

28 "German/Canadian Relations: Consultations at Official Level," memorandum, 23 November 1967, NA, RG 25, 20–1–2–GFR.

29 Ibid., and DEA, Ottawa, to Canadian embassy, Bonn, 18 December 1967, NA, RG 25, 20–1–2–GFR.

30 Excerpts of the Harmel Report are in Gellner, Canada in NATO, 90–1.

31 DEA document.

32 DEA document.

33 "Canada and the World: Policy Statement by the Prime Minister," 29 May 1968, Office of the Prime Minister, press release, 5–6.

34 DEA document.

35 See Spencer, "Canada and the Origins of the CSCE," 31, and Thordarson, Trudeau and Foreign Policy, 143.

36 Meeting of Defence Council, 21 October 1968, DND, DHist, 81/609.

37 Meetings of Defence Council, 7 and 21 October 1968, DND, DHist, 81/609.

38 Quoted in Spencer, "Canada and the Origins of the CSCE," 33–4.

39 "Instructions for NATO Ministerial Meeting," Privy Council files, Cabinet Minutes, 7 November 1968.

40 Harlan Cleveland, quoted in Eustace, Canada's European Force, 1964–71, 67.

41 Spencer, "Canada and the Origins of the CSCE," 34.

42 These included the Italian foreign minister, Pietro Nenni, in a meeting with Trudeau in Rome and British officials during the Commonwealth conference: Thordarson, Trudeau and Foreign Policy, 144–5.

43 Confidential source.

44 Granatstein and Bothwell, Pirouette, 17.

45 The interdepartmental task force, headed by John Halstead, had recommended that Canada "should continue to station troops in Europe since it was in Canada's economic and political, as well as military, interests to be actively involved in the continent." The task force also emphasized that forces in Europe supported the continuance of a transatlantic relationship which offset increasing dependence on the United States. See Eustace, Canada's European Force, 1964–71, 82–6; also Granatstein and Bothwell, Pirouette, 14–20, and Thordarson, Trudeau and Foreign Policy, 127–36. For the SCEAND report, see House of Commons, Standing Committee on External Affairs and National Defence, Minutes of Proceedings and Evidence, no. 35, 26 March 1969, 7–15.

46 DEA document.

47 See Granatstein and Bothwell, *Pirouette*, 3–35. For the inside view, see Head and Trudeau, *The Canadian Way*, 65–95. For the cabinet record, see "The Defence Policy Review and the Special Task Force on Europe," Privy Council files, Cabinet Minutes, 29 March 1969. Also, my interviews with Léo Cadieux, 20 October 1986, and Ross Campbell, 29 April 1987 and a brief reference by Sharp in *Which Reminds Me*, 173–5.

48 Harlan Cleveland, quoted in Granatstein and Bothwell, *Pirouette*, 26.

49 Granatstein and Bothwell, *Pirouette*, 27–8. The intensity of criticism from the NATO allies apparently again led Cadieux to consider resigning after the May meeting. He was apparently persuaded not to do so by his deputy minister, Elgin Armstrong, and the former defence minister, Paul Hellyer, who both argued that his presence was required to avert worse cuts to the defence budget and the forces in Europe.

50 DEA document.

51 Bleek, "Die bundesdeutsche-kanadische Krise 1969–1975," 128–32.

52 Ibid., 129, 131.

53 Franz Schedt, "Brandt in Kanada," *Osnabrücker Zeitung*, 8 April 1969.

54 "Brandt hofft auf ein Arrangement mit Kanada," *Frankfurter Allgemeine Zeitung*, 9 April 1969.

55 "Bundesminister des Auswärtigen, zu seinen Sondierungsgesprächen in Ottawa," *Kommentarübersicht*, 9 April 1969.

56 "Brandt hofft auf ein Arrangement mit Kanada," *Frankfurter Allgemeine Zeitung*, 9 April 1969.

57 "Report on Defence Policy Review – Phase II," Privy Council files, Cabinet Minutes, 20 May 1969.

58 "Brandt in Kanada," *Osnabrücker Zeitung*, 8 April 1969.

59 Cited in Flanagan, *NATO's Conventional Defences*, 16.

60 Sharp, *Which Reminds Me*, 175–6.

61 DEA document.

62 See Schmidt, *Balance of Power*, 55–88, 194–201; Bark and Gress, *Democracy and Its Discontents*, 61–2; and Flanagan, *NATO's Conventional Defences*, 16.

63 Confidential source.

64 DEA documents.

65 German Army Training Establishment Shilo, *10 Years: German Soldiers in Shilo 1973–1983*; interview at CFB Shilo, 23 August 1989; "Panzersoldaten in Kanada," 86–8.

66 Confidential sources.

67 DEA document. While the German decision to train troops in Canada could apparently be taken by the German defence minister without reference to his cabinet colleagues, Canadian approval of such an agreement would have to go to cabinet and also involve the Department of External Affairs.

68 The United States withdrew from the agreement in 1991 while the Netherlands acceded to it in 1987. In 1995, the Italian air force began to use Goose Bay and

late in the year an agreement was reached between Canada and the allies for a ten-year extension of the memorandum of understanding.

69 DND, *EIS: Military Flight Training*, chapter 5.

70 Ibid., 5–67 and 5–74.

71 DND, *Socio-Economic Impacts of Allied Training in Canada*, 8, 17–18; Government of Newfoundland, *Fact Sheet on Allied Military Training at Goose Bay* (1995).

72 DND, *Socio-Economic Impacts of Allied Training in Canada*, 15, 34.

73 DEA document.

74 DEA document.

75 "Possible Canadian-German Collaboration on the Construction of a Uranium Enrichment Plant in Canada," memorandum from European Division, DEA, to Economic Division, 19 December 1967, NA, RG 25, 20–1–2–GFR. German interest in scientific co-operation also led to an agreement, in July 1969, to use the rocket range at Churchill, Manitoba, to train members of the Bundeswehr.

76 Meeting of Defence Council, 11 March 1968, DND, DHist, 81/609.

77 Boyd, "Politics of Canadian Defence Procurement"; and ibid.

78 Meeting of Defence Council, 11 March 1968, DND, DHist, 81/609.

79 DEA document.

80 Meeting of Defence Council, 11 March 1968, DND, DHist, 81/609.

81 DEA document.

82 DEA document.

83 DEA document.

84 The Speaker's Office only offered to support the creation of a hospitality committee to welcome any German parliamentary delegation which chose to come to Canada. DEA document.

85 DEA document.

86 "A West German-Canada Pact," *Times* (London), 17 April 1971; "Kanadische Delegation kommt in die BRD," *Handelsblatt* (Hamburg), 7 April 1971.

87 Byers, "External Affairs and Defence," *Canadian Annual Review*, 1971, 263.

88 See Munson, *World Unmanned Aircraft*, 24–7. Information on the CL-289 drone is also found in Hausen, "Überlegung zum Aufklärungsdrohnensystem CL-289," 9-11. Further information from DEA files.

89 DEA document.

CHAPTER FOUR

1 *Foreign Policy for Canadians*, Europe booklet, 14.

2 Ibid., 23.

3 Spencer, "Canada and the Origins of the CSCE," 35.

4 Ibid. A thorough account of Canada's role on arms control and confidence-building in the CSCE process to the mid-1980s is found in Legault and Fortmann, *Diplomacy of Hope*, 466–524.

5   Spencer, "Canada and the Origins of the CSCE," 25–30.
6   Interview, John Halstead, 25 January 1991.
7   Interview, Thomas Delworth, April 1991.
8   Spencer, "Canada and the Origins of the CSCE," 38, 42.
9   Ibid., 38.
10   Ibid., 39, 57–72.
11   Basket One focused on specific security questions in Europe and Basket Two on issues of economic co-operation as well as co-operation in science, technology, and the environment.
12   Spencer, "Canada and the Origins of the CSCE," 62.
13   DEA files. On Sharp's visit to Bonn: Bleek, "Die bundesdeutsch-kanadische Krise 1969–1975," 136.
14   Spencer, "Canada and the Origins of the CSCE," 41. (Spencer mistakenly identifies the ambassador in Bonn in 1969 as John Starnes.)
15   Bleek, "Die bundesdeutsch-kanadische Krise 1969–1975," 136.
16   DEA document.
17   DEA document.
18   DEA document.
19   DEA document.
20   Granatstein and Bothwell, *Pirouette*, 189–96.
21   DEA document. In the event, difficult negotiations with the German Democratic Republic on family reunification meant that Canada did not establish diplomatic relations with the GDR until 1975. Even then, Canada always conducted those relations through its embassy in Warsaw.
22   "Kanadas aktivierte Ostpolitik," *Neue Zürcher Zeitung*, 17 November 1971.
23   Interview with Sharp quoted in DEA document.
24   DEA document.
25   DEA document.
26   DEA document.
27   See Rattinger, "MBFR-Stagnation und weitere Aussichten," 331–43. Some discussion of the FRG's policy is also found in Schilling, "Neue Strukturen der MBFR Verhandlungen," 404–14.
28   See Legault and Fortmann, *Diplomacy of Hope*, 422–65, 482.
29   See von Groll, "Die Genfer KSZE Verhandlungen," 159–66.
30   Genscher, *Aussenpolitik*, 73.
31   DEA document.
32   See Lyon, "Canada at Geneva, 1973–5," 124, 120–1.
33   Interview, John Halstead, 25 January 1991. Halstead, who became assistant under-secretary for European and defence affairs in 1971, was the official most responsible for directing policy on the CSCE.
34   Holsti, "Who Got What and How," 142.
35   David Binder, "Carter Sees Belgrade as Vehicle for Rights," *International Herald Tribune*, 26 May 1977; also Laux, "Human Contacts, Information,

Culture, and Education," 263–4, and Skilling, "The Belgrade Follow-up," 283–307.

36 Lyon, "Canada at Geneva, 1973–5," 117, 121. For further discussion of Canada's role in the confidence-building talks at Geneva, see Legault and Fortmann, *Diplomacy of Hope*, 482–92.

37 "'Vor allem die Schranke zwischen den Menschen durchbrechen' Kanada legt in Belgrad auf Familienzusammenführung grossen Wert," *Frankfurter Allgemeine Zeitung*, 8 October 1977.

38 DEA document.

39 DEA document.

40 Lyon, "Canada at Geneva, 1973–75," 125, and "Conference on Security and Cooperation in Europe: Final Act," printed in Spencer, ed., *Canada and the Conference on Security and Co-operation in Europe*, 366–7.

41 The number of ethnic Germans allowed to leave the Soviet Union increased from 364 in August 1975 to 1,129 in April 1976; from Poland the number increased from 358 in August 1975 to 2,528 in May 1976. There were also modest improvements in the number of Germans from the GDR who were allowed to leave and in the number of Germans from both the GDR and the FRG who were able visit family members on the other side. See "Verwirklichung der KSZE-Beschlüsse," *Der Bundesminister des Auswärtigen Informiert* (Bonn: Presse- und Informationsamt der Bundesregierung), no. 1022B (July 1976).

42 DEA files. See also discussion in Skilling, "The Belgrade Follow-up," 291–7.

43 Skilling, "The Belgrade Follow-up," 295.

44 A sense of the complexity of the negotiations can be gained from Ferraris, ed., *Report on a Negotiation*.

45 See Head and Trudeau, *The Canadian Way*, 292–309, and Granatstein and Bothwell, *Pirouette*, 363–76.

46 "Reflections on Peace and Security," DEA, Statements and Speeches 83/18, 27 October 1983.

47 For instance, "Wenig Echo auf Trudeaus Abrüstungsinitiative," *Neue Zürcher Zeitung*, 16 December 1983.

48 Granatstein and Bothwell, *Pirouette*, 375–6.

49 DEA document.

50 DEA document.

51 DEA document.

52 Confidential source.

53 Confidential source.

54 DEA document.

55 Granatstein and Bothwell, *Pirouette*, 371.

56 Interview, Colonel Roland Foerster, November 1991.

57 Confidential sources.

58 Confidential source. In November 1982, Genscher had expressed confidence in the CSCE process and emphasized that it was important that the current

Madrid follow-up conference should not fail through inadvertence because the FRG regarded it as a key vehicle for influencing its relationship with the GDR. DEA document.

59   A good discussion and thoughtfully sceptical analysis of the impact of the peace initiative on the Reagan administration is Fischer, "The Trudeau Peace Initiative."

60   On Canada's role in the Stockholm talks, see Legault and Fortmann, *Diplomacy of Hope*, 523–63.

61   Kissinger, *Diplomacy*, 733–61, especially 759–60. Mitchell Sharp also admitted to early scepticism about the CSCE process which he says he viewed as a "forlorn hope" in 1973: *Which Reminds Me*, 216–17.

CHAPTER FIVE

1   DEA document.

2   Sharp, *Which Reminds Me*, 219.

3   DEA document.

4   Granatstein and Bothwell, *Pirouette*, 162–4.

5   DEA document. Also noted in a speech to the Canadian Club in Toronto by G.G. Crean, Canada's ambassador in Bonn, on 8 January 1973: cited in DEA document. Brandt's speech was public and Canada was also specifically mentioned in the meeting's communiqué.

6   DEA document.

7   DEA document. The mission in Berlin was actually reopened in the course of 1974–5. Relations with the GDR were also established in 1975.

8   "Scheel will Kanadas Interessen in Europa vertreten," *Die Welt* (Bonn), 1 October 1973; also DEA document.

9   Granatstein and Bothwell, *Pirouette*, 164–6. For Trudeau's view of the Third Option strategy vis-à-vis Europe: Head and Trudeau, *The Canadian Way*, 265–72.

10   Ibid., 415. Granatstein and Bothwell were apparently read sections of the German Foreign Office files relating to Trudeau's March 1975 state visit which seemed to confirm that some ministry officials had concerns about the Canadian initiative.

11   DEA document.

12   *Direction of Trade Statistics Yearbook 1982*, 167.

13   See Nerlich, "Washington and Bonn," 367–78.

14   DEA document. G.G. Crean had outlined German motivations in his speech of 8 January 1973 to the Canadian Club: cited in DEA document. Aspects of an expanded European-Canadian economic relationship were also discussed in the German newspaper, *Handelsblatt* (Hamburg). It reported that a German trade delegation which had visited Canada in 1973 believed the government's new Foreign Investment Review Agency to be a possible impediment to expanded German investment in Canada. "Kanada wirbt um die Gunst der Europäer," *Handelsblatt* (Hamburg), 25 October 1974.

15 See Marshall, "Canada's Forces Take Stock in Defence Structure Review," 26.

16 After Trudeau's return to Canada, the prime minister remarked in the House of Commons that "it was impressed upon me by some of my NATO colleagues how disappointed they would be should any Canadian government at any time take steps to lessen the effectiveness of the Canadian military contribution." Canada, House of Commons, *Debates*, 5 June 1975, 6337. See also Rempel, "Canadian Defence Policy and NATO's Northern Flank," 104–11.

17 DEA document.

18 Robert Held's article described Trudeau as a political leader of some stature who had "changed Canada's image in the world" in barely eight years: "Der Gast aus Ottawa," *Frankfurter Allgemeine Zeitung*, 1 March 1975.

19 Interview, John Halstead, 25 January 1991.

20 "Trudeau mit Ergebnissen seiner Bonner Gespräche zufrieden," *Frankfurter Allgemeine Zeitung*, 5 March 1975; "Schmidt für engere Beziehungen Kanadas zur EG," *Stuttgarter Zeitung*, 5 March 1975; Granatstein and Bothwell, *Pirouette*, 168. Schmidt also apparently strongly supported Canada's membership in the G-7: see Head and Trudeau, *The Canadian Way*, 197.

21 Granatstein and Bothwell, *Pirouette*, 168–70.

22 Confidential source.

23 See Head and Trudeau, *The Canadian Way*, 272–3. Also Sokolsky, "Taking Canada More Seriously," 44; interview, John Halstead, 25 January 1991.

24 DEA document.

25 Trudeau made two state visits (1975 and July 1978) and three unofficial visits (October 1978, 1980, and 1981) to Germany to meet with Schmidt; Schmidt made two state visits (1977 and 1981) and four private visits to Canada. The two also met on at least eight other occasions: NATO meeting, May 1975; European security meeting, Helsinki, July 1975; summit, Jamaica, December 1975; G-7 summit, Puerto Rico, June 1976; G-7 meeting, London, June 1977; G-7 summit, Rome, September 1978; G-7 meeting, Venice, June 1980; and G-7 summit, Versailles, June 1982.

26 See Leyton-Brown, "External Affairs and Defence," *Canadian Annual Review*, 1976, 316; Klaus Dreher, "Bonn und Ottawa für engere Kooperation," *Süddeutsche Zeitung* (Munich), 23 July 1976; Bernt Conrad, "Kanada will näher an Bonn und die EG heranrücken," *Die Welt* (Bonn), 14 July 1976.

27 MacEachen's speech at a dinner hosted by Foreign Minister Genscher, cited in DEA document. German press reports of MacEachen's visit spoke of nearly totally convergent views on the wide variety of issues discussed between the foreign ministers: "Genscher bezeichnet Beziehungen zu Kanada als 'exemplarisch,'" *General Anzeiger* (Bonn), 25 May 1976.

28 Thus, in 1977 there were seven visits by Canadian ministers to the Federal Republic and two by German ministers to Canada as well as numerous visits

by parliamentarians in both directions and by provincial and Land officials.
DEA document.

29 DEA document.

30 Granatstein and Bothwell, *Pirouette*, 169–71.

31 DEA document.

32 Information on Trudeau-Schmidt talks from confidential sources.

33 Schmidt, *Men and Powers*, 123–4, 181–7.

34 Confidential source.

35 Leyton-Brown, "External Affairs and Defence," *Canadian Annual Review*, 1977, 256–9. Canada's desire for an acceptable compromise on the uranium question was reflected in the German press: "Kanadas Regierung will Europa nicht verprellen," *Handelsblatt* (Hamburg), 11 July 1977; Heinz Mörsberger, "Kanzlers Erfolg in Kanada," *Stuttgarter Zeitung*, 13 July 1977.

36 DEA document.

37 Confidential source.

38 Strempel, "Europa als Test für Kanadas Dritte Option," 399–410.

39 DEA document. Also *Jane's All the World's Aircraft, 1994–95*, 189.

40 *Jane's All the World's Aircraft, 1994–95*, 189–95.

41 "Kanadische Flugzeugerkundung," *Süddeutsche Zeitung* (Munich), 25 February 1977, and "Wirbelwind für Kanadas Luftwaffe?" *Rhein-Neckar Zeitung* (Heidelberg), 23 March 1978.

42 For a discussion of the performance characteristics of these aircraft in the competition, see *Jane's All the World's Aircraft, 1994–95* and (for the F-14) *Jane's All the World's Aircraft, 1992–93*.

43 Boyd, "Politics of Canadian Defence Procurement," 143; also Atkinson and Nossal, "Bureaucratic Politics and the New Fighter Aircraft Decisions," 531–58.

44 Operating from an aircraft carrier, the combat air patrol endurance time of the F/A-18 was only about 1 hour and 45 minutes at a range of about 150 nautical miles from the carrier as compared with the Tornado's time of some two hours at a distance of 300 to 400 nautical miles from base. Likewise, the ferry range of the Tornado was listed as 2100 nautical miles while that of the F/A-18 was 1800 nautical miles. See *Jane's All the World's Aircraft, 1994–95*, 189–95 and 586–90.

45 DEA document.

46 Interview, Colonel Rolf Klages, August 1991.

47 DEA document.

48 DEA document.

49 DEA document.

50 DEA document.

51 DEA document.

52 DEA document.

53 DEA document.

54 Confidential source.

55 "Notes for a Speech," DEA, Statement, 6 December 1979.

56 Quoted in Leyton-Brown, "External Affairs and Defence," *Canadian Annual Review*, 1980, 218.

57 There had been little time for Clark and Schmidt to develop a relationship. No time had been set aside for an introductory bilateral meeting during the Tokyo summit in June 1979. Clark had made a brief stop in Lahr during his visit to Africa in August but efforts to link the two men by telephone were unsuccessful. DEA document.

58 DEA document.

59 DEA document.

60 DEA document. Trudeau stopped over in Bonn for talks with Schmidt en route to the Middle East. The June visit to Europe also included pre-summit discussions in London and Paris.

61 Frost and Stent, "NATO's Troubles with East-West Trade," 179–200; *Strategic Survey, 1982–83*, 52–7; Stent-Yergin, *East-West Technology Transfer*, 29–30.

62 On the National Energy Program, see Clarkson, *Canada and the Reagan Challenge*, 55–82.

63 Confidential source. Schmidt's sympathy for the NEP is also noted by Clarkson: ibid., 163.

64 Confidential source.

65 DEA document.

66 Other major actions advocated included opening a consulate general in Munich and organization of a German mission to the east coast to investigate supplying equipment for offshore development. There were some seven other recommendations, most of a more minor nature. DEA document.

67 DEA document.

68 DEA document.

69 DEA document.

70 DEA document.

71 DEA document.

72 By the early 1980s, some 1500 firms in Canada were majority- or partly owned by German firms. DEA document.

73 DEA document.

74 See, for instance, Pentland, "L'option européenne du Canada dans les années 80," 39–58.

75 For a discussion of the Aurora purchase, see Tucker, *Canadian Foreign Policy*, 143–74. On the politics of the F/A-18 procurement decision, see Atkinson and Nossal, "Bureaucratic Politics and the New Fighter Aircraft Decisions," 539.

76 DEA, *Canada's Export Development Plan for the Federal Republic of Germany*, 10; cost of the Leopard tank purchase from Leyton-Brown, "External Affairs and Defence," *Canadian Annual Review*, 1976, 359.

77 DEA document.

78 These sectors were automotive parts, computers and communications-related products, defence electronics/avionics, timber frame housing, manufactured wood products, fisheries products, sporting goods, apparel, co-operation with German firms in third countries, and industrial co-operation: DEA, *Canada's Export Development Plan for the Federal Republic of Germany.*

79 Interview with an Alberta government official who was involved in the meeting.

80 In October Schmidt was forced out of office by the defection of his junior coalition partner – the Free Democrats – and Helmut Kohl and the Christian Democrats took office.

81 DEA, *Canada's Export Development Plan for the Federal Republic of Germany*, 10.

82 While the export development plan was approved by a cabinet committee in 1983, it focused almost exclusively on trading relations and did not outline the integrated economic, political, and military strategy which was necessary.

CHAPTER SIX

1 Discussed in Eayrs, *In Defence of Canada: Growing Up Allied*, 207–11.

2 "United States, United Kingdom and Canadian Assurances," London Conference, 28 September–3 October 1954, *Foreign Relations of the United States 1952–54* (Washington: United States Government Printing Office 1983), vol. 5, 1351–2. Specifically, Canada gave no indication that its commitment to the North Atlantic alliance was in any way linked to a Canadian military presence in Europe. By contrast, the United States had made this linkage implicit while the British commitments had already been made explicitly in treaty form.

3 The defence budget was more than quadrupled between 1949 and 1952, jumping from $384.9 million in 1949/50 to $1971.2 million in 1952/3: Eayrs, *In Defence of Canada: Growing Up Allied*, 197.

4 Ibid., 212–15.

5 These were composed of eight weak divisions, two each from the United States, France, Britain, and Belgium.

6 "Das kanadische Verteidigungsprogramm 1953/54," German ambassador, Ottawa, to Foreign Office, Bonn, 13 November 1953, AA, 230–00/40, vol. 3.

7 Each of the original 12 squadrons had 16 aircraft. By the mid-1950s there were some 25 aircraft per squadron. In 1956, the air division re-equipped 4 of its squadrons with the CF-100s, with 18 aircraft per squadron. A top secret departmental memorandum from 1957 lists the air division's strength as some 200 F-86s in 8 squadrons and 72 CF-100s in 4 squadrons: "Memorandum for the Minister: Canadian Defence Programme," 17 September 1957, DND, DHist, Raymont Papers, #761.

8 For the briefing by Air Marshal W.A. Curtis on the Paris meeting, see Meeting of Chiefs of Staff Committee, 25 June 1951, DND, DHist.

9 Eayrs, *In Defence of Canada: Growing Up Allied*, 223.

10 Trade figures from "Notes on Germany Briefing Paper," 2 November 1956, NA, RG 25, vol. 186, 10,934–B–40; "Kanada's Stellung in der Welt und die deutsch-kanadische Beziehungen," in "Informations und Besprechungsmappe-Stattsbesuch des kanadischen Premierministers John G. Diefenbaker" [Briefing notes for Prime Minister Diefenbaker's November 1958 visit to the FRG], AA, 305 82.21.

11 For more detailed discussion, see Rempel, "The Canadian Army and the Commitment-Capability Gap: Central Europe, 1956–1961."

12 Canadian minister, Bonn, to DEA, 23 June 1950, DEA files, 50,173–40, pt. 1 (10,935–40).

13 For the outline of the Canadian proposal, see Memorandum for the Minister, 3 September 1954, and for the earlier proposals, "NATO, the EDC and Armament Control," memorandum for the minister, 16 July 1954, both in NA, RG 24, vol. 21066, file CSC 1224.1, pts. 1–3. For discussion of the Canadian ideas by the British Foreign Office and Imperial General Staff, see Mager, *Die Stationierung der britischen Rheinarmee: Grossbritanniens EVG-Alternative*, 102–3.

14 For further discussion, see Rempel "The Anglo-Saxon Powers and the German Rearmament Question."

15 Canada's permanent representative to the North Atlantic Council, Paris, to secretary of state for external affairs, 10 September 1954 (telegram 682), NA, RG 24, vol. 21066, file CSC 1224.1, vol. 1.

16 Ibid.

17 For Pearson's discussion of his role at the conference, including an account of pre-conference discussions with the French and British prime ministers, see *Mike*, vol. 2, 89–90.

18 Cited by Bercuson, "Allies or Occupiers?" 2–6.

19 Ibid.

20 Memorandum for the under-secretary, 3 October 1951, NA, RG 25, 86–87/160, file 11,381–40, vol. 1. A note on the memorandum indicates the meeting between DEA and DND officials took place on 4 October.

21 Supplementary Instructions, Simonds to Walsh, 6 November 1951, DND, DHist, Raymont Papers.

22 Cabinet Decision, 5 February 1952, NA, RG 24, vol. 17, 605.

23 Canadian ambassador, Bonn, to chancellor, FRG, 2 October 1951, NA, RG 24, vol. 17, 605.

24 Cited by Bercuson, "Allies or Occupiers?" 6–9.

25 Ibid., 9–18. Bercuson suggests that Claxton acted far beyond his own authority when, without consulting cabinet, he told Simonds, who was then in London, to tell General Eisenhower that unless the dispute was cleared up quickly, Canada might act unilaterally, either to keep the troops in Canada or to send the brigade under an arrangement made directly with the West German government.

26 Supplementary Instructions, Simonds to Walsh, 6 November 1951, DND, DHist, Raymont Papers.

27 Ibid.

28 These newspaper reports included: "Canadian Brigade at Its Own Expense: Breach in Occupation Policy," *Hamburg Abendblatt*, 1 November 1951; "Differences of Opinion Concerning a Canadian Brigade," *Frankfurter Allgemeine Zeitung*, 2 November 1951. The translations of these articles are in NA, RG 25, 86–87/160, file 11,381, vol. 3. Similar articles appeared in 1953 coinciding with the dispatch of the RCAF to Germany: for instance, "Wir sind keine Besatzungstruppe," *Frankfurter Rundschau*, 29 April 1953. The Canadian embassy also reported in October 1952 that a Social Democratic member of the Bundestag (Herr Hoecker) had held up the Canadian policy as one other allied states should emulate. Complaining about the past requisitioning of German property by the allies, Hoecker noted, to the "enthusiastic applause" of the Bundestag: "With a Canadian military formation I have an example that there is a non-European military power who can act differently. The 27th Canadian Infantry Brigade has given an excellent example in this connection ... The Canadian government said: if the Western European Nations come to hate the troops of their allies the whole North-Atlantic Defence Community will collapse ... I only wish that the American, the British and the French Governments would also take this point of view." Cited in communication of Canadian embassy, Bonn, to under-secretary of state for external affairs, 11 October 1952, NA, RG 25, 86–87/160, file 11,381–40, vol. 2.

29 German minister, Ottawa, to Foreign Office, Bonn, 25 May 1951, AA, III Länderabteilung, 230–00/40, vol. 1.

30 Canadian ambassador, Paris, to secretary of state for external affairs, Ottawa, 7 February 1952, NA, RG 25, 84–85/150, file 10,935–F–40, pt. 1.

31 German minister, Ottawa, to Foreign Office, Bonn, 28 April 1952, AA, 223–00/40 1951–1953, Abteilung 2.

32 Dankwort's assertion that Canada favoured full NATO membership for the Federal Republic was highlighted in the text sent from Ottawa to Bonn and also apparently by the reader of the report in Bonn. German minister, Ottawa, to Foreign Office, Bonn, 2 January 1953, AA, 211 Band 45, 91.20.

33 Chancellor, FRG, Bonn, to Canadian ambassador, Bonn, 14 November 1951, NA, RG 25, 86–87/160, file 11,381–40, vol. 2.

34 "General Review of Events in Germany," Canadian ambassador, Bonn, to secretary of state for external affairs, Ottawa, 6 August 1952, DEA files, 50,173–40, vol. 3 (10,935–40).

35 Memorandum for the minister, 3 September 1954, DEA files, 10,935–F–40, and memorandum for the minister, 16 July 1954, NA, RG 24, vol. 21066, file CSC 1224.1, pts. 1–3. The Germans themselves seem to have been unaware of the specifics of Canada's position in September 1954. The Canadian ambassador in Bonn at the time, Charles Ritchie, was called in by Herbert Blankenhorn, Adenauer's chief foreign policy adviser, to explain the comments Pearson had made in a speech a few days earlier. Pearson had called for the "association of

Germany" with NATO, and Blankenhorn wanted to know whether this phrase
in any way implied "that Canada envisaged Germany as a 'junior partner in
the Alliance.'" Canadian ambassador, Bonn, to secretary of state for external
affairs, Ottawa, 10 September 1954, NA, RG 24, vol. 21066, file CSC 1224.1, vol. 1.
Pearson's speech, delivered in Toronto on 7 September, is summarized in
Eayrs, *In Defence of Canada: Growing Up Allied*, 359.
36 Meeting of Chiefs of Staff Committee, 23 July 1959, DND, DHist.
37 See "Text of Part IV of the Final Act of London – Annex D of Memorandum
to the Cabinet," 18 October 1954, NA, RG 24, vol. 21066, CSC 1224.1, vol. 1.
38 Canada's commitment is summarized in the memorandum, "The Development of Nuclear Weapons for Canadian Forces in NATO (Europe)," no date
(c. 1962–3), DND, DHist, Raymont Papers, #625.
39 Foulkes (now retired) envisaged that eventually no Canadian troops would be
permanently based abroad: see his testimony before the Senate's Special Committee on National Defence, *Minutes of Proceedings and Evidence*, no. 15,
22 October 1963. For discussion of the mobile force concept, see Rempel, "Canadian Defence Policy and NATO's Northern Flank,' chapter 1.
40 Debate over the strengthening of the Canadian brigade and note of Speidel's
suggestion that it be expanded into a small division is found in Memorandum
of the Chief of the General Staff to the Chairman of the Chiefs of Staff, 12 February 1960, DND, DHist, Raymont Papers, #211. Discussion of SACEUR's proposals in 1960 for a greater Canadian effort is found in "Reply to NATO.
Questions on Forces in Europe; MC-70 Country Study," Privy Council files,
Cabinet Minutes, 22 March 1960. See also Meeting of Chiefs of Staff Committee, 22 March 1962, DND, DHist, and Memorandum for the Minister from the
Chief of the General Staff, 29 April 1963, DND, DHist, 112.1.009 (D38). Also
expanded discussion in Rempel, "The Canadian Army and the Commitment-
Capability Gap: Central Europe, 1956–1961."
41 Discussed in "Memorandum to the Defence Council: NATO Defence Ministers Briefing," Meeting of Defence Council, 18 May 1965, pt. 2, DND, DHist.
42 Summarized from ibid., and an attached document, "NATO Defence Planning
Committee – NATO Defence Planning – Draft Report to Ministers – Report
by the Defence Planning Working Group," 30 April 1965, 5–6.
43 "Memorandum to the Defence Council: NATO Defence Ministers Briefing,"
Meeting of Defence Council, 18 May 1965, pt. 2, DND, DHist.
44 Ibid.
45 Ibid., 3–6.
46 The air division had been run down from 144 aircraft to 108 through attrition.
Even so, options for as few as 72 and 92 aircraft had been mooted within the
department: Meeting of Chiefs of Staff Committee, 2 July 1964, DND, DHist;
Meeting of Defence Council, 26 June 1966, and "The Air Division – Future
Posture, 1965–64," memorandum for Defence Council, 6 April 1965, DND,
DHist.

47 During Hellyer's visit to Bonn in 1964, the German defence minister thanked Canada for leaving the mechanized brigade in the NATO front line: personal correspondence with Paul Hellyer.
48 DEA document.
49 Flanagan, *NATO's Conventional Defences*, 15. See also the testimony of the chief of the general staff, Lieutenant-General Geoffrey Walsh, in Canada, House of Commons, Special Committee on National Defence, *Minutes of Proceedings and Evidence*, no. 5, 11 July 1963, 129–44.
50 Bundesministerium der Verteidigung, *Weissbuch 1969: Zur Verteidigungspolitik der Bundesregierung*, 16–17, 19.
51 In 1969 eight priority areas were identified for improving conventional defences and in 1973 NATO's Defence Planning Committee decided to focus on improvements in six specific areas. See Flanagan, *NATO's Conventional Defences*, 20–1.
52 See Evraire, *Canada's NATO Brigade*. Half of the BAOR's smaller brigades were equipped only with 105-mm self-propelled guns and had no integral Honest John battery. Moreover, instead of five principal manoeuvre units as in 4 CMBG (armour, artillery, and three infantry), British brigades generally only had four battalion-sized units.
53 Memorandum to the cabinet, 9 June 1966, Meeting of Defence Council, 20 June 1966, DND, DHist.
54 The German ambassador in Ottawa reported to Bonn in March 1961 that Allard's appointment was important because he was a firm supporter of a continued Canadian military presence in the FRG and had stated this to several members of the embassy staff. "It is certainly in our interests," the ambassador argued, for Germans both inside and outside the military sphere to develop the closest contacts with Allard. He had himself personally offered the general his congratulations on his appointment. German ambassador, Ottawa, to Foreign Office, Bonn, 21 March 1961, AA, 301 91–20, vol. 3.
55 Healey criticized Canada both in the NATO meeting and privately: Rempel, "Canadian Defence Policy and NATO's Northern Flank"; interview, Léo Cadieux, 20 October 1986; and interview, Ross Campbell, 29 April 1987.
56 "Press Note Distributed by the British Information Service," 3 December 1969, in Gellner, *Canada in NATO*, 106; Ranger, "Defense," 248.
57 "Report on Defence Policy Review – Phase II," Privy Council files, Cabinet Minutes, 20 May 1969.
58 The M-113 was also acquired to equip lighter brigades in Canada but its air transportability was limited in practical terms.
59 While the F-5 Freedom Fighter was procured by both the Netherlands and Norway, the Canadian air force rejected the deployment of the CF-5 in Europe. The CF-5 was not an aircraft the air force had wanted. It had been procured because budget constraints prevented the acquisition of the more capable F-4 Phantom. The result was what the *Toronto Star* called the "most

irresponsible waste of public funds in Canadian peacetime history" with most of the aircraft going into storage immediately upon delivery. Deployment of the CF-5 in Europe is discussed in Meeting of Defence Council, 15 September 1969, DND, DHist, 81/609. See also Hellyer, *Damn the Torpedoes*, 130–2, and Porter, *In Retreat*, 102–4.

60 Meeting of Defence Council, 16 June 1969, DND, DHist.

61 Cited in Arsenault, "The DDH–280 Program," 127.

62 Privy Council files, Cabinet Minutes, 20 May 1969.

63 Meeting of Defence Council, 16 June 1969, DND, DHist. Either the costs of acquiring a full range of battlefield helicopters for 4 CMBG substantially increased in the months after June or the initial estimates presented to the Defence Council were far too low. Porter reports that in the early 1970s cabinet was presented with (and rejected) an option of purchasing battlefield helicopters which would have cost $400 million: *In Retreat*, 153.

64 See above, 47–55.

65 "Annex B: Lighter Equipped Forces for NATO" in "Force Structure – Mobile Command," memorandum to Defence Council, 11 January 1966, DND, DHist.

66 Privy Council files, Cabinet Minutes, 20 May 1969.

67 Privy Council files, Cabinet Minutes, 13 August 1969.

68 Figures cited in "Memorandum to the Cabinet: 1969/70 Defence Review," 29 April 1968, DND, DHist, 73/1223, file 770. See also ibid.

69 Privy Council files, Cabinet Minutes, 13 August 1969.

70 Meeting of Defence Council, 16 June 1969, DND, DHist.

71 Canada, House of Commons, *Debates*, 3 June 1969, 9327. These three brigades, grouped into a division under the German II Corps, had a rapid deployment and blocking mission in each of the German army's three corps. Elements from these brigades were also assigned to Allied Command Europe's mobile force for deployment on the NATO flanks. Since they lacked any armour they had little counterattack capability.

72 Privy Council files, Cabinet Minutes, 13 August 1969.

73 "NATO: Restriction of Defence Expenditures," memorandum to the prime minister, 16 November 1967, NA, RG 25, 20–1–2–GFR, vol. 4.

74 The chief of defence staff discussed this question with the prime minister in April 1969: Allard, *Memoirs*, 289–92.

75 Introduction Speech to the Purpose and Rationale of Defence Forces – CDS Special Conference, Kingston, Ontario, 29 August 1967, DND, DHist, 73/1223, file 769.

76 Sharp, *Which Reminds Me*, 175.

CHAPTER SEVEN

1 See Hahn, *Between Westpolitik and Ostpolitik*, 56.

2 Quoted in ibid., 68.

3 Ibid., 56, 68–9.
4 Confidential source.
5 DND, *Defence in the 70s*, 35.
6 "Land Forces Europe – Post 74," presentation to Defence Council, 26 January 1972, DND, DHist, 81/609. The cost for 131 Scorpion light tanks was set at $33.6 million, considerably below the cost of a new main battle tank.
7 Ibid.
8 "Army Structure Model," memorandum to chief of defence staff, 20 July 1979, DND, DHist, 81/609.
9 Interview, Colonel Rolf Klages, August 1991.
10 See discussion by Stewart, *Canada's European Force, 1971–1980*, 37–46, and Porter, *In Retreat*, 162.
11 Porter, *In Retreat*, 162. Dextraze apparently followed up the failure of this plan with a proposal to lease some 72 Leopard tanks after the Centurion was retired between 1974 and 1976. This option was at first rejected and then later superseded by the decision, after the Defence Structure Review, to purchase 128 Leopard Is for use in Europe. Porter sets the cost (quoted to the cabinet in 1972) of 160 Leopards at $55 million. However, a cabinet memorandum from November 1964 listed the current cost of a main-battle-tank programme (presumably to equip one brigade – as called for in the 1964 white paper) as $96 million. The cost of the 128 Leopards eventually purchased in 1976 was $187 million: figures for the envisaged tank purchase are from "Integrated Defence Program – 1967," Meeting of Defence Council, 12 July 1966, DND, DHist; figures for actual Leopard purchase from Leyton-Brown, "External Affairs and Defence," *Canadian Annual Review*, 1976, 359.
12 Interview. Richardson's ideas, which were apparently floated first as a substitute for the land force commitment and later as an augmentation of that commitment, are discussed in Stewart, *Canada's European Force, 1971–1980*, 47, 80–1.
13 DEA document.
14 Dropping the nuclear role actually produced savings for the land forces because there was no need to replace the Honest John rockets with the Lance surface-to-surface missiles as the other NATO allies were doing.
15 Granatstein and Bothwell (*Pirouette*, 29) argue that Canada's rhetorical support for NATO nuclear strategy had not changed and that its forces continued to serve as part of allied formations which could provide the Canadians with nuclear support; nevertheless Canada was the only alliance member in central Europe not to assign a portion of its forces to nuclear tasks.
16 Interview, John Anderson, January 1991.
17 See Rühl, "Die Vorwärtsverteidigung der NVA und der sowjetischen Streitkräfte in Deutschland bis 1990," 501–8. For a summary of Rühl's findings, see Rühl, "Offensive Defence in the Warsaw Pact," 442–50.
18 Information from interviews in the Federal Republic and Canada, 1990 and 1991.

19 Flanagan, *NATO's Conventional Defences*, 47–52. Later in the 1970s and 1980s, the French army was reorganized and the larger divisions were reconfigured into smaller, but more numerous, ones. As a result of this reorganization, the French II Corps deployed three divisions instead of two while the back-up corps in France was subdivided into two smaller corps.

20 DEA document.

21 Confidential sources.

22 Cited by Hahn, *Between Westpolitik and Ostpolitik*, 70.

23 DEA document.

24 Granatstein and Bothwell, *Pirouette*, 254, and interview at German II Corps headquarters, Ulm, 13 December 1990.

25 The German army's airborne brigades, while they seemed on the surface to be an exception, were assigned very specific missions within the larger German corps organizations.

26 Interview, Lieutenant-General Richard Evraire, December 1991. See also Evraire, *Canada's NATO Brigade*.

27 General Jacques Dextraze, "The Defence Structure Review and NATO," in Stewart, ed., *Canadian Defence Policy: Selected Documents*, 53–5; also Stewart, *Canada's European Force, 1971–1980*, 101–2. "Army Structure Model," memorandum to chief of defence staff, 20 July 1979, and "Land Forces Europe – Post 74," presentation to Defence Council, 26 January 1972, DND, DHist, 81/609.

28 "Army Structure Model," memorandum to chief of defence staff, 20 July 1979, DND, DHist, 81/609. The chief of defence staff had originally proposed that a third mechanized infantry battalion be provided for 4 CMBG as part of the fly-over commitment. This augmentation plan, which would have raised the war-time strength of 4 CMBG to 6600 men, was not adopted.

29 As part of this enhanced emphasis on NATO, the ceiling for Canada's forces in Europe was raised from 5000 to 5400 personnel. Likewise, early in 1977 the government decided to increase the current ceiling on armed forces personnel (78,800) by 4000 to 5000.

30 Similar problems, though on a much larger scale, would be faced by American units deploying by air to Europe.

31 Interview, Lieutenant-General Richard Evraire, December 1991.

32 Interview, Lieutenant-General Jack Dangerfield, 6 December 1991, and subsequent correspondence in 1995.

33 Several senior officers noted that the enthusiasm of the German II Corps for lending Canada Leopard tanks from its reserve stocks may have been motivated in part by a desire to influence future deployment options for 4 CMBG. Certainly, the Leopard purchase and other equipment acquisitions were influential in determining with which force a particular allied formation could most easily inter-operate. Interviews in Europe, November and December 1990 and December 1991.

34 The brigade had some 1000 dismounted infantrymen while German and American tank brigades had about 300–450 men and German and American

armoured infantry brigades some 600–750. Interviews; also German Ministry of Defence, *White Paper 1985*, 192 and 194; Rogers, "U.S. Army's Division 86," 19–20. Kenneth Macksey's book, *First Clash*, published with the support of DND provides good descriptions of the wartime capabilities of 4 CMBG.

35 Flanagan, *NATO's Conventional Defences*, 51–8.

36 Austria's forces were oriented primarily to territorial or partisan style defence. As such, its army fielded only one mechanized division designed to "cover" full mobilization and was not expected to hold up a Warsaw pact offensive against southern Germany for more than 24 hours. Interviews.

37 The scope of the military mission envisaged for the 4th Division led the Ministry of Defence to reinforce its strength with an extra mechanized brigade, assigned to the division in the early 1980s from the German territorial army. The 4th Division was thus one of only two "four-brigade divisions" in the German army.

38 Most information in this section was compiled in the autumn of 1990 and the autumn of 1991 in interviews at Brussels, CFB Lahr and Baden-Söllingen, and II Corps headquarters at Ulm.

39 Rühl, "Die Vorwärtsverteidigung der NVA und der sowjetischen Streitkräfte in Deutschland bis 1990," 505.

40 Interview, Lieutenant-General Richard Evraire, December 1991.

41 For the American Seventh Army in the CENTAG sector this meant that by the late 1980s sufficient equipment was pre-positioned in southern Germany for an additional two divisions and one armoured cavalry regiment. This brought the Seventh Army (composed of both the V and VII Corps) to a wartime strength of 7 mechanized and armoured divisions and 3 armoured cavalry regiments. The Wartime Host Nation Support agreement is discussed in the German Defence Ministry's *White Paper 1985* at 114–15. The role of the German territorial army in providing logistics support and rear-area security to the German field army and the allied corps is discussed in Munro, "The West German Territorial Army," 166–70.

42 Prior to the 1984 election, Mulroney had promised to increase defence spending by 4 per cent annually in real terms: Canada, House of Commons, *Debates*, 9 February 1984, 1219.

43 Whereas the Liberals had envisaged a 3-per-cent real increase in spending for 1984/5, the Conservative budget of November 1984 reduced this to 2.75 per cent and lowered appropriations even farther for 1985/6 to an increase of 2 per cent in real terms. Cited in Byers, *Canadian Security and Defence*, 43.

44 For further discussion on the commitment-capability dilemma, see Rempel, "Canada's Troop Deployment in Germany," 243 (note 22); Rempel, "Canadian Defence Policy and NATO's Northern Flank," 155–80; and Rempel, "The Canadian Commitment in Germany," 280–5.

45 Discussion of the political and military aspects of security on the northern flank is found in Rempel, *Strategic Change on NATO's Northern Flank*. Proposals for a northern defence orientation are summarized and discussed in Rempel, "Canadian Defence Policy and NATO's Northern Flank," 134–55.

46 This discussion of events associated with the Nielsen defence review in 1985 is largely based on interviews conducted in Canada and Germany in 1990 and 1991. Persons interviewed include General Gerard Thériault, Lieutenant-General Jack Dangerfield, John Anderson, Colonel Goetz Sperling, and Colonel Gerry Hirter. Another account of the 1985 review is Langille, *Changing the Guard*, 58–79.

47 As chairman of a government task force on spending priorities, Nielsen apparently advocated relatively dramatic reductions in domestic spending but after negative public reaction to the press leaks on potential cuts, cabinet support for such changes rapidly evaporated. Nielsen's standing within the cabinet dropped dramatically thereafter, culminating in his retirement from the cabinet in June 1986.

48 General Rogers had also argued in the past that the CAST brigade should be given priority in modernization over 4 CMBG. Confidential source.

49 Confidential source. In his memoirs, Gotlieb refers to the Nielsen visit without mentioning the specifics of its purpose. Of any initiatives presented to the Americans by government ministers or provincial governments without involving the embassy, Gotlieb writes: "federal ministers might seek têtes-à-têtes and adopt an independent line with their opposite members [*sic*] – for example, in the field of defence. Or, in addition to making unaccompanied calls in Washington, a minister might work in such secrecy (as was the case for Brian Mulroney's secrecy-obsessed minister of national defence, Erik Nielsen) as to make it impossible for the ambassador or the foreign ministry to know what stance he was actually taking during meetings on issues of the very highest order." Gotlieb, *'I'll be with you in a minute'*, 128.

50 Confidential source.

51 One senior Canadian official reported that, according to Nielsen, Heseltine had been very intense at their bilateral meeting and stated with some emotion: "I beg you Minister not to pursue that idea [proposed defence plan] further." Interviews. Field Marshal Bramall was already in Canada (en route to a NATO chiefs of staff conference in Banff, 12–15 September) at the time of Nielsen's visit to the United Kingdom and was telephoned by Heseltine who informed him of the substance of the Nielsen visit. Heseltine apparently told Bramall that he wanted to discuss the matter further once Bramall returned to London so that he could provide a substantive response to the Nielsen proposal. Confidential source.

52 DEA files. The strategic and political problems associated with a West German military role on the northern flank are discussed in Rempel, *Strategic Change on NATO's Northern Flank*, 40–7.

53 DEA files. Some discussion of Danson's review of the CAST role is found in Stewart, *Canada's European Force, 1971–1980*, 115; also Rempel, "Canadian Defence Policy and NATO's Northern Flank," 134–7.

54 Interview, Lieutenant-General Jack Dangerfield, 6 December 1991.

55 Interview.

56 Interviews.

57 See Kempling, "The Brave New Army," 31–9; also Rempel, "The Canadian Commitment in Germany," 285–9.

58 Confidential source.

59 DND, *Challenge and Commitment*.

60 Interview.

61 A senior Canadian officer at CENTAG in 1989, Colonel J.C. Lemieux, described this as a "sensitive" time in relations with the allies: interview, 31 October 1990.

62 Interview, Lieutenant-Colonel J.C Arbuckle, December 1990.

63 Interview, Lieutenant-General Brian Smith, autumn 1990.

64 Prior to 1991, Canada's CF-18s had been tasked to a primary offensive mission. On 1 January 1991, the tasking shifted to a primary air-defence emphasis. It remained so oriented until the withdrawal of Canadian fighters from Europe at the end of 1992. Interviews.

65 DEA document.

66 Canada, Senate, Sub-Committee on National Defence, *Manpower in Canada's Armed Forces*. The sub-committee recommended a phased increase of the forces in Europe from 5400 personnel to 10,000 by 1987.

CHAPTER EIGHT

1 DND, *Canadian Defence Policy*, 14. Development assistance bore 23.3 per cent of government spending cuts in 1989/90 and 17.3 per cent in 1990/1, In total, defence and foreign aid accounted for 60.5 per cent of the government's spending reductions in 1989/90 and 45.7 per cent in 1990/1. See Clarke, "Overseas Development Assistance: The Neo-Conservative Challenge"; also Treddenick, "The Defence Budget."

2 For information on the progression of Canadian and German defence spending as a percentage of GNP/GDP, see Appendix Five.

3 "Speech at Humber College on Canada and the New Europe," DEA, Statements and Speeches 90/9, 26 May 1990, 1–2.

4 Ibid., 2, 3.

5 Canada, Department of External Affairs and International Trade, *Annual Report 1990–1991*, 8.

6 See the discussion in Sokolsky, "Parting of the Waves?; also Jockel, *Security to the North*, 161–78.

7 For further discussion, see Rempel, "Canada's Troop Deployments in Germany: Twilight of a Forty-Year Presence?" 213–47.

8 Cited in "Genscher for 'New Quality in U.S.-European Ties,'" 1.

9 Interview, Thomas Delworth, April 1991.

10 Confidential sources. Also Paul Buteux, "Maintaining Link with Europe Key to Canada's Foreign Policy," *Financial Post* (Toronto), 14 January 1991.

11 See Huysman, "Airmobility in NATO," 45–50.
12 The Senate committee recommended an air-mobile brigade force posture based on a minimum of one air support battalion with "at least" one combat helicopter squadron with about 16 aircraft: Senate, Special Committee on National Defence, *Canada's Land Forces*, 67–9, 115–20, 131–3. See also Sharp, "Conventional Arms Control in Europe," 425.
13 Confidential sources.
14 Interview, Major-General Klaus Naumann, autumn 1990.
15 In the attack role then assigned to Canada's CF-18s in Germany, it was estimated by one senior Canadian officer that 60 to 65 per cent of training was conducted below the 300-metre level. In the air-defence role assumed by the CF-18s in January 1991, it was estimated that 15 per cent of training would need to be conducted below that level. For further discussion, see Rempel, "Canada's Troop Deployments in Germany: Twilight of a Forty-Year Presence?" 232–3.
16 Confidential sources.
17 "Decision Soon on Troops in Europe, McDougall Says," *Globe and Mail* (Toronto), 9 June 1991; "Retreat from Europe," *Ottawa Citizen*, 25 May 1991; "NATO Partners Would Back Closing Bases," *Globe and Mail* (Toronto), 31 May 1991; "Meaner and Leaner," *Maclean's*, 17 June 1991, 20–8.
18 Interview.
19 "New Defence Policy Expected in June," *Globe and Mail* (Toronto), 22 May 1991.
20 Confidential source. Mulroney's pledge was quoted in DND, *Statement of the Honourable Marcel Masse, September 17, 1991*.
21 DND, *Statement of the Honourable Marcel Masse, September 17, 1991*.
22 Confidential sources and correspondence with Thomas Delworth, October 1994.
23 Confidential source.
24 Cited in "Canadian Troop Pullout Upsets Allies in NATO," *Globe and Mail* (Toronto), 5 March 1992.
25 See, for instance, Létourneau and Roussel, "Le Canada et l'OTAN" and Haglund and Mager, "Bound to Leave?"
26 Interview.
27 "Canada's Pullout Frustrates NATO," *Winnipeg Free Press*, 27 February 1992.
28 Confidential source.
29 Confidential sources.
30 "Allies Urge Canada to Leave Troops in Europe," *Times* (London), 29 February 1992; "Canada Adamant on European Pull-Out" and Klepak, "Canada's Pull-Out May Mean More than Losing a Brigade," *Jane's Defence Weekly*, 11 April 1992, at 607 and 614 respectively; Cohen, "Security and NATO."
31 For a discussion of public and media reaction in Canada to the withdrawal decision, see Nossal, "Succumbing to the Dumbbell."

32 Karl Feldmeyer, "Abschied von Europa bis Ende 1994," *Frankfurter Allgemeine Zeitung*, 18 April 1992.

33 Thränert, "Eine gemeinsame Aussen- und Sicherheitspolitik für die EG – Chancen und Risken," 7–14. Thränert's arguments with respect to "Canadian-ization" picked up on a thesis first put forward by David Haglund: see, for instance, Haglund, "A Tale of Two 'Canadianizations,'" 69–76. See also Michael Stürmer, "Ein Ahornblatt im Wind," *Frankfurter Allgemeine Zeitung*, 18 July 1992, and Létourneau, "Kanada: Weg von der NATO?" 303–12.

34 German Ministry of Defence, *White Paper 1994*, 56–7.

35 Such views were expressed in France by, among others, President Mitterrand and Prime Minister Michel Rocard: see, for instance, Menon, "France," 204. See also Mitterrand's comments at the founding of the Euro-Corps in April 1992, cited in Rempel, "German Security Policy in the New European Order," 180.

CHAPTER NINE

1 Some of the arguments in this chapter were first put forward in an earlier arti-cle: Rempel, "German Security Policy in the New European Order."

2 In 1991–2 it was decided to establish a Franco-German Defence Council to complement the bilateral Security Council which had been created in the 1980s: see Foster, "The Franco-German Corps," 63–7.

3 See the article by the foreign minister, Klaus Kinkel: "Die Westeuropäische Union – eine Schicksalgemeinschaft," *Bulletin*, no. 59 (4 June 1992): 582–4.

4 French desires for a stronger European union were expressed to German offi-cials soon after the fall of the Berlin Wall in November: Teltschik, *329 Tage*, 26. An English account of unification diplomacy is found in Pond, *Beyond the Wall*.

5 Teltschik, *329 Tage*, 35–6.

6 The negotiations produced the Maastricht Treaty and with its entry into force late in 1993, the European Community changed its name to the European Union.

7 The movement to strengthen European defence co-operation was a continua-tion of a process begun in the early 1980s to strengthen the "European pillar" of the alliance and enhance military co-operation with France. Even before the collapse of the Soviet threat, strong Atlanticists like Helmut Schmidt had come to look favourably on the idea that a Franco-German alliance might be sufficient in and of itself to guarantee the security of central Europe.

8 Taft, "The NATO Role in Europe and the US Role in NATO," 14–19.

9 Confidential source. For an outline of the British position, see Weston, "Chal-lenges to NATO," 9–14.

10 For further discussion, see Rempel, *The European Security and Defence Identity and Nuclear Weapons*.

11 Garton Ash, *In Europe's Name*. This very thorough book addresses the history of the FRG's Ostpolitik from the Cold War era into the post–Cold War period and thus covers the main aspects of unification diplomacy as well.

12 *BBC Summary of World Broadcasts: Eastern Europe*, 4 March 1993, A2 (Hungary), 18 March 1993, A2 (Czechoslovakia), and 1 April 1993, A3 (Poland).

13 See Teltschik, *329 Tage*, 182; also German Information Service, "Genscher Proposes East-West Cooperative Security Structures."

14 For further discussion, see Rempel, *Alternatives to Nuclear Deterrence in the Post-Cold War Period*.

15 Kinkel, "NATO's Enduring Role in European Security," 3–7.

16 See Wettig, "Moscow's Perception of NATO's Role," 123–33. Divisions between Western countries and Moscow over the future role of NATO in eastern Europe and over Russia's visions of the future role of the CSCE emerged in December 1994 at the CSCE summit in Budapest. *Globe and Mail* (Toronto), 5 and 6 December 1994.

17 Social Democratic Party, *Protokoll: Parteitag Wiesbaden 16.-19. November 1993*, 987.

18 Ibid., 986.

19 The American ambassador expressed this view to Horst Teltschik, Chancellor Kohl's senior foreign policy adviser, as early as 16 November 1989 – one week after the fall of the Wall. Similarly, on 22 November, the United States secretary of state, James Baker, in a meeting with the German foreign minister, Hans-Dietrich Genscher, became the first allied foreign minister to support German unification without reservation, when he declared that reunification remained United States policy. This position was in marked contrast to the initial positions of both Britain and France which made their unease with the evolving policy of the Federal Republic very apparent through their statements (by Prime Minister Thatcher in particular) and actions (for example, President Mitterrand's December 1989 visit to East Germany). See Teltschik, *329 Tage*, 32–3, 48, 96, and 115–16; also Pond, *Beyond the Wall*, 153–224, especially 156–69.

20 In addition to the accounts of Teltschik and Pond (ibid.), see Alexander Moens' analysis of American policy: "American Diplomacy and German Unification," 531–45.

21 Helmut Kohl, "Die Zukunft der deutsch-amerikanischen Partnerschaft," *Bulletin*, no. 59 (4 June 1992): 577–82.

22 Interview with Klaus Kinkel, "Der Europäische Weg ist absolut alternativlos," *Süddeutsche Zeitung* (Munich), 19 May 1992.

23 Cited by Czempiel, "Ansätze und Perspektiven der Aussen- und Sicherheitspolitik der Europäischen Gemeinschaft," 28–9.

24 See "Die Nato im euro-atlantischen Formtief," *Neue Zürcher Zeitung*, 12/13 June 1993; also Rühe, "Europe and the Alliance," 12–15.

25 Interviews, Bonn, August 1993.

26 An unpublished paper by Senator Richard Lugar was the most notable example of congressional support for an expanded NATO: "NATO: Out of Area or Out of Business." On the evolution of American policy on expanded NATO membership, see: "NATO Favours U.S. Plan for Ties with the East, But Timing is Vague," *New York Times* (London), 22 October 1993; "War Games in Poland Proposed," *Washington Post*, 8 January 1994; and "Clinton Pledges Role in 'Broader Europe'," *Washington Post*, 10 January 1994.

27 See: "EC Seeks to End Paralysis on Bosnia," 21 June 1993, "Bonn Fights Back as Allies Try to Pin Blame for War," 22 June 1993, and "Kohl Retreats to Patch EC Bosnia Policy," 23 June 1993, all three articles in the *Times* (London).

28 A discussion of polls done in 1990–1 on the continued value of the American military presence in Germany is found in Asmus, "A Unified Germany," 89–92. Poll results from a Rand study done in 1991 are cited in "Die Mehrheit der Deutschen befürwortet den Abzug aller amerikanischen Truppen," *Frankfurter Allgemeine Zeitung*, 12 May 1992.

29 Excerpts from the ambassador's telegram were printed in both the *Süddeutsche Zeitung* (Munich) and (in greater detail) the *Financial Times* (London): "Cracks Are Appearing in the Alliance," 2 December 1994.

30 Ibid.

31 In 1993 the new Liberal government of Jean Chrétien changed the title of the Department of External Affairs to Foreign Affairs. For many Liberals this change was a declaratory assertion of Canada's distinct identity and independence, since it diluted the notion that Commonwealth states (most especially the United Kingdom) were anything but foreign countries.

32 "Address to the Parliamentary Debate on Canada's Foreign Policy Review," DEA, Statements and Speeches 94/11, 15 March 1994, 1.

33 Welch, "The New Multilateralism and Evolving Security Systems," 84.

34 German Ministry of Defence, *White Paper 1994*, 40–1.

35 Canada, Department of Foreign Affairs, *Canada in the World*, 2.

36 The most notable of these in 1994 was the *Canada 21* report (*Canada 21: Canada and Common Security in the Twenty-First Century*). Its findings were based on the views of a cross-section of Canadian political figures, former civil servants, former military officers, and academics. Beyond the emphasis on multilateral diplomacy and concentration on foreign development assistance, the study's basic recommendation in the defence sphere was that the Canadian Forces should be configured solely for peacekeeping and made available to the United Nations. In this sense, it reflected a fairly widespread view that beyond peacekeeping and certain peacetime sovereignty protection roles, the Canadian Forces in fact have little utility. In critiquing the report, one analyst noted that readers "will search in vain for realistic analysis of the prospects for security in the future ... or of the most plausible ways in which Canada can contribute to global security": Gray, *Canadians in a Dangerous World*, 31.

37 Canada, Parliament, Special Joint Committee Reviewing Canadian Foreign
Policy, *Canada's Foreign Policy: Principles and Priorities for the Future*, 2.
38 "Address to the 49th General Assembly of the United Nations," DEA, Statements and Speeches 94/55, 29 September 1994.
39 Canada, Parliament, Special Joint Committee Reviewing Canadian Foreign
Policy, *Canada's Foreign Policy: Principles and Priorities for the Future*, 30.
40 For an interesting discussion see, for instance, *Globe and Mail* (Toronto),
12 November 1994.
41 "Address to the Parliamentary Debate on Canada's Foreign Policy Review,"
DEA, Statements and Speeches 11, 15 March 1994; *Globe and Mail* (Toronto),
12 November 1994.
42 For a concise discussion of this point, see Buteux, "Sutherland Revisited," 5–9.
43 Figures from: Canada, Department of Finance, *Budget Plan 1996*, 36; Canada,
Parliament, Special Joint Committee Reviewing Canadian Foreign Policy,
Canada's Foreign Policy: Principles and Priorities for the Future, 58; Canada, Parliament, Special Joint Committee on Canada's Defence Policy, *Security in a
Changing World*, 27; *Globe and Mail* (Toronto), 12 November 1994.
44 "Address in the House of Commons on Canada's Role in Peacekeeping," DEA,
Statements and Speeches 94/52, 21 September 1994.
45 DND, *1994 Defence White Paper*, 27.
46 Ibid., 12–14.
47 Ibid., 36. The Norwegian commitment encompassed the pledge of an infantry
battalion group and included some military equipment (including artillery
and over-snow vehicles) pre-positioned in Norway, which will now be withdrawn.
48 Ibid., 46; Canada, Parliament, Special Joint Committee on Canada's Defence
Policy, *Security in a Changing World*, appendices, 17.
49 DND, *1994 Defence White Paper*, 12–13.
50 For a discussion of the requirements of the land forces, see *Committee of 13:
Report on the Review of Canadian Defense Policy*, 43–65.
51 "Huge Arms Purchase on Hold," *Globe and Mail* (Toronto), 26 July 1995. In
particular it appeared that the cabinet had decided to abandon the idea of purchasing four Upholder class submarines from the United Kingdom which will
mean that the Canadian navy will eventually have no sub-surface capability.
Coming just two years after the Chrétien government's politically driven and
ill-considered decision to cancel the EH-101 helicopter deal with Britain (and
Italy), this decision certainly did not raise Canada's standing or credibility in
British or European eyes. "Canada Could Lose Chance at Four Subs, Britain
Says," *Globe and Mail* (Toronto), 2 August 1995.
52 Canada, Department of Foreign Affairs, *Canada's Merchandise Trade (Imports
and Exports)*. By 1995/6, two-way trade had plummeted farther. Only 9 per
cent of Canada's imports came from the EU by that year while a mere 5 per
cent of exports went to that destination. Only 2 per cent of the EU's total

trade was now with Canada: *Globe and Mail* (Toronto), 26 June 1996. See also Ostry and Alexandroff, "The Challenge of Global Trade, Investment and Finance for Canada," 51–2.

53 In November 1994, Canada's ambassador to Germany warned that it was foolish for Canada to turn its back on Europe and Germany in favour of the "glamour markets" of Asia. He noted that a change in German investment by one decimal point would bring more wealth to Canada than would a tripling of trade with Vietnam. Cited in fall 1994 issue of *Perspectives on Canada and Germany* published by the German embassy in Ottawa.

54 Interviews, Ottawa and Bonn, 1990.

55 The official purpose of Canada's overseas development assistance is to "support sustainable development in developing countries" on the basis of the following programme priorities: basic human needs; women in development; infrastructure services; human rights, democracy, good governance; private sector development; and the environment. The focus of Canadian aid on regions of the world of the greatest political, economic, and strategic importance to Canada is nowhere to be found in this statement. See Canada, Department of Foreign Affairs, *Canada in the World*, 40–7.

56 Ostry and Alexandroff, "The Challenge of Global Trade, Investment and Finance for Canada," 55. Also Department of Finance figures for General Government Gross Financial Liabilities for the seven leading industrialized countries.

Bibliography

PRIMARY SOURCES

Canada

ARCHIVAL

Department of External Affairs (DEA)
  Classified documents accessed under the programme for academic research. Cited
    simply as DEA document.
  Declassified documents, in particular the 50,000 series – Relations with the Federal
    Republic of Germany to 1963.
Department of National Defence (DND), Directorate of History (DHist) files, in
  particular:
  Meetings of the Chiefs of Staff Committee (to 1964)
  Meetings of the Defence Council (1964–1972)
  Raymont Papers
National Archives of Canada (NA)
  Record Group (RG) 2, Privy Council Office: Cabinet Minutes, Cabinet Defence
    Committee Minutes, 1945–1960
  Record Group (RG) 24, Department of National Defence
  Record Group (RG) 25, Department of External Affairs, files relating to Canada's
    European policy and relations with Germany
Privy Council Office files, Cabinet Minutes, 1960–1971

PUBLISHED
Department of External Affairs. *Annual Report 1989/90*. Ottawa 1990.

- *Canada's Export Development Plan for the Federal Republic of Germany*. Ottawa, October 1983.
- *Foreign Policy for Canadians*. Ottawa 1970.
- Statements and Speeches. 1990–4.

Department of External Affairs and International Trade. *Annual Report 1990–1991*. Ottawa 1991.

Department of Finance. *Budget Plan 1995*. Ottawa, February 27, 1995.

Department of Foreign Affairs. *Canada in the World*. Ottawa 1994.

Department of Foreign Affairs, Policy Staff. *Canada's Merchandise Trade (Imports and Exports)*. Ottawa, June 1995.

Department of National Defence. *Canadian Defence Policy*. Ottawa, April 1992.
- *Challenge and Commitment: A Defence Policy for Canada*. Ottawa 1987.
- *Defence Canada 80*. Ottawa 1981.
- *Defence in the 70s: White Paper on Defence*. Ottawa 1971.
- *EIS: Military Flight Training*. Vol. 1. Ottawa, January 1994.
- *1994 Defence White Paper*. Ottawa 1994.
- *The Socio-Economic Impacts of Allied Training in Canada*. Operational Research and Analysis Report 614. Ottawa, August 1993.
- *Statement by the Honourable Marcel Masse, September 17, 1991*. Ottawa 1991.
- *White Paper on Defence – March 1964*. Ottawa 1964.

House of Commons. Special Committee on National Defence, *Minutes of Proceedings and Evidence*, 1963–1965.

Parliament. Special Joint Committee of the Senate and the House of Commons on Canada's Defence Policy. *Security in a Changing World*. Ottawa 1994.
- Special Joint Committee Reviewing Canadian Foreign Policy. *Canada's Foreign Policy: Principles and Priorities for the Future*. Ottawa 1994.

Senate. Special Committee on National Defence. *Canada's Land Forces*. Ottawa 1989.
- Sub-Committee on National Defence. *Manpower in Canada's Armed Forces*. Ottawa 1982.

Federal Republic of Germany

ARCHIVAL

Bundesarchiv, Militärischen-Abteilung [Federal Archives, Military Division], Freiburg: German-Canadian relations to 1962

Politischen Archiv, Auswärtiges Amt (AA) [Political Archives, Foreign Office], Bonn: relations with Canada to 1962; Canadian relations with NATO to 1962

PUBLISHED

The Basic Law of the Federal Republic of Germany. Wolfenbüttel, Germany: Roco Druck 1989.

Bundesministerium der Verteidigung. *Weissbuch 1969: Zur Verteidigungspolitik der Bundesrepublik*. Bonn: Presse- und Informationsamt der Bundesregierung 1969.

- *Weissbuch 1970: Zur Sicherheit der Bundesrepublik Deutschland und zur Lage der Bundeswehr.* Bonn: Presse- und Informationsamt der Bundesregierung 1970.
Bulletin. Bonn: Presse- und Informationsamt der Bundesregierung, 1955–1992.
Federal Ministry of Defence. *White Paper 1985: The Situation and the Development of the Federal Armed Forces.* Bonn: Federal Republic Publications 1985.
- *White Paper 1994.* Bonn: Federal Ministry of Defence 1994.
German Army Training Establishment Shilo (GATES). *10 Years: German Soldiers in Shilo, 1973–1983.* CFB Shilo: GATES Information Booklet 1983.
Kommentarübersicht. Bonn: Presse- und Informationsamt der Bundesregierung.
Perspectives on Canada and Germany. Ottawa: German Embassy 1994–1995.

SECONDARY SOURCES

Allard, Jean. *Memoirs of General Jean Allard.* Vancouver: University of British Columbia Press 1988.
Aron, Raymond. *Peace and War: A Theory of International Relations.* London: Weidenfeld & Nicolson 1966.
Arsenault, J.W. "The DDH-280 Program: A Case Study of Governmental Expenditure Decision-Making." In David Haglund, ed. *Canada's Defence Industrial Base.* Kingston ON: Ronald P. Frye 1988. Pp. 118–36.
Asmus, Ronald. "Germany and America: Partners in Leadership." *Survival* 23 (November/December 1991): 546–66.
- "A Unified Germany." In Robert A. Levine, ed., *Transition and Turmoil in the Atlantic Alliance.* New York: Crane Russak 1992.
Atkinson, Michael, and Kim Richard Nossal. "Bureaucratic Politics and the New Fighter Aircraft Decisions." *Canadian Public Administration* 24 (winter 1981): 531–58.
Bandulet, Bruno. *Adenauer zwischen West und Ost: Alternativen der deutschen Aussenpolitik.* München: Weltforum-Verlags 1970.
Bark, Dennis, and David Gress. *A History of West Germany.* I: *From Shadow to Substance 1945–1963.* II: *Democracy and Its Discontents 1963–1988.* Oxford: Basil Blackwell 1989.
Barre, Raymond. "The 1987 Alistair Buchan Memorial Lecture." *Survival* 29 (July-August 1987): 291–300.
Bercuson, David. "Allies or Occupiers?: The Canadian Forces in Germany." Paper delivered to the Canadian Historical Association, Quebec City, June 1989.
Bland, Douglas. *The Administration of Defence Policy in Canada, 1947–1985.* Kingston ON: Ronald P. Frye 1987.
Bleek, Wilhelm. "Die bundesdeutsche-kanadische Krise 1969–1975." In Josef Becker and Rainer-Olaf Schutze, eds. *Im Spannungsfeld des Atlantischen Dreiecks: Kanadas Aussenpolitik nach dem Zweiten Weltkrieg.* Bochum: N. Brockmeyer 1989.
Bluth, Christoph. "SDI: The Challenge to West Germany." *International Affairs* 62 (spring 1986): 247–64.

Boyd, Frank L., Jr. "The Politics of Canadian Defence Procurement: The New Fighter Aircraft Decision." In David Haglund, ed. *Canada's Defence Industrial Base.* Kingston ON: Ronald P. Frye 1988. Pp. 137–58.

Brandt, Willy. "German Foreign Policy." *Survival* 11 (November 1969): 370–2.

– *A Peace Policy for Europe.* New York: Holt, Rinehart and Winston 1969.

British Broadcasting Corporation. *Summary of World Broadcasts: Eastern Europe,* 1990–1993.

Bull, Hedley. *The Anarchical Society: A Study of Order in World Politics.* London: Macmillan 1977.

Burns, E.L.M. *A Seat at the Table.* Toronto: Clarke, Irwin 1972.

Buteux, Paul. "NATO and the Evolution of Canadian Defence and Foreign Policy." In David B. Dewitt and David Leyton-Brown, eds. *Canada's International Security Policy.* Scarborough: Prentice-Hall Canada 1995. Pp. 153–70.

– *The Politics of Nuclear Consultation in NATO, 1965–1980.* Cambridge: Cambridge University Press 1983.

– "Sutherland Revisited: Canada's Long-Term Strategic Situation." *Canadian Defence Quarterly* 23 (September 1994): 5–9.

Byers, R.B. *Canadian Security and Defence: The Legacy and the Challenges.* London: International Institute of Strategic Studies, winter 1985.

– "Defence and Foreign Policy in the 1970s: The Demise of the Trudeau Doctrine." *International Journal* 33 (spring 1978): 312–38.

– "External Affairs and Defence." In *Canadian Annual Review for 1971.* Toronto: University of Toronto Press 1972.

Canada 21 Council. *Canada 21: Canada and Common Security in the Twenty-First Century.* Toronto: Centre for International Studies, University of Toronto, 1994.

Clarke, Robert E. "Overseas Development Assistance: The Neo-Conservative Challenge." In Maureen Appel Molot and Fen Osler Hampson, eds. *Canada among Nations 1989: The Challenge of Change.* Ottawa: Carleton University Press 1990. Pp. 193–206.

Clarkson, Stephen. *Canada and the Reagan Challenge.* Toronto: James Lorimer 1985.

Cohen, Andrew. "Security and NATO." In Fen Osler Hampson and Christopher Maule, *Canada among Nations 1993–94: Global Jeopardy.* Ottawa: Carleton University Press 1994. Pp. 251–65.

Committee of 13. *Committee of 13: Report on the Review of Canadian Defense Policy.* Quebec: Centre Québécois de relations internationales, Université Laval, 1994.

Crane, Brian. *An Introduction to Canadian Defence Policy.* Toronto: Canadian Institute of International Affairs 1964.

Czempiel, Ernst-Otto. "Ansätze und Perspektiven der Aussen- und Sicherheitspolitik der Europäischen Gemeinschaft." In Oliver Thränert, ed. *Die EG auf dem Weg zu einer gemeinsamen Aussen- und Sicherheitspolitik.* Bonn: Friedrich Ebert Stiftung, January 1993.

Dahrendorf, Ralf. *Society and Democracy in Germany.* New York: Anchor Books 1969.

Dalma, Alfons. "The Risks of a Détente Policy to Central Europe." In Arnold Wolfers, ed. *Changing East-West Relations and the Unity of the West*. Baltimore MD: Johns Hopkins University Press 1964.

Dewitt, David, and John Kirton. *Canada as a Principal Power: A Study in Foreign Policy and International Relations*. Toronto: John Wiley 1983.

Direction of Trade Statistics Yearbook 1982. Washington DC: International Monetary Fund 1982.

Donneur, André P. "La fin de la guerre froide, le Canada et la sécurité européenne." *Études Internationales* 23 (March 1992): 169–80.

Duchêne, François. *Beyond Alliance*. Paris: The Atlantic Institute 1965.

Eayrs, James. "Future Roles of the Armed Forces of Canada." *Behind the Headlines* 28 (April 1969).

– *In Defence of Canada: Growing Up Allied*. Toronto: University of Toronto Press 1980.

Eden, Anthony. *Full Circle*. Boston: Houghton Mifflin 1960.

Eustace, Marilyn. *Canada's European Force, 1964–1971: Canada's Commitment to Europe*. Kingston ON: Centre for International Affairs, Queen's University, 1982.

Evraire, Richard. *Canada's NATO Brigade: A History*. Lahr: Moritz Schauenburg 1983.

Ferraris, Luigi Vittorio, ed. *Report on a Negotiation: Helsinki-Geneva-Helsinki: 1972–1975*. Alphen aan den Rijn: Sijthoff & Noordhoff 1979.

Fischer, Beth A. "The Trudeau Peace Initiative and the End of the Cold War: Catalyst or Coincidence?" *International Journal* 49 (summer 1994): 613–34.

Flanagan, Stephen. *NATO's Conventional Defences: Options for the Central Region*. London: Macmillan 1988.

Foster, Edward. "The Franco-German Corps: A 'Theological' Debate?" *RUSI Journal* 137 (August 1992): 63–7.

Frost, Ellen, and Angela Stent. "NATO's Troubles with East-West Trade." *International Security* 8 (summer 1983): 179–200.

Garton Ash, Timothy. *In Europe's Name: Germany and the Divided Continent*. New York: Random House 1993.

Gates, David. "Area Defence Concepts: The West German Debate." *Survival* 28 (July/August 1986): 322–36.

Gellner, John. *Canada in NATO*. Toronto: Ryerson Press 1970.

Genscher, Hans-Dietrich. *Aussenpolitik: Im Dienste von Sicherheit und Freiheit*. Stuttgart: Verlag Bonn Aktuell 1976.

"Genscher for 'New Quality in U.S.-European Ties.'" *The Week in Germany* (German Information Center, New York), 6 April 1990.

Glazebrook, George P. deT. "The Middle Powers in the United Nations' System." *International Organization* 1 (June 1947): 307–15.

Gnesotto, Nicole. "Die französischen Parteien und die sicherheitspolitische Zusammenarbeit mit der Bundesrepublik Deutschland." In Karl Kaiser and Pierre Lellouche, eds. *Deutsch-französische Sicherheitspolitik auf dem Weg zur Gemeinsamkeit?* Bonn: Europe Union Verlag 1986. Pp. 57–67.

Gotlieb, Allan. *Canada and the Economic Summits: Power and Responsibility*. Toronto: Centre for International Studies 1987.

– *'I'll be with you in a minute Mr. Ambassador': The Education of a Canadian Diplomat in Washington*. Toronto: University of Toronto Press 1991.

Granatstein, J.L., and Robert Bothwell. *Pirouette: Pierre Trudeau and Canadian Foreign Policy*. Toronto: University of Toronto Press 1990.

Gray, Colin S. *Canadian Defence Priorities: A Question of Relevance*. Toronto: Clarke Irwin 1972.

– *Canadians in a Dangerous World*. Toronto: The Atlantic Council of Canada 1994.

Grosser, Alfred. *Deutschlandbilanz: Geschichte Deutschlands seit 1945*. Munich: Carl Hanser Verlag 1970.

Hahn, Walter. *Between Westpolitik and Ostpolitik: Changing West German Security Views*. Beverly Hills: Sage 1975.

Haglund, David. "A Tale of Two 'Canadianizations': Some North American Perspectives on Transatlantic Relations." In Oliver Thränert, ed. *Transatlantic Relations in Transition*. Bonn: Friedrich Ebert Stiftung, January 1993. Pp. 69–76.

Haglund, David, and Olaf Mager. "Bound to Leave? The Future of the Allied Stationing Regime in Germany." *Canadian Defence Quarterly* 21 (February 1992): 35–43.

– eds. *Homeward Bound?: Allied Forces in the New Germany*. Boulder CO: Westview 1992.

Hanrieder, Wolfram. *Germany, America, Europe: Forty Years of German Foreign Policy*. New Haven CT: Yale University Press 1989.

– ed. *Helmut Schmidt: Perspectives on Politics*. Boulder CO: Westview 1982.

Hausen, Wulf. "Überlegung zum Aufklärungsdrohnensystem CL-289." *Wehrtechnik*, no. 1 (1992): 9–11.

Hawes, Michael. *Principal Power, Middle Power or Satellite? Competing Perspectives on the Study of Canadian Foreign Policy*. Toronto: Research Programme in Strategic Studies, York University, 1984.

Head, Ivan, and Pierre Trudeau. *The Canadian Way: Shaping Canada's Foreign Policy, 1968–1984*. Toronto: McClelland & Stewart 1995.

Hellyer, Paul. *Damn the Torpedoes: My Struggle to Unify Canada's Armed Forces*. Toronto: McClelland & Stewart 1990.

Hill, Roger. *Political Consultation in NATO*. Toronto: Canadian Institute of International Affairs 1978.

Hillmer, Norman, and Garth Stevenson, eds. *Foremost Nation: Canadian Foreign Policy in a Changing World*. Toronto: McClelland & Stewart 1977.

Hockin, Tom. "External Affairs and Defence." In *Canadian Annual Review for 1966*. Toronto: University of Toronto Press 1967.

Hoffmann, Stanley. *Janus and Minerva*. Boulder CO: Westview 1987.

Holmes, John. *The Shaping of Peace: Canada and the Search for a New World Order, 1943–1957*. Vol. 2. Toronto: University of Toronto Press 1982.

Holsti, Kalevi J. "Who Got What and How: The CSCE Negotiations in Retrospect." In Robert Spencer, ed. *Canada and the Conference on Security and Co-operation in Europe*. Toronto: Centre for International Studies, University of Toronto, 1984.

Holsti, Ole, P.T. Hopmann, and John Sullivan. *Unity and Disintegration in International Alliances*. New York: John Wiley 1973.

Huysman, Pieter. "Airmobility in NATO: The New MND(C)," *RUSI Journal* 139 (April 1994): 45–50.

Iggers, George. *The German Conception of History: The National Tradition of Historical Thought from Herder to the Present*. Scranton PA: Wesleyan University Press 1983.

James, Harold. "The Roots of the German Identity." *Encounter* 72 (January 1989): 23–33.

Jane's All The World's Aircraft for the years 1963–1964, 1992–93, and 1994–95. London: Jane's Publishing 1963, 1992, 1994.

Jesse, Ekhard. "The German Question: Anglo-American, French and West German Perspectives." *West European Politics* 12 (April 1989): 143–50.

Jockel, Joseph. *Security to the North: Canada-U.S Defense Relations in the 1990s*. East Lansing: Michigan State University Press 1991.

Jockel, Joseph T., and Joel J. Sokolsky. "Dandurand Revisited: Rethinking Canada's Defence Policy in an Unstable World." *International Journal* 48 (spring 1993): 380–401.

Joffe, Josef. *The Limited Partnership: Europe, the United States and the Burdens of the Alliance*. Cambridge MA: Ballinger 1987.

Kaiser, Karl. "Die deutsch-amerikanischen Sicherheits-beziehungen in Europa nach dem kalten Krieg." *Europa-Archiv*, no. 1 (1992): 7–17.

– *German Foreign Policy in Transition: Bonn between East and West*. London: Oxford University Press 1969.

Kelleher, Catherine. "The Federal Republic of Germany." In Douglas Murray and Paul Viotti, eds., *The Defense Policies of Nations: A Comparative Study*. Baltimore MD: Johns Hopkins University Press 1989.

Kempling, S.H. "The Brave New Army: The Militia of 2002." *Canadian Defence Quarterly* 17 (winter 1987–8): 31–9.

Keating, Tom, and Larry Pratt. *Canada, NATO and the Bomb: The Western Alliance in Crisis*. Edmonton: Hurtig 1988.

Kinkel, Klaus. "NATO's Enduring Role in European Security." *NATO Review* 40 (October 1992): 3–7.

Kissinger, Henry. *Diplomacy*. New York: Simon and Schuster 1994.

Klepak, Harold. "Canada's Pull-Out May Mean More than Losing a Brigade." *Jane's Defence Weekly*, 11 April 1992: 614.

Kolboom, Ingo. "Im Westen nichts Neues? Frankreichs Sicherheitspolitik, das deutsch-französische Verhältnis und die Deutsche Frage." In Karl Kaiser and Pierre Lellouche, eds., *Deutsch-französische Sicherheitspolitik auf dem Weg zur Gemeinsamkeit?* Bonn: Europe Union Verlag 1986. Pp. 68–89.

Kovrig, Bennett. "'European Security' in East-West Relations: The History of a Diplomatic Encounter." In Robert Spencer, ed. *Canada and the Conference on Security and Co-operation in Europe*. Toronto: Centre for International Studies, University of Toronto, 1984.

Kronenberg, Vernon. *All Together Now: The Organization of the Department of National Defence in Canada*. Toronto: Canadian Institute of International Affairs 1973.

Langille, Howard Peter. *Changing the Guard: Canada's Defence in a World of Transition*. Toronto: University of Toronto Press 1990.

Laux, Jeanne Kirk. "Human Contacts, Information, Culture, and Education." In Robert Spencer, ed. *Canada and the Conference on Security and Co-operation in Europe*. Toronto: Centre for International Studies, University of Toronto, 1984.

Legault, Albert, and Michel Fortmann. *A Diplomacy of Hope: Canada and Disarmament, 1945–1988*. Kingston & Montreal: McGill-Queen's University Press 1992.

Létourneau, Paul. "Kanada: Weg von der NATO?" *Europa-Archiv* 47 (10 June 1992): 303–12.

– "La révision de la politique de défense canadienne." *Études Internationales* 19 (June 1988): 345–55.

Létourneau, Paul, and Stéphane Roussel. "Le Canada et l'OTAN: le seuil de découplage a-t-il été franchi?" *Canadian Defence Quarterly* 21 (February 1992): 29–34.

Leyton-Brown, David. "External Affairs and Defence." *Canadian Annual Review* for the years 1976, 1977, and 1980. Toronto: University of Toronto Press 1977, 1979, 1982.

Lowenthal, Richard. "The German Question Transformed." *Foreign Affairs* 63 (winter 1984): 303–15.

Lyon, Peyton. "Canada at Geneva, 1973–5." In Robert Spencer, ed. *Canada and the Conference on Security and Co-operation in Europe*. Toronto: Centre for International Studies, University of Toronto, 1984.

– "The Trudeau Doctrine." *International Journal* 26 (winter 1970–1): 19–37.

Liska, George. *Nations in Alliance: The Limits of Interdependence*. Baltimore MD: Johns Hopkins University Press 1968.

Mackness, William. *Big Government and the Constitution Crisis*. Toronto: Mackenzie Institute 1991.

Macksey, Kenneth. *First Clash: Combat Close Up in World War Three*. Toronto: Stoddart 1985.

McLin, Jon B. *Canada's Changing Defense Policy 1957–1963: The Problems of a Middle Power in Alliance*. Baltimore MD: Johns Hopkins University Press 1967.

Mager, Olaf. *Die Stationierung der britischen Rheinarmee: Grossbritanniens EVG-Alternative*. Baden-Baden: Nomos Verlagsgesellschaft 1990.

Marshall, C.J. "Canada's Forces Take Stock in Defence Structure Review." *International Perspectives* (January/February 1976): 26–30.

Meinecke, Friedrich. *The German Catastrophe*. Cambridge MA: Harvard University Press 1950.

Menon, Anand. "France." In Alexander Moens and Christopher Anstis, eds. *Disconcerted Europe: The Search for a New Security Architecture*. Boulder CO: Westview 1994.

Middlemiss, D.W., and Joel J. Sokolsky. *Canadian Defence: Decisions and Determinants*. Toronto: Harcourt Brace Jovanovich 1989.

Mitrany, David. *A Working Peace System: An Argument for the Functional Development of International Organization*. London: Oxford University Press 1943.

Moens, Alexander. "American Diplomacy and German Unification." *Survival* 23 (November/December 1991): 531–45.

Morgan, Roger. *West Germany's Foreign Policy Agenda*. Georgetown: Center for Strategic and International Studies 1978.

Morgenthau, Hans. *Politics among Nations*. 3rd edition. New York: Alfred A. Knopf 1963.

Munro, Neil. "The West German Territorial Army." *Armed Forces* 6 (April 1987): 166–70.

Munson, Kenneth. *World Unmanned Aircraft*. London: Jane's Publishing 1988.

Nerlich, Uwe. "Washington and Bonn: Evolutionary Patterns in the Relations between the United States and the Federal Republic of Germany." In Karl Kaiser and Hans-Peter Schwarz, eds. *America and Western Europe: Problems and Prospects*. Lexington MA: D.C. Heath 1978.

Nossal, Kim Richard. *The Politics of Canadian Foreign Policy*. Toronto: Prentice-Hall Canada 1989.

– "Succumbing to the Dumbbell: Canadian Perspectives on NATO in the 1990s." In Barbara McDougall et al. *Canada and NATO: The Forgotten Ally?* Washington DC: Brassey's 1992. Pp. 17–32.

Ørvik, Nils, ed. *Semi-Alignment and Western Security*. New York: St Martin's Press 1986.

Ostry, Sylvia, and Alan Alexandroff. "The Challenge of Global Trade, Investment and Finance for Canada." In Canada, Parliament, Special Joint Committee Reviewing Canada's Foreign Policy, *Canada's Foreign Policy: Position Papers*. Ottawa 1994.

"Panzersoldaten in Kanada." *Wehrtechnik*, no. 1 (1984): 86–8.

Painchaud, Paul, ed. *De Mackenzie King à Pierre Trudeau: quarante ans de diplomatie canadienne 1945–1985*. Quebec: Les Presses de l'université Laval 1989.

Payne, Keith, and Michael Rühle. "The Future of the Alliance: Emerging German Views." *Strategic Review* 19 (winter 1991): 37–45.

Pearson, Lester B. *Democracy in World Politics*. Toronto: Saunders 1955.

– *Mike: The Memoirs of the Rt. Hon. L.B. Pearson*. Vols. 1 & 2. Toronto: University of Toronto Press 1972 and 1973.

– *Peace in the Family of Man: The Reith Lectures*. Toronto: Oxford University Press 1969.

Pentland, Charles. "L'option européenne du Canada dans les années 80." *Études Internationales* 14 (March 1983): 39–58.

Pond, Elizabeth. *Beyond the Wall: Germany's Road to Unification*. New York: The Brookings Institution 1993.

- "The Security Debate in West Germany." *Survival* 28 (July/August 1986): 322–36.

Porter, Gerald. *In Retreat: The Canadian Forces in the Trudeau Years.* Toronto: Deneau and Greenberg 1979.

Prittie, Terence. *Konrad Adenauer 1876–1967.* Chicago: Cowles 1971.

Preston, Richard. "Military Influence on the Development of Canada." In H.J. Massey, ed. *The Canadian Military: A Profile.* Toronto: Copp Clark 1972. Pp. 49–86.

Ranger, Robin. "Defense." In *Britannica Book of the Year, 1970.* Chicago: University of Chicago Press 1971.

Rattinger, Hans. "MBFR-Stagnation und weitere Aussichten." *Aussenpolitik* 30 (3/1979): 331–43.

Rautenberg, Hans-Jürgen, and Norbert Wiggershaus. *Die Himmeroder Denkschrift vom Oktober 1950: politische und militärische Überlegungen für einen Beitrag der Bundesrepublik Deutschland zur westeuropäischen Verteidigung.* Karlsruhe: G. Braun 1985.

Reford, Robert. *Canada and Three Crises.* Toronto: Canadian Institute of International Affairs 1968.

Reid, Escott. *Radical Mandarin: The Memoirs of Escott Reid.* Toronto: University of Toronto Press 1989.

- *Time of Fear and Hope: The Making of the North Atlantic Treaty, 1947–1949.* Toronto: McClelland & Stewart 1977.

Rempel, Roy. *Alternatives to Nuclear Deterrence in the Post–Cold War Period: The Implications for Europe.* Winnipeg: Centre for Defence and Security Studies, University of Manitoba, August 1994.

- "The Anglo-Saxon Powers and the German Rearmament Question." Unpublished paper presented to the Society for Historians of American Foreign Relations, Bentley College, Waltham, Massachusetts, June 1994.

- "Canada, Germany and Alliance Relations in the Crisis Years of 1958–61: A Study in the Nature of Alliance Politics." *Militärgeschichtliche Mitteilungen* 53 (1994): 85–100.

- "Canada's Troop Deployment in Germany: Twilight of a Forty-Year Presence?" In David Haglund and Olaf Mager, eds. *Homeward Bound?: Allied Forces in the New Germany.* Boulder CO: Westview 1992. Pp. 213–47.

- "The Canadian Army and the Commitment-Capability Gap: Central Europe, 1956–1961." *Canadian Defence Quarterly* 25 (September 1995): 22–6.

- "The Canadian Commitment in Germany." In Michael K. Hawes and Joel J. Sokolsky, eds. *North American Perspectives on European Security.* Lewiston & Queenston: Edwin Mellen Press 1989.

- "Canadian Defence Policy and NATO's Northern Flank." Master's thesis, University of Manitoba, 1987.

- *The European Security and Defence Identity and Nuclear Weapons.* Winnipeg: Centre for Defence and Security Studies, University of Manitoba, October 1995.

- "German Security Policy in the New European Order." In Alexander Moens and Christopher Anstis, eds. *Disconcerted Europe: The Search for a New Security Architecture.* Boulder CO: Westview 1994. Pp. 159–96.

– *The Meaning of the German Question in the New Europe.* Winnipeg: Centre for Defence and Security Studies, University of Manitoba, 1993.
– "The Need for a Canadian Security Policy." *Canadian Defence Quarterly,* 19 (April 1990): 38–42.
– *Strategic Change on NATO's Northern Flank: The Dilemma for the Nordic States and NATO.* Winnipeg: Program of Strategic Studies, University of Manitoba, May 1988.
Richardson, James. *Germany and the Atlantic Alliance: The Interaction of Strategy and Politics.* Cambridge MA: Harvard University Press 1966.
Rogers, Pat. "U.S. Army's Division 86." In *Combat: War and Weapons 1986.* New York: Modern Day Periodicals 1986. Pp. 19–20.
Ross, Douglas, and Frank Langdon. "Towards a Canadian Maritime Strategy in the North Pacific Region." *International Journal* 42 (autumn 1987): 848–89.
Rothstein, Robert. *Alliances and Small Powers.* New York: Columbia University Press 1968.
Roy, R.H. "The Canadian Military Tradition." In H.J. Massey, ed. *The Canadian Military: A Profile.* Toronto: Copp Clark 1972. Pp. 6–48.
Rühe, Volker. "Europe and the Alliance: Key Factors for Peace and Stability." *NATO Review* 41 (June 1993): 12–15.
Rühl, Lothar. "Die Vorwärtsverteidigung der NVA und der sowjetischen Streitkräfte in Deutschland bis 1990." *Österreichische Militär Zeitschrift,* no. 6 (1991): 501–8.
– "Offensive Defence in the Warsaw Pact." *Survival* 23 (September/October 1991): 442–50.
Schilling, Walter. "Neue Strukturen der MBFR Verhandlungen." *Aussenpolitik* 31 (4/1980): 404–14.
Schmidt, Helmut. *A Grand Strategy for the West: The Anachronism of National Strategies in an Interdependent World.* New Haven CT: Yale University Press 1985.
– *The Balance of Power: Germany's Peace Policy and the Superpowers.* London: William Kimber 1971.
– *Men and Powers: A Political Retrospective.* New York: Random House 1989.
– "The Zero Solution: In the German Interest." *Atlantic Community Quarterly* 25 (1987–88): 244–52.
Schulte, Birgitte. "Sicherheit für die Deutschen nur mit den Nachbaren." *Europäische Sicherheit,* no. 10 (1991): 568–70.
Schweitzer, C.C., et al., eds. *Politics and Government in the Federal Republic of Germany: Basic Documents.* Worcester, England: Berg 1984.
Sharp, Jane. "Conventional Arms Control in Europe." In *SIPRI Yearbook, 1991: World Armaments and Disarmament.* London: Oxford University Press 1991.
Sharp, Mitchell. "Canada-U.S. Relations: Options for the Future." *International Perspectives* (autumn 1972).
– *Which Reminds Me … A Memoir.* Toronto: University of Toronto Press 1994.
Skilling, H. Gordon. "The Belgrade Follow-up." In Robert Spencer, ed. *Canada and the Conference on Security and Co-operation in Europe.* Toronto: Centre for International Studies, University of Toronto, 1984.

Smith, Roland. *Soviet Policy toward West Germany.* London: International Institute for Strategic Studies, winter 1985.

Smouts, Marie-Claude. "The External Policy of François Mitterrand." *International Affairs* 59 (spring 1983): 155–67.

Snyder, Glenn. "The Security Dilemma in Alliance Politics." *World Politics* 36 (July 1984): 461–95.

Sokolsky, Joel J. "Parting of the Waves? The Strategy and Politics of the SSN Decision." In David Haglund and Joel J. Sokolsky, eds. *The U.S-Canada Security Relationship: The Politics, Strategy and Technology of Defense.* Boulder CO: Westview 1989. Pp. 267–95.

– "Taking Canada More Seriously." *RUSI Journal* 127 (December 1982).

Social Democratic Party of Germany. *Protokoll: Parteitag Wiesbaden 16.-19. November 1993.* Bonn: Vorstand der SPD 1993.

Social Democratic Party of Germany. Bundestags Fraktion. "Streitkräften – Personnel-, Rüstungs- und Finanz-plannung der Bundeswehr." *Politik* 5 (August 1988).

Spencer, Robert. "Canada and the Origins of the CSCE, 1965–73." In Robert Spencer, ed., *Canada and the Conference on Security and Co-operation in Europe.* Toronto: Centre for International Studies, University of Toronto, 1984.

Stent-Yergin, Angela. *East-West Technology Transfer.* Georgetown: Center for Strategic and International Studies 1980.

Stewart, Larry. *Canada's European Force, 1971–1980: A Defence Policy in Transition.* Kingston ON: Centre for International Relations, Queen's University, 1980.

– ed. *Canadian Defence Policy: Selected Documents, 1964–1981.* Kingston ON: Centre for International Relations, Queen's University, 1982.

Strategic Survey, 1982–83. London: International Institute for Strategic Studies 1983.

Strauss, Franz-Josef. *Die Erinnerungen.* Berlin: Wolf Jobst Verlag 1989.

Strempel, Ulrich. "Europa als Test für Kanadas Dritte Option." *Aussenpolitik* 29 (4/1978): 399–410.

Sutherland, R.J. "Canada's Long-Term Strategic Situation." *International Journal* 17 (summer 1962): 199–223.

Taft, William H., IV. "The NATO Role in Europe and the US Role in NATO." *NATO Review* 40 (August 1992): 14–19.

Taylor, A.J.P. *The Struggle for the Mastery of Europe: 1848–1918.* Oxford: Clarendon Press 1954.

Teltschik, Horst. *329 Tage: Innenansichten der Einigung.* Berlin: Siedler Verlag 1991.

Thordarson, Bruce. *Trudeau and Foreign Policy: A Study in Decision-Making.* Toronto: Oxford University Press 1972.

Thränert, Oliver. "Eine gemeinsame Aussen- und Sicherheitspolitik für die EG – Chancen und Risken." In Oliver Thränert, ed. *Die EG auf dem Weg zu einer gemeinsamen Aussen- und Sicherheitspolitik.* Bonn: Friedrich Ebert Stiftung, January 1993. Pp. 7–14.

Tomlin, Brian, ed. *Canada's Foreign Policy: Analysis and Trends.* Toronto: Methuen 1978.

Treddenick, John M. "The Defence Budget." In David Dewitt and David Leyton-Brown, eds. *Canada's International Security Policy*. Scarborough: Prentice-Hall Canada 1995. Pp. 413–54.

The True North Strong and Free? Proceedings of a Public Inquiry into Canadian Defence Policy and Nuclear Arms. West Vancouver: Gordon Soules 1987.

Tucker, Michael. *Canadian Foreign Policy: Contemporary Issues and Themes*. Toronto: McGraw-Hill Ryerson 1980.

Vano, Gerard S. *Canada: The Strategic and Military Pawn*. New York: Praeger 1988.

von Groll, Götz. "Die Genfer KSZE Verhandlungen." *Aussenpolitik* 25 (2/1974): 159–66.

Wallace, William. "Foreign Policy and National Identity in the United Kingdom." *International Affairs* 67 (January 1991): 65–80.

Welch, David A. "The New Multilateralism and Evolving Security Systems." In Fen Osler Hampson and Christopher Maule, eds. *Canada among Nations 1992–93: A New World Order?* Ottawa: Carleton University Press 1992. Pp. 67–93.

Weston, Sir John. "The Challenges to NATO: A British View." *NATO Review* 40 (December 1992): 9–14.

Wettig, Gerhard. "Moscow's Perception of NATO's Role." *Aussenpolitik* 45 (2/1994): 123–33.

Whetten, Lawrence. *Germany's Ostpolitik: Relations between the Federal Republic and Warsaw Pact Countries*. London: Oxford University Press 1971.

Windsor, Philip. *Germany and the Management of Détente*. New York: Praeger 1971.

Wörner, Manfred. "Die Atlantische Allianz und die europäische Sicherheit." *Europa-Archiv*, no. 1 (1992): 1–6.

Yost, David. "France and West-European Defence Identity." *Survival* 23 (July/August 1991): 327–51.

Zuckerman, William. "The Germans: What is the Question?" *International Affairs* 61 (1984–85): 465–70.

INTERVIEWS

Several dozen interviews (many of which are confidential) were conducted in Canada and Europe, mostly during 1990 and 1991. Information offered on the record is identified in the notes.

Index